ELIZABETH I

PROFILES IN POWER

General Editor: Keith Robbins

ELIZABETH I
Christopher Haigh

LLOYD GEORGE
Martin Pugh

ELIZABETH I

Christopher Haigh

LONGMAN
London and New York

Longman Group UK Limited,
Longman House, Burnt Mill, Harlow,
Essex CM20 2JE, England
and Associated Companies throughout the world.

Published in the United States of America
by Longman Inc., New York

First published 1988

British Library Cataloguing in Publication Data

Haigh, Christopher
Elizabeth I. —— (Profiles in power)
1. Elizabeth I, *Queen of England*
2. Great Britain —— Queens —— Biography
I. Title
942.05'5'0924
ISBN 0-582-02390-4   CSD
ISBN 0-582-00534-5   PPR

Library of Congress Cataloging-in-Publication Data

Haigh, Christopher.
Elizabeth I.

(Profiles in power)
Bibliography: p.
Includes index:
1. Elizabeth I, Queen of England, 1533-1603.
2. Great Britain —— Kings and rulers —— Biography.
3. Great Britain —— History —— Elizabeth, 1558-1603.
I. Title.   II. Series: Profiles in power (London, England)
DA355.H17   1988   942.05'5'0924 [B]   87-29853
ISBN 0-582-02390-4
ISBN 0-582-00534-5 (pbk.)

Set in 10½/12pt AM Comp Edit Baskerville

Produced by Longman Singapore Publishers (Pte) Ltd.
Printed in Singapore.

CONTENTS

. . . . .

PREFACE

This is not a biography of Elizabeth I – there are too many of them already. Instead, as one of the first titles in the 'Profiles in Power' series, the book seeks to analyse Elizabeth's exercise of political power. Recent historical work – on the continuing strength of Catholicism and the commitment of zealous Protestants; on the influence of the aristocracy; on the machinations of politicians in Council, Court, and Parliament; and on the planning and conduct of military and naval campaigns – has changed the context in which Elizabeth should be seen. We have also been led towards a fuller and more subtle understanding of what was expected of women in the sixteenth century, and of how some of them coped with the ideal foisted upon them by men. Elizabeth's problems as queen now seem (at least to me) both different from and more difficult than those which her scholarly biographers have studied – not only what she should do about marriage, the succession, religion, political malcontents and threats from abroad, but also how she could reach her own decisions and have them enforced. Elizabeth faced not only problems of policy, but problems of power, and this 'Profile' examines how she wielded the limited power she had.

I am grateful (I think!) to Keith Robbins for inviting me to write this book, and to Longman for helping it towards prompt completion. The views expressed here were shaped in conversations with Simon Adams, Patricia Crawford, Geoffrey Elton, Michael Graves, Alison Wall and Penry Williams, and influenced by those Oxford students who commented on the argument outlined in my lectures in 1987: I thank all those, named and unnamed, who have contributed towards the book. Finally, I am grateful to Lucy and Emily Haigh, for good-humoured reminders that a word-processor should also be used for computer games.

C.A.H.

(N.B. In the Notes and References at the end of chapters and in the Bibliographical Essay University Presses are indicated solely by place, e.g. Oxford for Oxford University Press)

FOR LUCY AND EMILY

INTRODUCTION

On Sunday 30 April 1536, Elizabeth Tudor was clutched in her mother's arms as her parents argued through a window at Greenwich Palace. The child, 2½ years old, was lifted up by Queen Anne, to apply emotional pressure to an angry King Henry VIII: the pleadings failed. Later that day, arrests of Anne's servants and friends began, and on Tuesday 2 May the Queen herself was interrogated by councillors and sent to the Tower of London. On Monday 8 May, Anne was tried for alleged treason, and convicted on evidence which was patently incredible. On Wednesday 17 May, Anne's marriage to the King was declared null by the Archbishop of Canterbury (on grounds which were never divulged), and Princess Elizabeth was made illegitimate – thus losing her claim to the crown of England. Two days later, Anne was beheaded on Tower Green, before a silent crowd of about a thousand. On Saturday 20 May, Elizabeth's father was betrothed to Jane Seymour, and ten days later they were married. It had taken Henry VIII a month to dispose of a wife on a charge of treason, sweep some of her friends to the block with her, bastardise her child, and acquire a new queen. Here was the power of the Tudor monarchy in action, with the King bending his Council, the Church, and the law to do his will.

But the fall of Anne Boleyn was not quite as it seemed, and Henry was almost as much a victim of events as was his former queen.[1] The dissolution of the royal marriage had been plotted for weeks by an alliance of conservative peers and courtiers, friends of Henry's divorced (and deceased) first wife, and the Imperial ambassador. A new candidate for the King's hand, Jane Seymour, had been carefully coached to attract his attention, frustrate his desires, and turn him against his queen.

1

The conspirators had intended to have the Boleyn marriage annulled, but a more drastic solution was proposed from an unexpected source. Thomas Cromwell, once a political ally of the Boleyns and now the King's leading administrator, determined to dispose of Anne for good – probably because she stood in the way of his projected alliance with the Emperor Charles V. He planned charges of multiple adultery (and incest) against the Queen, which would also enable him to remove some of Anne's political allies. Jane and her friends soured Henry against Anne, and Cromwell turned courtly dalliance into evidence of adultery and conspiracy to murder.

We do not know if Henry VIII was brought to swallow the allegations against Anne. Perhaps the attractions of Jane made him willing to suspend his disbelief; perhaps a man nervous of his own virility was made to believe his wife had mocked him with other men. But Henry certainly behaved as if the stories were true: he wept and raged against Anne, and he supervised the arrangements for her trial and execution. If Henry accepted the claims, he may have been one of the few at Court who did. The evidence produced against Anne was flimsy, based on a confession induced by torture and the misrepresentation of innocent relationships. The precise charges of adultery cannot have been true, since on almost all the alleged occasions the accused were not in the same places – but such issues were not explored by a court which knew what was required. The trials of Anne and her accomplices showed that, in treason cases at least, the Crown got its way. But the Crown wanted this way only because of a factional plot, which had poisoned the King's mind, seduced his affections, and pressured him to abandon a wife whom he had loved almost to the end.

Once Henry had decided that Anne had to go, there was little chance he would be prevented from disposing of her. His councillors were unlikely to raise objections: many had risen to greatness by the King's favour, and all feared its loss (or worse) if they crossed his will. The Church would do nothing: Henry had already denied papal authority and declared himself supreme head of the Church in England; the conservative bishops objected to Anne's heretical ideas; and the reformist bishops no doubt feared that to identify themselves with Anne would wreck their Reformation. So Thomas Cranmer, Archbishop of Canterbury, heard Anne's last confession and obediently dissolved her marriage. The law, too, was no obstacle. Anne was tried before a court which comprised her uncle, the Duke of Norfolk, as Lord Steward, her cousin, the Earl of Surrey, as Earl Marshal, a jury of twenty-six peers, and the Lord Chancellor and judges – but no one risked the King's anger, or invited suspicion of complicity in Anne's offences, or challenged the court which had already found her alleged paramours guilty. Within a few weeks, Parliament, too, followed the King's wishes and excluded Elizabeth from the succession to the throne, in favour of the children of Jane Seymour or any future queen.

The fate of Elizabeth's mother showed the vulnerability, as well as the power, of the Tudor monarchy. By a combination of constitutional authority and personal intimidation, Henry VIII had been able to enforce his wish to dispose of Anne – but he had been manœuvred by councillors and courtiers into wishing to dispose of her. No matter how great the formal power of the King of England, it was exercised under the informal influence of the politicians who surrounded him. By control of access to the King's presence, by selection of the documents he was to see, by the doctoring of reports and the whispering of half-truths, those about Henry had the opportunity to manage him.[2] Factional manipulation of the King destroyed Anne Boleyn in May 1536, as it destroyed Cardinal Wolsey's power in 1529, Anne's conservative enemies in June 1536 and in 1538, and Thomas Cromwell in 1540. Henry may have learned caution from the fall of Cromwell, for factional attempts to bring down Archbishop Cranmer in 1543, Bishop Gardiner in 1544, and Queen Katherine Parr in 1546 were unsuccessful. But as the King's health failed late in 1546, the Howard dynasty was overwhelmed by a Court coup from reformers in the Privy Chamber, who gained control of the young heir to the throne – Jane Seymour's son Edward.

We know very little of Elizabeth's attitude towards her dead mother. She was said to have gloried in her father, but she was certainly not ashamed of her mother. Elizabeth sometimes used Anne Boleyn's falcon badge, and as queen her own symbol of the phoenix may have signified her recovery from the disaster of Anne's execution. Elizabeth herself had a ring which carried her mother's portrait, and she appointed as her first Archbishop of Canterbury Anne's chaplain, Matthew Parker – who believed that Anne had commended her daughter to his spiritual care. If Elizabeth had forgotten the detailed events of 1536 by the time she became queen in November 1558, she was soon reminded of them. In September 1559 a Scottish theologian, Alexander Alesius (who had been on the fringe of the English Court in 1536), sent her a narrative version of her mother's fall, including a description of the parental argument in which Elizabeth had been held up to Henry VIII in supplication.[3] Elizabeth must surely have learned from her mother's fate – learned that a woman in politics was at risk from emotional entanglements, and that a ruler of England could be made the tool of Court intrigues.

Elizabeth's fortunes after the execution of her mother also had much to teach her. At first, she had been merely the acknowledged bastard daughter of the King, appearing in the royal party on state occasions; after the Succession Act of 1544, she had been third in line to the throne. From 1547, with the accession of her young half-brother Edward, she was second in succession and a figure of political promise: she had to protect first her virginity and then her single status from the attentions of the ambitious Thomas Seymour. From 1553, when her Catholic half-sister Mary became queen, Elizabeth was heir presumptive to the kingdom – and focus of the aspirations of Mary's opponents. In these years, Elizabeth had to learn personal distrust and political caution. The plots against Queen Mary led to suspicion of Elizabeth, and she spent much of her sister's reign in custody or isolation. But she avoided public disloyalty and provable complicity in the conspiracies, while maintaining her popularity with critics of the regime. Elizabeth learned to walk a political tightrope with great skill: she managed to please (or not displease) Mary just enough to retain her place in the succession, while not alienating her own (mainly Protestant) support.

By the autumn of 1558 it was plain that Queen Mary did not have long to live, and that her sister would succeed to the throne. Elizabeth's agents formed plans to overcome any resistance, making discreet contacts with reliable magnates and commanders of garrisons. As rumours of Mary's illness spread, so Elizabeth's callers and correspondents grew in number and crowds gathered around her house at Hatfield. On 17 November, Mary died and Elizabeth was proclaimed queen without opposition. Eleven days later she took formal possession of the Tower of London, where her mother had been executed twenty-two years before. In those years, Elizabeth had risen from bastard child of an adulterous traitress to Queen of England: she was indeed a political phoenix, and was aware of her good fortune. A little before her accession, she had been visited by a Spanish envoy, who was struck by her confidence and authority: she was acting like a powerful ruler. But Elizabeth was herself a child of the weakness of Tudor kingship, and of its vulnerability to manipulation. She, above all others, knew the precariousness of the royal position and the constraints upon royal power. Her own reign would be a constant test of the political skills she had acquired in adversity.

. . .

NOTES AND REFERENCES

1. My account of Anne's fall relies heavily upon Ives E W 1986 *Anne Boleyn*. Blackwell, pp. 335–418
2. See the discussion of factional manipulation through the Privy Chamber in Starkey D R 1985 *The Reign of Henry VIII: personalities and politics*. George Philip
3. *Calendar of State Papers Foreign, 1558–59*, p. 527

Chapter 1

THE QUEEN AND THE THRONE

The monarchy of Elizabeth I was founded upon illusion. She ruled by propagandist images which captivated her courtiers and seduced her subjects – images which have misled historians for four centuries. The first illusion was that Elizabeth had inherited chaos and disaster; the second was that she inaugurated a golden age of national harmony and achievement. The themes were set out almost immediately she ascended the throne. On 14 January 1559, eight weeks after her accession, the new Queen's coronation procession took place through London. It passed by a carefully orchestrated series of pageants and tableaux, which provided the capital with a visual manifesto for the new government. The tableau at Cornhill showed a child, representing Elizabeth, supported by four characters dressed as virtues, who crushed down their opposite vices. As the official account of the procession, rushed out by the government printer, put it, 'pure religion did tread upon superstition and ignorance; love of subjects did tread upon rebellion and insolency; wisdom did tread upon folly and vainglory; justice did tread upon adulation and bribery'. The glories of the future triumphed over the failures of the past. Elizabeth's supporters had, by press and pulpit, been rubbishing her predecessor's government for some weeks: now, all was going to be different – and better! In the pageant at Fleet Street the promise of truth and harmony was declared for all to see: a queen dressed in Parliament robes sat consulting the estates of her realm, under the biblical slogan 'Deborah, the judge and restorer of the house of Israel'.[1] Elizabeth was signalling – and justifying – a decisive break with the past.

For, although it suited her to exaggerate the extent, Elizabeth's really was a new regime. Under the pretence that

7

Mary's Privy Council had been too large and factious, Elizabeth dismissed two-thirds of its members and replaced them with her own relations, servants, and political allies – led by William Cecil, Nicholas Bacon, and Thomas Parry. In the royal Household, in the Court, the change-over was even more marked: Elizabeth surrounded herself with those she knew she could trust, her late mother's relatives and her own domestic staff. The Queen had thus created a rather narrowly based government, defined by personal loyalty to herself and ideological loyalty to Protestantism – for in dismissing the Marians she had dismissed most of the Catholics, and in reappointing some of Edward VI's ministers she had recruited Protestants. But the novelty and homogeneity of the regime should not be over-emphasised: Elizabeth's 'new men' were mainly experienced administrators from Edward's era, and the realities of political power had forced her to retain some conservative councillors. Some of the less partisan of Mary's bureaucrats – Winchester, Mason, and Petre – stayed in office, and, more importantly, so did the great regional magnates, the Earls of Derby, Shrewsbury, Pembroke, and Arundel. It was a government which typified Elizabeth's approach to politics: under the banner of novelty she assembled an alliance of experienced men, and behind the public face of Protestantism she made the necessary compromise with conservatism. The rhetoric of monarchy was one thing: the politics of power was quite another.

But the continuities in power were masked by the rhetoric of reform, and the public image was one of sparkling novelty. Elizabeth sought support by discrediting her predecessor's rule and dissociating herself from it. The problems of the realm were determinedly blamed upon the previous government, and its reliance upon Catholicism and Spain; a change of ruler would bring solutions. Elizabeth had to differentiate her regime from Mary's because they had something very obvious in common: they were both women, and some men had related the difficulties of Mary's reign to her sex. Thomas Becon had cried to God in 1554, 'Thou hast set to rule over us a woman, whom nature hath formed to be in subjection unto man, and whom thou by thine holy apostle commandest to keep silence and not to speak in the congregation. Ah, Lord! to take away the empire from a man, and to give it to a woman, seemeth to be an evident token of thine anger toward us Englishmen.'[2] Becon had republished his words in 1563, with no indication that a Protestant queen was any better than a Catholic, or that Elizabeth was any less of a punishment than Mary had been. Rule by a woman was the antithesis of proper order, and was bound to lead to disaster.

Elizabeth, like Mary before her, had an image problem – what was the appropriate image of a female ruler? In sermons and prescriptive literature, sixteenth-century Englishmen propounded an ideal of womanhood, and it was an ideal which left little room for an unmarried female ruler: a woman should be a wife, and she should be silent, obedient, and domestic. A woman might rule her own kitchen, but surely not her own kingdom; outside the kitchen, she should be under the authority of a man, because she was physically, intellectually, and emotionally inferior to men. A woman's role was essentially passive and subservient; throughout Elizabeth's reign, the preachers continued to insist that it was contrary to nature for a woman to exercise authority over men in a family. If a woman could not rule a household, how could Elizabeth rule a realm?

Elizabeth I was dogged by the fact that she was 'only' a woman. The men she worked with saw her in terms of the stereotype female, flawed and ineffective. In 1560, William Cecil was furious when a messenger discussed with the Queen a dispatch from her ambassador in Paris, 'being too much for a woman's knowledge'. In 1592, it was discovered that the Lord Deputy in Ireland had been abusing her roundly: 'This fiddling woman troubles me out of measure'; 'Ah, silly woman, now she shall not curb me, she shall not rule me'; 'God's wounds, this it is to serve a base, bastard, pissing kitchen woman! If I had served any prince in Christendom, I had not been so dealt withal.'[3] When things went wrong it was the Queen's gender which was often blamed: in 1597, the Earl of Essex told the French ambassador that 'they laboured under two things at this Court, delay and inconstancy, which proceeded from the sex of the queen'. Lower down the social scale, ordinary people found it difficult to believe that they really were governed by a female: in 1591, an Essex man was claiming that she was no more than a puppet – 'the queen is but a woman, and ruled by noblemen'. A little later, a London woman saw Elizabeth for the first time and exclaimed, 'Oh Lord, the queen is a woman!' – how could it be?[4]

Elizabeth herself sometimes affected the 'mere woman' role.

She described herself to the 1563 House of Commons as 'being a woman, wanting both wit and memory', and admitted that reticence would be 'a thing appropriate to my sex'. In 1576 she told an emissary from the Spanish Netherlands that his master thought 'he has only to do with a woman', and, a few years later, in her own private prayers, she was 'a weak woman'.[5] This was, of course, conventional rhetoric and tactical role-play, but even the Queen could not flout the convention and ignore the required role. However the issue was obscured, there was a contradiction between the ideal of a monarch and the ideal of a woman: a monarch should rule, a woman should obey. John Knox had found the contradiction so blatant as to make the rule (or 'regiment') of a woman 'monstrous', an unnatural perversion of the right order of things. In 1558 he had published *The First Blast of the Trumpet* to argue his case and justify the deposition of Mary, and was considerably embarrassed when another woman succeeded to the English throne. Knox wriggled around his earlier argument, writing that, although female rule was unnatural, God had made an exception so that Elizabeth could restore the Gospel. There was a heavy hint that Elizabeth's religion might compensate for her gender. John Calvin had a similar view: sometimes God gave a woman special qualities above her sex to serve his divine plan. This was an argument which Elizabeth herself was to use: she was not a 'mere' woman, she was a special woman, an exception from the rules binding ordinary females. Perhaps this was how William Cecil came to see her, as an exception, an interruption of the natural flow of things. But the proper flow would be restored: he prayed that God would 'send our mistress a husband, and by time a son, that we may hope our posterity shall have a masculine succession'.[6]

One consequence of the Tudor ideal of woman was the assumption that Elizabeth would marry – that was what women did. It was agreed that Elizabeth needed a husband. Philip II of Spain charitably offered himself, to relieve his sister-in-law of the burden of rule: 'It would be better for herself and her kingdom if she would take a consort who might relieve her of those labours which are only fit for men.'[7] Some historians, especially recent feminist writers, have seen the pressure to marry as the result of male chauvinism, a determination that Elizabeth should marry herself to a king who could then rule for her. This is probably untrue: William Cecil, Nicholas Bacon, and the others who urged her to marry had nothing to gain, and much influence to lose, from a king. If they judged that Elizabeth herself could not govern, they would rather govern for her than hand over power to another man. When marriage to a foreign prince was considered, Elizabeth's councillors based negotiations upon the marriage treaty between Mary and Philip of Spain, which had deliberately excluded the husband from rule. They sought not a consort for the Queen but a father for her son – not a sovereign, but a stud.

A husband for the Queen was a means to an end; the end was a secure succession, and the necessary means was a marriage. In 1559 the House of Commons petitioned Queen Elizabeth to marry and produce an heir – and then went on to discuss the limitations to be placed on the powers of her husband. In 1563 the House of Lords asked 'that it please your Majesty to dispose yourself to marry, where you will, with whom you will, and as shortly as you will' – but, after a token reference to the Queen's happiness, the reasons for marriage related to the production of an heir. Also in 1563, the Commons beseeched 'God to incline your Majesty's heart to marriage, and that he will so bless and send such good success thereunto that we may see the fruit and child that may come thereof'.[8] The Parliaments of 1566 and 1576 again petitioned for marriage, but again for the same reason, an heir to the throne. A royal husband was an unfortunate necessity: the real aim was a royal son.

At least for tactical purposes of public argument, Queen Elizabeth accepted that she had a duty to marry for the good of the realm. In 1563, 1566, and 1576, she told Parliament that, although for herself she preferred the single state, yet for the sake of her subjects she would marry. In 1576, Lord Keeper Bacon declared that 'Her Majesty hath called me to say that, albeit of her own natural disposition she is not disposed or inclined to marriage, neither would she ever marry if she were a private person, yet for your sakes and for the benefit of the realm she is contented to incline and dispose herself to the satisfaction of your humble petition, so that all things convenient may concur that be meet for such a marriage.'[9] But by then it was unlikely that anybody believed her, and probable that she did not believe herself. By 1576, and perhaps by 1563, the Queen's marriage had become her chosen weapon in diplomatic intrigue, rather than her chosen solution to the succession problem.

But, early in the reign at least, there was no shortage of volunteers to sire the Queen's anticipated heir. Elizabeth was, as Secretary Walsingham put it later, 'the best marriage in her parish',[10] and some had high hopes of winning her. In the first weeks of her reign, the Earl of Arundel borrowed heavily from an Italian merchant, and used the money in lavish entertainments and to bribe Elizabeth's women friends and servants to persuade her to marry him. In May 1559, Sir William Pickering was making a bid for the Queen's affections, and when Elizabeth fussed over him Londoners were soon wagering four to one he would be king. Eric XIV of Sweden sent his brother to plead for Elizabeth's hand and to throw money about to get it – and there were more restrained early enquiries from the Earl of Arran, the Dukes of Holstein and Saxony, and the Archduke of Austria. In 1561 the London Stationers' Company was ordered to confiscate any printed pictures of Elizabeth with a suitor, especially those with King Eric. The queue of candidates had become a diplomatic embarrassment, and the Queen's courtships something of a scandal. But most disreputable of all was the Dudley affair, which for a while cast Elizabeth as the trollop of Europe, and threatened the political stability of England. Either the Queen was very foolish in the extent of her flirtation, or she seriously contemplated marriage to Robert Dudley. But she pulled back – or was forced back – twice within a few months.

In August and September 1560, with Robert's wife apparently dying of breast cancer, Elizabeth and Dudley were widely thought to be planning marriage. William Cecil made preparations to resign as Secretary of State if they married, but he also struggled to defeat the project. He spread a rumour that Amy Dudley was not really ill at all, but that Elizabeth and Dudley were plotting to poison her; he even told the story to the Spanish ambassador, and added that Dudley was bringing disaster to the realm. This tactic had two results: the ambassador was prompted to warn the Queen off the marriage; and, when Amy died, as she did in September, Robert was suspected to have organised her murder. There was outrage at Court and in the country, and, for a while at least, a Dudley marriage became politically impossible. But Elizabeth and Dudley, or perhaps Dudley alone, had devised a desperate way of marrying despite internal opposition. In mid-January 1561, the Spanish ambassador was told by a Dudley ally that the

Queen and Robert would move towards the restoration of Catholicism in England if Philip II would support their marriage and help them deal with any consequences. This astonishing proposal was in the air until mid-April, with Dudley and his ally Paget working on the Queen and preparing to receive an emissary from the Pope. But Cecil moved again to block Elizabeth and Dudley's plans. It may have been Cecil who leaked the story publicly, to raise popular fears of popery, and he created the impression of a papist conspiracy by arresting leading Catholic gentry and priests and charging them with illegal masses.

There was a public outcry in London, which presumably convinced Elizabeth that Dudley's 'Spanish strategy' was impossible. She denied to the Spanish ambassador that she had ever planned to restore Catholic religion, the Privy Council decided not to admit the Papal Nuncio, and by early May 1561 it was all over. As Cecil reported, 'When I saw this Romish influence towards, about one month past, I thought it necessary to dull the papists' expectations by discovering of certain mass-mongers and punishing them.'[11] Cecil's tactics had been brilliant: he had wrecked Robert Dudley's chances of becoming king, by displaying to Elizabeth the extent of aristocratic and popular hostility to a Dudley marriage – but he had also consigned Elizabeth to the role of Virgin Queen. It was probably at this point that Elizabeth decided not to marry – or, at least, recognised the likelihood that she would not. There were still twenty years of international courtships to go, but, with a brief exception in 1579, they were diplomatic manœuvres for political advantage. The Queen's political terms for her suitors were always far too high, and cannot have been seriously intended. She offered herself to the highest diplomatic bidder, but since no one could afford her price she became a royal tease rather than a royal tart.

Elizabeth probably intended to remain single. In 1563, she told an imperial envoy that 'If I am to disclose to you what I should prefer if I follow the inclination of my nature, it is this: beggar-woman and single, far rather than queen and married!'[12] Three years later, she told the Spanish ambassador that if she could find an acceptable way of settling the succession without marriage, she would certainly stay single. Of course, the Queen played politics when she said she would not marry as much as when she said she would, but her reluctance was widely known. The French ambassador reported in 1569 that the English nobles were generally convinced that the Queen would not marry, and William Cecil was by then seeking other means to solve the succession problem. By 1572, Robert Dudley, the most careful observer of Elizabeth's diplomatic flirtations, had concluded that 'Her Majesty's heart is nothing inclined to marry at all, for the matter was ever brought to as many points as we could devise, and always she was bent to hold with the difficultest'. As Dudley had noticed, in any marriage negotiations Elizabeth looked for the snags rather than the advantages. By 1575, Francis Walsingham, marriage-negotiator-in-chief, regarded the cause as, essentially, lost:

> I do daily more and more discover her Majesty's affection towards marriage to be such as until necessity shall press thereto, for the saving of her crown and the avoiding of the contempt of her people, I can no way hope to see that take effect that we have all over just cause to desire, and therefore to God we must commit it and ourselves to become better reformed Christians than we are, for our sins are the true cause of these her Majesty's indispositions.[13]

The marriage issue was kept open, but as a political weapon, to entice suitors and to tame claimants to the throne. The threat that Elizabeth might marry and produce a child was a way to make Mary Queen of Scots behave herself – in so far as Mary could. Elizabeth told a Scottish emissary in 1564 that 'I am resolved never to marry, if I be not thereto necessitated by the queen my sister's harsh behaviour toward me'. Melville alleged he had replied, 'Your Majesty thinks that if you were married you would be but queen of England, and now you are both king and queen!' There was probably something in this. Elizabeth did get used to keeping her own counsel and exercising power alone; she loved to be the single centre of attention. She told Robert Dudley, by then Earl of Leicester, in 1566 that 'If you think to rule here, I will take a course to see you forthcoming. I will have but one mistress, and no master!'[14] It was certainly clear that Leicester would not be her master, for, after her early indiscretions, she had concluded that a Dudley match was too undignified. In 1565 Elizabeth confided to the French ambassador that 'as for the earl of Leicester, I have always loved his virtues, but the aspiration to greatness and honour which is in me could not suffer him as a companion and husband'. She was even more emphatic in 1575: 'Dost thou think me so unlike myself and unmindful of my royal majesty that I would prefer my servant, whom I myself have raised, before the greatest prince of Christendom, in the honour of a husband!'[15] She would not marry Robert Dudley, a mere subject.

But if marriage to a subject was too demeaning, marriage to a foreign prince was too dangerous. It would force a permanent choice of allies (and perhaps enemies), bringing fixed foreign entanglements; and, since most eligible suitors were Catholic princes, it would probably entail religious concessions which would provoke her Protestant subjects. The Alençon matchmaking, the one occasion after 1560–61 when Elizabeth may have seriously considered marriage, was stopped in 1579 by a public outcry against the French prince's Catholicism. Whether she chose her husband within the realm or outside, a match would be divisive. William Camden, whose view of Elizabeth probably reflected that of his mentor William Cecil, wrote later that

> Some were of opinion that she was fully resolved in her mind that she might better provide both for the commonwealth and her own glory by an unmarried life than by marriage, as forseeing that if she married a subject she would disparage herself by the inequality of the match, and give occasion of domestical heartburnings, private grudges and commotions; if a stranger, she would then subject both herself and her people to a foreign yoke and endanger religion.[16]

The reigns of both her father and her sister had shown how domestic politics and foreign relations could be disrupted by the monarch's choice of spouse, and Elizabeth often preferred prevarication to the risk of making a wrong decision.

John Clapham, another Cecilian writer, suspected that devious political pressures had been at work. He thought that Elizabeth had not married 'by reason either that she best liked a single life and thereby also to govern more absolutely, or that, having a purpose to marry, she was dissuaded from it by some particular favourites who sought their own advancement'.[17] It was certainly true that Leicester had attempted to disrupt the Queen's cross-Channel courtships, as threats to his own position in Court politics. Clapham may also have been right that Elizabeth wished 'to govern more absolutely', refusing to share her power with a husband. A woman who spent her adult life struggling against the conventional ideal of womanhood presumably found it difficult to do the most conventional womanly thing of all. Elizabeth strove to show that she was not as other women; how could she admit that she was just the same as the rest, and submit herself to a husband? She would compromise her claim to exceptional status, undermine the images upon which she had based her rule, and weaken her authority over her male subjects. Elizabeth had refused to be a mere woman, and was not going to be a mere wife.

Some historians, notably A. F. Pollard,[18] have argued that Elizabeth did not marry because that course offered no solution to the succession problem: she knew she could not bear children. But there is very little evidence to support this view. Spanish ambassadors bought information from the Queen's laundresses, and were assured that Elizabeth had a regular menstrual cycle. As late as March 1579, when the Queen was 45, Lord Burghley consulted her doctors and female servants, and concluded that she was still able to have children. Indeed, the risk of pregnancy was more of a threat than the risk of failure. Perhaps 10 per cent of childbirths resulted in the mother's death, and two of Elizabeth's stepmothers, Jane Seymour and Catherine Parr, had died in childbirth. If Elizabeth had done so, she would have bequeathed either a succession struggle or a long royal minority. So a marriage might have aggravated the succession problem, and to Elizabeth other solutions probably seemed preferable. In 1566 William Cecil wrote a memorandum on the importance of pursuing both a marriage and a settlement of the succession. He concluded, 'The mean betwixt these is to determine effectually to marry, and, if it succeed not, then proceed to discussion of the right of succession.'[19]

As Elizabeth's reluctance to marry became clear, so she came under intense pressure to declare the succession to the throne. This was partly the fault of her own family and its publicists: Tudor propaganda had portrayed the monarchy as the key to social stability, and had argued that civil wars were a necessary consequence of a disputed succession. Especially after the Queen's attack of smallpox in October 1562, there was a widespread fear of conflict if she died without an agreed heir. The Privy Council had split three ways in support of different claimants, and Elizabeth had made matters worse by asking for Robert Dudley to be made protector of the realm. William Cecil expected trouble, writing of the 1563 Parliament that 'I think somewhat will be attempted to ascertain the realm of a successor to this crown, but I fear the unwillingness of her Majesty to have such a person known will stay the matter.'[20] And so it was to be.

The House of Lords and the House of Commons both petitioned Elizabeth to name an heir in 1563. The Lords drew attention to her recent illness and the uncertainty it had produced:

> Most gracious sovereign Lady, the lamentable and pitiful state and condition wherein all your nobles and counsellors of late were, when it pleased God to lay his heavy hand over you, and the amazedness that most men of understanding were, by the bruit that grew by that sickness, brought unto, is one cause of this petition.

If the Queen died before the succession was made clear, it would

> be the occasion of very evident and great danger and peril to all states and sorts of men in this realm, by the factions, seditions and intestine war that would grow through want of understanding to whom they should yield their allegiances and duties.[21]

Elizabeth's refusal to name an heir led to a good deal of criticism. The preacher Thomas Sampson proposed in 1565 that 'if there should be such difficulty in the queen that she would not of herself incline to help this misery, then is the wisdom and power of the Parliament to be showed, so that they do what may be done to have this matter of succession decided'. In the Commons in 1566 it was said that 'it toucheth the Council in honour and conscience to move her Majesty to provide a known successor', and that 'the Queen's Majesty, the Council and this House shall answer for all the innocent blood that shall be spilt in this cause'.[22] After Elizabeth had tried to stifle debate on the succession in the 1566 Parliament, broadsheets were distributed in London criticising the Queen and, unfairly, William Cecil for the failure to name an heir. The Queen was coming to be seen as irresponsible, and careless of the welfare of her subjects.

Elizabeth consistently refused to name a successor, and tried to prevent discussion of the issue. She was furious in 1566 when a group of nobles held a meeting on the succession at Arundel's house. In the same year, she instructed Parliament not to debate the problem: 'For if you should have liberty to treat of it, there be so many competitors – some kinsfolks, some servants and some tenants; some would speak for their master, and some for their mistress, and every man for his friend – that it would be an occasion of a greater charge than a subsidy.'[23] Of course the Queen was right that debate over successors was divisive, and suppression of speculation made sense; in 1581 a statute forbade prophecies and astrological calculations of when Elizabeth would die and who would succeed. But such considerations hardly explain why Elizabeth was so adamant, and why she risked unpopularity by inaction, for the divisiveness of debate paled in comparison with the divisiveness of an unresolved succession when the Queen died. It is true that, in the end, her procrastination worked and the problem solved itself: Elizabeth outlived some claimants, and others disqualified themselves, but this good fortune could not have been anticipated.

Elizabeth risked instability after her death for the sake of stability in her own lifetime. The uncertainty of the succession strengthened her position by making her survival essential and focusing loyalty upon her. 'Oh, how wretched are we, who cannot tell under what sovereign we are to live!' cried Bishop Jewel – 'God will, I trust, long preserve Elizabeth to us in life and safety', was his conclusion. In 1578, the Queen was almost killed by an accidental shot, and the balladeers drew the political lesson:

> And told again, if that mishap had happened on her
>   Grace,
> The stay of true religion, how parlous were the case:
> Which might have turned to bloody wars, of strange and
>   foreign foes,
> Alas! how had we been accursed, our comfort so to lose.[24]

Elizabeth refused to create a reversionary interest, and she remained afraid of plots to advance a known successor. 'I know the inconstancy of the people of England, how they ever mislike the present government and have their eyes fixed upon that person that is next to succeed', she said in 1561. She told the Scottish ambassador of the conspiracies to put her on the throne, in the reign of her sister Mary, and he reported that 'If it were certainly known in the world who would succeed her, she would never think herself in sufficient security.' When, in 1566, a parliamentary delegation pressed her to name her heir, she retorted, 'I am sure there was not one of them that ever was a second person, as I have been.' Mary Tudor had been in danger because of plots for Elizabeth, and Elizabeth had been endangered by Mary's suspicion – 'And so shall never be my successor.'[25]

Elizabeth knew her own capacity for jealousy, and recognised that she would not trust a named heir: 'Think you that I could love my winding-sheet, when, as examples show, princes cannot even love their children who are to succeed them?' she had asked in 1561. In the following year it was being said in London that the Queen would not settle the succession, 'because she is persuaded that if there were any heir apparent known the people would be more affectionated to him than to her'.[26] In 1566 she told the Privy Council that she would not be a lame duck queen, or see her councillors trooping off to negotiate with her successor. However she dressed it up in terms of the public interest and the safety of her successor, the key reason for Elizabeth's refusal to name an heir was her own political security. She dared not name a figurehead for the coup which might overthrow her. Her position was vulnerable: she would not nominate an alternative focus of loyalty, and complicate still further the problem of being a woman ruler in a man's world.

Elizabeth sought to present herself, woman though she was, as a fit occupant of the throne of England, and she did not propose to confuse the issue by recruiting a husband or an heir. She and her propagandists tried to define the attributes of female monarchy, and to escape from the restrictive ideal of womanhood. This was not done by an attack upon the sixteenth-century stereotype of a woman. Elizabeth accepted the image, and often derided her own sex: when congratulated in 1598 for her ability in foreign languages, she retorted 'it was no marvel to teach a woman to talk; it were far harder to teach her to hold her tongue!'[27] She did not seek to change the ideal, but to escape from it, by suggesting that she was no ordinary woman. It is striking that in poetry and portraiture she was invariably represented as an adored goddess or an untouchable virgin, never as a mere female. She was the moon-goddess, Cynthia, Diana, or Belphoebe; the virginal Astraea or a Vestal Virgin; pure ermine or the unique phoenix.

Queen Elizabeth immediately staked out her claim to be

different, and her unmarried status was part of the difference. She told her first Parliament, 'And, in the end, this shall be for me sufficient, that a marble stone shall declare that a queen, having reigned such a time, lived and died a virgin.' Others took up the theme, and extended it. In 1582, Thomas Bentley dedicated *The Monument of Matrons* to Elizabeth as the virgin bride of Christ and mother of the Church. Elizabeth was not just *a* virgin, but competed with the Virgin Mary to be *the* virgin. In 1600, John Dowland's *Second Book of Airs* set songs to Elizabeth against prayers to Mary, and proposed 'Vivat Eliza for an Ave Maria'. Soon after her death in 1603, an engraving of the late Queen was inscribed

She was, she is, (what can there more be said?)
In earth the first, in heaven the second Maid.

Elizabeth was, indeed, beyond human comparison, as a ballad of 1587 claimed:

A monarch maiden Queen
Whose like on earth was never seen.[28]

But Elizabeth was not simply a virgin; she was in some sense married to everyone, to the kingdom of England. She may have said this to her first Parliament, and flourished her coronation ring in token of her commitment, but even if the story was apocryphal it was a popular one and widely believed. Certainly, in 1599 the Queen herself referred to 'all my husbands, my good people'. Nor was she just a wife, she was a mother too. In 1559, she may have declared that 'every one of you, and as many as are Englishmen, are children and kinsmen to me'. She told the Commons in 1563 that 'though after my death you may have many stepdames, yet shall you never have any a more natural mother than I mean to be unto you all'. Her position as virgin mother was a common metaphor in her speeches to Parliament, and in her private prayers – 'Preserve then the mother and the children, whom thou hast given to her, so shall we serve thee yet better for the good of thy poor Church', she asked in about 1579.[29] So Elizabeth presented herself in female roles which were elevated far above those of other women. She was not just a virgin, but a virgin of Mary-like significance; not just a wife, but the wife of the realm; not just a mother, but the mother of the English people and the English Church. Nor was she just a daughter: she was the daughter of Henry VIII.

Elizabeth deliberately invoked her father's memory, and identified herself with him: the Count of Feria noticed this even before Mary's death. When, in her coronation procession, Elizabeth heard someone in the crowd cry out 'Remember old King Henry VIII!', she deliberately drew attention to it by smiling, and the incident was stressed in the official account. She told Parliament in 1559 that 'we hope to rule, govern and keep this our realm in as good justice, peace and rest, in like wise as the king my father held you in'.[30] Elizabeth had set up Henry as her model, and others publicised his virtues; in 1560 Sir Thomas Chaloner, diplomat and old friend of William Cecil, dedicated his *In laudem Henrici Octavi carmen panegiricum* to the new Queen. Elizabeth herself claimed the courage of her father, as in speeches to Parliament in 1566 and to an envoy from the Spanish Netherlands in 1576. When she received visitors in the Privy Chamber at Whitehall, she would pose in front of the Holbein mural of the Tudor dynasty, under the dominating figure of Henry.

Elizabeth was a special woman, never a 'mere' woman. She determinedly contrasted herself with the rest of her sex, stressing their frailty but claiming to be an exception because she was queen. In 1563, she told the Commons that, 'being a woman, wanting both wit and memory', perhaps she should be silent, 'but yet the princely seat and kingly throne wherein God (though unworthy) hath constituted me' gave her confidence. She was a monarch, chosen by God and endowed by him with all the skills she needed: she was not to be pushed around! 'Though I be a woman', she told a parliamentary delegation in 1563,

> yet I have as good a courage answerable to my place as ever my father had. I am your anointed queen. I will never be by violence constrained to do anything. I thank God I am indeed endued with such qualities that if I were turned out of the realm in my petticoat I were able to live in any place of Christendom.

She had been given these abilities because she was the instrument of God. In a prayer she wrote in about 1579, Elizabeth thanked God for 'making me (though a weak woman) yet thy instrument to set forth the glorious gospel of thy dear son Christ Jesus'.[31] To be God's instrument, she had been made as good as any man: she claimed in 1581 that 'I have the heart of a man, not of a woman, and I am not afraid of anything'. By 1586, indeed, she was better than some men: her career had 'taught me to bear with a better mind these treasons, than is common to my sex – yea, with a better heart perhaps than in some men!' Elizabeth was a woman with masculine courage – indeed, with courage greater than ordinary men. In her famous speech to the assembled troops at Tilbury in 1588, her claim to superiority was made ringingly clear: 'I know I have the body of a weak and feeble woman, but I have the heart and stomach of a king, and of a king of England too!'[32] Elizabeth was a political hermaphrodite, not only a queen, but a king as well.

As a virgin wife and mother, daughter of Henry VIII, instrument of God, and with the courage of a king, Elizabeth had risen above her sex; she had transcended the limitations of the ideal of womanhood. To Lord Burghley, late in his life, she was 'the wisest woman that ever was, for she understood the interests and dispositions of all the princes in her time, and was so perfect in the knowledge of her own realm that no counsellor could tell her anything she did not know before'. She was almost superhuman, and she was certainly superwoman. As William Camden put it, 'by these manly cares and counsels, she surpassed her sex'; Robert Cecil was less charitable – she was 'more than a man, and, in truth, sometime less than a woman'. Elizabeth had projected herself as a wonder, exempt from the conventions of her gender, and so she was accepted: a ballad at her death recorded;

> She ruled this nation by herself
> And was beholden to no man;
> Oh, she bore the sway of all affairs
> And yet she was but a woman.[33]

All this was possible, a woman could rule and rise above her natural weaknesses, because she had been chosen by God. Elizabeth cast herself as God's own instrument, and so responded to Calvin's argument that God might choose a female ruler for some special task. She had a strong sense of specific selection, and felt God's favour upon her. She told the Council at the beginning of her reign that 'the burthen that is fallen upon me maketh me amazed; and yet, considering I am God's creature, ordained to obey his appointment, I will thereunto yield, desiring from the bottom of my heart that I may have assistance of his grace to be the minister of his heavenly will in this office now committed to me'. Elizabeth's own view reflected John Foxe's argument that she had been protected and preserved through the reign of Mary, so that she could restore the Gospel. In the prayers she wrote about 1579, she asked God to keep her 'under the shadow of the wings of thy divine power, as thou hast done with a mighty hand since my childhood'. God had made her queen: 'It is thou who hast raised me and exalted me through thy providence to the throne', 'pulling me from the prison to the palace, and placing me a sovereign princess over thy people of England.'[34]

The proof that she was God's own queen lay in her success, which Elizabeth claimed as a sign of his favour. The Queen told Parliament in 1576 that 'I cannot attribute these haps and good successes to my device, without detracting much from the divine providence', and argued that 'These seventeen years God hath both prospered and protected you with good success under my direction.' She made much the same point to her last Parliament, in 1601: 'It hath pleased God (to whose honour it is spoken, without arrogation of any praise or merit to myself) by many hard escapes and hazards, both of diverse and strange natures, to make me an instrument of his holy will in delivering the state from danger and myself from dishonour.' Elizabeth's sex thus became, paradoxically, a propaganda weapon: if a woman could rule effectively, it must be because she had God's particular support. Lord Keeper Puckering used the argument at the opening of the 1593 Parliament: God 'enableth the weakest sex, and maketh them to admire it that ere now were wont to doubt their success'.[35] Because she had God's aid, the Queen had been able to confound those sceptical of a woman's ability to rule.

Elizabeth I's consciousness of divine favour gave her the psychological strength to beat the patriarchal system, to be more than a woman and to rule over men. But although she might be chosen by God in some special sense, all rulers held authority by divine appointment. She also gained confidence from her membership of the international union of princes, and she had a high sense of royal dignity. In 1582, she chastised a group of Dutch emissaries: 'You shoemakers, carpenters and heretics, how dare you speak in such terms to a man of royal blood like the duke of Alençon! I would have you know that when you approach him or me you are in the presence of the two greatest princes in Christendom.'[36] Elizabeth's legitimism was an important prop to her monarchy: whatever her sex, she was rightful ruler. This was a convenient domestic principle, but it caused her problems in foreign policy, for it sometimes clashed with the broader interests of the state. She continued to regard Mary Stuart as a queen, even after her abdication in 1567, and she seems to have been genuinely horrified by the Scottish lords' treatment of their monarch. Elizabeth's refusal to remove Mary from the English succession in 1572, her reluctance to have Mary tried in 1586, and her real anger and grief when Mary was executed in 1587 (anger the more intense because she knew she had to agree), reflect her recognition of Mary's royal status.

Elizabeth had declared in 1565 that 'she would not, to be a prince of a world, maintain any subject in any disobedience against the prince, for besides the offence of her conscience which should condemn her, she knew that Almighty God might justly recompense her with the like trouble in her own realm'. In fact, she reluctantly supported Protestant rebels in Scotland, France, and the Netherlands, but she feared that any infringement of another ruler's rights implied a diminution of her own. Elizabeth insisted upon the dignity of princes, as part of the maintenance of her own power, and she cloaked her female status in the garb of royalty. During her last illness in 1603, Robert Cecil told her she 'must' go to bed: 'Little man, little man!' she retorted, 'The word "must" is not to be used to princes!' Elizabeth was a woman, but above all she was a monarch: as she said a few weeks before her death, 'my sex cannot diminish my prestige'.[37]

· · · ·

NOTES AND REFERENCES

1. Nichols J 1823 *The Progresses and Public Processions of Queen Elizabeth* (3 vols). Nichols, vol. 1 pp. 38–60
2. Becon T 1844 *Prayers and Other Pieces*, Ayre J (ed.), Parker Society, p. 227
3. Wernham R B 1966 *Before the Armada*. Cape, p. 237; Harrison G B (ed.) 1938 *The Elizabethan Journals, 1591–1603* (3 vols). Routledge & Kegan Paul, vol. 1 p. 126
4. de Maisse A H 1931 *A Journal of All That Was Accomplished by Monsieur de Maisse*. Nonsuch, p. 115; Emmison F G 1970 *Elizabethan Life: disorder*. Essex County Council, p. 57; Barton A 1981 Harking back to

Elizabeth: Ben Jonson and Caroline nostalgia, *English Literary History* 48: 711

5. Hartley T E (ed.) 1981 *Proceedings in the Parliaments of Elizabeth I, 1558–1581.* Leicester, p. 94; Read C 1925 *Mr Secretary Walsingham and the Policy of Queen Elizabeth* (3 vols). Oxford, vol. 1 p. 320; Haugaard W P 1981 Elizabeth Tudor's *Book of Devotions, Sixteenth Century Journal* 12: 96

6. Smith L B 1975 *Elizabeth Tudor: portrait of a queen.* Hutchinson, p. 120

7. *Calendar of Salisbury Manuscripts* vol. 1 p. 158

8. Hartley T E (ed.) 1981 pp. 64, 110

9. Hartley T E (ed.) 1981 p. 464

10. Read C 1925 vol. 1 pp. 402–3

11. Read C 1955 *Mr Secretary Cecil and Queen Elizabeth.* Cape, p. 211. There is useful new material on these manœuvres and the public response to them in Bernard G W (forthcoming) A mid-Tudor chronicle, *Camden Miscellany.* (I am grateful to Dr Bernard for allowing me to see his transcript of this document.)

12. Neale J E 1979 *Queen Elizabeth I.* Panther edn, p. 143

13. Johnson P 1974 *Elizabeth I: a study in power and intellect.* Weidenfeld & Nicolson, p. 112; Read C 1925 vol. 1 p. 292

14. Melvil J 1683 *The Memoires* Scott G (ed.), p. 49; Naunton R 1641 *Fragmenta regalia, or observations on the late Queen Elizabeth, her times and favorits,* p. 6

15. Williams N 1967 *Elizabeth, Queen of England.* Weidenfeld & Nicolson, pp. 129–30; Smith L B 1975 p. 125

16. Camden W 1675 *The History of the Most Renowned and Victorious Princess Elizabeth,* p. 269

17. Read E P, Read C (eds) 1951 *Elizabeth of England: certain observations concerning the life and reign of Queen Elizabeth by John Clapham.* Pennsylvania, p. 68

18. Pollard A F 1919 *The History of England from the Accession of Edward VI to the Death of Elizabeth* (2nd edn). Longmans, Green, pp. 181, 244, 326

19. Read C 1955 p. 357

20. Read C 1955 p. 266

21. Hartley T E (ed.) 1981 pp. 59–60

22. MacCaffrey W T 1968 *The Shaping of the Elizabethan Regime.* Princeton, p. 210; Hartley T E (ed.) 1981 pp. 135, 138

23. Hartley T E (ed.) 1981 p. 148
24. Levine M 1966 *The Early Elizabethan Succession Question, 1558–1568*. Stanford, p. 19;   Firth C H 1909 The ballad history of the reigns of the later Tudors, *Transactions of the Royal Historical Society* 3rd series 3: 96
25. Read C 1955 p. 229;   Neale J E 1979 pp. 113–14;   Hartley T E (ed.) 1981 p. 147
26. Neale J E 1979 p. 113;   Bernard G W (forthcoming)
27. de Maisse A H 1931 p. 110
28. Neale J E 1953 *Elizabeth I and her Parliaments, 1559–1581*. Cape, p. 49;   Heisch A 1980 Queen Elizabeth I and the persistence of patriarchy, *Feminist Review* 4: 46–7;   Yates F A 1975 *Astraea: the imperial theme in the sixteenth century*. Routledge & Kegan Paul, pp. 78–9
29. Camden W 1675 p. 27;   Harington J 1804 *Nugae Antiquae* (2 vols). Park T (ed.). Vernon & Hood, vol. 1 p. 178;   Heisch A 1980: 50;   Haugaard W P 1981: 96
30. Nichols J 1823 vol. 1 p. 58;   Taylor-Smither L J 1984 Elizabeth I: a psychological profile, *Sixteenth Century Journal* 15: 66
31. Hartley T E (ed.) 1981 pp. 94, 148;   Haugaard W P 1981: 96
32. Williams N 1967 p. 290;   Neale J E 1957 *Elizabeth I and Her Parliaments, 1584–1601*. Cape, p. 118;   Neale J E 1979 p. 302
33. Smith L B 1975 p. 81;   Camden W 1675 p. 32;   Harington J 1804 vol. 1 p. 345;   Williams N 1967 p. 354
34. Williams N 1967 p. 51;   Haugaard W P 1981: 93–4
35. Neale J E 1953 pp. 364–5;   Neale J E 1957 pp. 248, 428–9;   Neale J E 1976 *The Elizabethan House of Commons*. Fontana edn, p. 348
36. Smith L B 1975 pp. 62–3
37. Read C 1955 p. 345;   Smith L B 1975 p. 61;   *Calendar of State Papers Venetian, 1592–1603*, p. 533

Chapter 2

THE QUEEN AND THE CHURCH

When Elizabeth became queen, she was immediately cast as a 'pushy' woman. Philip II's agent, the Count of Feria, reported on her bossiness, and an imperial envoy was contemptuous: 'Like a peasant on whom a barony has been conferred, she, since she came to the throne, is puffed up with pride and imagines that she is without peer.'[1] She *was* bossy, she was something of a fishwife (or fish-virgin), partly because she had to establish immediate authority over sceptical men and partly because she had a sense of her own destiny. In the collection of private devotions she composed about 1579, Queen Elizabeth presented herself as God's instrument for the restoration of the Gospel, as mother of the Church in England, and as protectress of religious refugees. It is true that in her prayers she dressed herself as she would like God to see her, rather than as she actually was. But her self-image was as patroness of the Gospel and she took her religious duties seriously.

It has been usual for historians to suppose that Elizabeth cared little for religion, except as a political weapon in the maintenance of order, but this is probably unfair. She was a political realist, but this does not mean that she was indifferent to spiritual things: she cared about right religion, but she would not take foolish risks for it. There is some evidence of real personal commitment, and she certainly preserved a public face of piety. In 1544, she had spent perhaps four months translating and producing a fair copy of Marguerite of Navarre's mildly Protestant *Mirror of a Sinful Soul*, and in her teenage years she cultivated an image of godly austerity at Court. As queen, she attended morning service every day in her chapel, and her dutifulness was much commented upon by visitors. Her own book of private devotions was a highly personal collection of prayers in English, French, Italian, Latin, and Greek, adorned with Hilliard miniatures of herself and her suitor Alençon. Her prayers show her sense of personal sin, and her awareness of dependence upon God. She asked for the support of the Holy Spirit to do God's will: 'So shall this my kingdom through thee be established with peace; so shall thy Church be edified with power; so shall thy Gospel be published with zeal; so shall my reign be continued with prosperity; so shall my life be prolonged with happiness; and so shall my self at thy good pleasure be translated into immortality.'[2]

There can be little doubt of Elizabeth's personal Protestantism. Her private prayers were Protestant, embodying reformed assumptions on salvation by Christ's imputed merits and justification by faith alone. She recognised that she differed in religion from most of her fellow rulers, and thanked God that he had 'from my earliest days kept me back from the deep abysses of natural ignorance and damnable superstitions, that I might enjoy the great sun of righteousness which brings with its rays life and salvation, while still leaving so many kings, princes and princesses in ignorance under the power of Satan'. It is true that she had conformed to Catholic requirements in the reign of Mary, but her devotions were ostentatious only when she was most suspected. Perhaps she contemplated a move back towards Catholicism in 1561 as a means to make a Dudley marriage possible, but if she did she soon abandoned the idea. Elizabeth claimed to be an idealist, to have put true religion before political calculation; she asked the 1576 Parliament, 'If policy had been preferred before truth, would I, trow you, even at the first beginning of my rule, have turned upside down so great affairs, or entered into the tossing of the great waves and billows of the world?' Ten years later, she told a parliamentary delegation she had been consistently reformist: 'When first I took the sceptre, my title made me not forget the giver, and therefore [I] began, as became me, with such religion as both I was born in, bred in, and, I trust, shall die in.'[3]

Queen Elizabeth was publicly identified with the Protestant movement, by others and by herself. Soon after her accession the Scottish reformer Alexander Alesius greeted her as a Protestant heroine and successor to Anne Boleyn, the progenitor of the Protestant cause in England. The Protestant Duchess of Suffolk wrote with enthusiasm, 'If the Israelites might joy in their Deborah, how much more we English in our Elizabeth.'[4] Ballads presented her accession as the triumph of the Gospel and the deliverance of the godly from persecution, themes given historical perspective by John Foxe in 1563. Protestant books were immediately dedicated to the new Queen – the Geneva edition of the Psalms in 1559, the Geneva Bible in 1560, and books of piety and polemic throughout the reign. Protestant authors assumed Elizabeth's commitment to their cause, because the Queen had signalled her allegiance. She had walked out of her Christmas mass in 1558 at the elevation of the host, and she had absented herself from mass and scorned the monks' procession at the opening of Parliament in 1559. In 1572 she ordered Sir Francis Knollys to tell the Commons that 'as she is termed the defender of the faith, so she will be found the protector of true Protestants'. Elizabeth had deliberately adopted a Protestant image: in 1581 Sir Walter Mildmay described her as 'a princess known by long experience to be a principal patron of the Gospel, virtuous, wise, faithful, just'.[5]

Some of this was political posturing to ensure the loyalty of the godly, but the posture was effective because it was close to the truth. Elizabeth had, as she claimed, taken great risks in 1559 to introduce the Gospel. Although advice had been sought at the beginning of the reign from those favourable to reform, they had counselled caution. The author of the 'Device for Alteration of Religion' warned that, if Elizabeth reintroduced official Protestantism, the Pope would excommunicate her, the French would invade England, the Irish might rebel, and English Catholics would cause trouble. Richard Goodrich and Sir Nicholas Throckmorton advised against hasty action, and Armagil Waad reminded the Queen 'how dangerous it is to make alteration in religion, especially in the beginning of a prince's reign'.[6] But, despite later appearances, Elizabeth was a Protestant, and those close to her were Protestants. She proposed to attract popularity by maligning her sister's rule, and by claiming to inaugurate a new era. If she wished to break with the past, she would have to dismiss Mary's councillors and her bishops, and she would have to replace them with Protestant Edwardians. So Elizabeth publicly threw in her lot with the Protestants: the first official sermon of the reign was preached by William Bill, a known Protestant; pulpits at Court and at St Paul's Cross were monopolised by Protestants; and Richard Cox, a returned exile, preached the sermon which opened Parliament. Elizabeth had chosen her future: she was going to have a Protestant Church of England.

But, as Norman Jones has shown,[7] the process of getting her Protestant Church turned out to be difficult. At first all went well. In February 1559 the Privy Council introduced into the House of Commons a Bill to restore the royal supremacy over the Church, and two Bills to restore the Protestant services of Edward's reign. By 21 February, these three had been amalgamated into a single Reformation Bill, and pushed through the Commons. But the Bill encountered resistance in the Lords: the restoration of the Book of Common Prayer was deleted, and the amended Bill simply told the Queen she could take the supremacy if she wished. Opposition had been led by the Catholic bishops, but they had received enough support from lay peers for official policy to be blocked. Protestant councillors recovered the initiative by a combination of political muscle and political luck: a rigged disputation on religion tried to show that the Catholic bishops were obscurantist and obdurate, and two of them were imprisoned, while their voting strength was further reduced by illnesses and death

After Easter the government played safe, proceeding in the Commons with two Bills, one on the supremacy and another on liturgy, and making them a little less offensive to conservatives; both passed through the House. The Supremacy Bill made the Queen supreme *governor* rather than supreme head, and repealed the heresy laws; it passed the Lords despite the opposition of the Catholic bishops, partly because conservative peers had been alienated by the contentious issue of Church lands. The Uniformity Bill had a much more difficult ride: it passed the Lords only by a three-vote margin, against the opposition of all the bishops, two privy councillors, and seven other peers. The conservative vote had been weakened by imprisonments, but also by royal concessions to make the Prayer Book less offensive. The words of administration at communion had been altered to allow a Catholic understanding of a real presence of Christ in the bread and wine; the vestments and ornaments at communion were to be those of the mass; abuse of the Pope was deleted from the Litany; and in church services ministers were to stand where Catholic priests had stood. These amendments had emphasised continuity with the Catholic past: a compromise settlement had been forced on a reformist queen by the resistance of conservatives in the Lords.

It was once argued that a compromise settlement had been

forced on a conservative queen by the resistance of radicals in the Commons. Sir John Neale suggested that Elizabeth had wanted a much more 'Catholic' Church, but, since the conservative bishops refused to accept a royal supremacy, she had to give in to the Protestant clamour for a more radical settlement.[8] Although the evidence is inconclusive, this view appears to be wrong. Neale attached significance to the peace negotiations at Cateau-Cambresis: he thought Elizabeth had to pursue a conservative policy, at least until a treaty had been signed and England was safely out of the war. But it was Elizabeth herself who had delayed the peace, by her unrealistic demand for the return of Calais, and the negotiations did not determine her parliamentary strategy. Indeed, it is not impossible that the state of war was deliberately prolonged by Elizabeth herself to weaken the resistance of conservative peers to her religious proposals. Neale also exaggerated the political weight of the Protestant radicals in the Commons. Only nineteen Marian exiles were elected to the 1559 Parliament, and some returned too late to play any active role. The radicals were not an organised pressure group able to dominate the Commons, which was usually controlled by the Council and its agents. The Queen's tactics had been designed to contain conservative opposition in the Lords, not radical pressure in the Commons. Above all, the Neale version of 1559 simply does not fit with what we know of the religion of Elizabeth and her advisors. Even if the Queen herself is dismissed as a politique, it is difficult to see that William Cecil, Nicholas Bacon, Francis Knollys, and the Earl of Bedford would have headed a regime aiming for anything less than a Protestant settlement. Elizabeth and those close to her wanted a Protestant Church of England, and that is what they tried to get.

But it was not precisely what they achieved, for Elizabeth was badly frightened by her clash with the Lords. It was not the determined speeches of the Catholic bishops which were the problem, but the votes of the Catholic nobles. The nine lay votes against the Uniformity Bill were an embarrassment, especially as two came from privy councillors; they were also a danger, since some came from powerful regional magnates. The Queen back-pedalled on the Book of Common Prayer, and then sought further means of conciliating conservative opinion. Only the most obviously hard-line Catholic bishops were removed from the bench, and those who had conformed under Edward VI were left in office for a time in the hope that they would knuckle under again and lend continuity to the episcopate. Some of the more radical Protestant ministers proposed to Elizabeth for bishoprics, Becon, Lever, Nowell, and Sampson, were passed over. The Queen's own royal injunctions introduced further liturgical modifications, which blurred the departure from the Catholic past: the communion table was to stand where the altar had been, and wafers were permitted at communion. In 1560, a Latin edition of the Prayer Book for use in colleges allowed reservation of the communion elements for the sick, and requiem celebrations for the dead. In 1561, a new edition of the ecclesiastical calendar restored fifty-nine abrogated saints' days.

When enforcement of even her moderated settlement encountered resistance in the parishes, Queen Elizabeth attempted further moves in a conservative direction – but now found that she was alienating her Protestant allies. In October 1559, she had a crucifix and candles restored to the altar of her chapel, and she seems to have decided to have roods (the great crosses which hung in chancels) restored to parish churches. The new Protestant bishops threatened to resign, and wrote a joint letter of protest to the Queen that images were contrary to the Second Commandment. There was then a tacit compromise: the bishops were not required to restore roods in their dioceses, but the Queen kept her own cross (which was thrown down by fanatics in 1562 and 1567, only to be restored on each occasion). Elizabeth also tried to enforce the wearing of full Catholic vestments, but many Protestant ministers found that even the surplice strained their conscience. Again, there was a compromise: the 'Bishops' Interpretations' in 1560 ordered that only the cope need be worn for communion, other vestments were quietly dropped, and there was little effort to enforce even copes.

It may have been these episcopal successes which prompted the Queen's suspiciously public espousal of Dudley's 'Spanish strategy' early in 1561. The leaked rumour that she was considering concessions to Catholics to gain the support of Spain may have been designed to shock the Protestants into obedience: if so, it failed. In the summer of 1561 she apparently contemplated banning clerical marriage (a particular bugbear of conservative parishioners and virgin queens), but was vigorously opposed by Cecil and Archbishop Parker. Instead, in August 1561, Elizabeth revenged herself on the Protestant higher clergy by driving wives and children from colleges and cathedral closes. But if she had suffered a series of defeats in 1559-61, she had minor victories over her bishops in 1563. She herself amended the Articles of Religion, after they had been agreed by the bishops. She added a sentence to Article 20 on the authority of the Church, which confirmed her right to alter liturgy (thus preserving the possibility of further concessions to Catholics); and she deleted Article 29, on the presence of the wicked at the Lord's Supper, which could be read as an attack on the real presence doctrine. From 1563 to 1571 (when the bishops restored Article 29), Elizabeth allowed the Church of England Thirty-eight, not Thirty-nine, Articles.

By her deliberate interventions, the Queen had blunted the Protestantism of her government's original programme. She had made concessions on the very issues which laypeople most noticed – the dress and movements of the priest, clerical marriage, the position of the altar – and believed most strongly – the real presence of Christ in the Eucharist. In doing so, she had raised the hopes of conservatives. There were persistent rumours of further religious change – in London and Coventry in 1561, in Cumbria in 1562, in Lancashire and elsewhere in 1565. Catholics came to think that the Queen might be won over, and in 1564-65 a spate of Catholic books dedicated to Elizabeth was published by exiles at Antwerp. But the concessions to Catholics brought Elizabeth into dispute with Protestants, and provoked demands for further reform: in his sermon at the opening of the 1571 Parliament, Bishop Sandys asked that the Church be purged of 'Judaical and heathenish rites'. The Queen's Protestant commitment, which had seemed so certain in 1559, was called into question. There was a suspicion, as was reported to the Commons in 1571, that the Queen 'is of another religion than is published', and there were further stories of a return to Catholicism in 1579-80, during the Alençon negotiations. There was uncertainty about the nature and the future of English religion. In 1567, before he set off as ambassador to the Holy Roman Emperor, the Earl of Sussex put the question bluntly: 'As to the question of religion, he wished to be quite clear about it before he left, because, although he was a native-born Englishman and knew as well as others what was passing in the country, he was at a loss to state what was the religion that really was observed here.'[9]

The ecclesiastical decisions of 1559–63 seemed to make no coherent sense, and the 'Elizabethan Settlement' had, apparently, settled nothing. But, to the surprise of everyone except the Queen, the uneasy compromise was maintained and Elizabeth tried to freeze her Church in the form it had reached by 1563. Elizabeth was perhaps the only determined 'Anglican' in England: she told the Commons in 1585, 'For as she found it at her first coming in, and so hath maintained it these twenty-seven years, she meant in like state, by God's grace, to continue it and leave it behind her.' She blocked what Protestants regarded as essential further reform. In 1566 and 1571 there was pressure in Parliament for ecclesiastical reform, from a coalition of councillors, bishops, and Protestant MPs managed by the Council's 'men of business' – but Elizabeth forbade discussion of some Bills (claiming infringement of prerogative) and vetoed another. More radical proposals were made in the Parliaments of 1584–85 and 1586–87, apparently by militant minorities: again, the Queen prohibited debate, declaring the programmes 'most prejudicial to the religion established, to her crown, to her government and to her subjects'. She had made her determination clear in a message to the Commons in 1585: 'Resolutely, she will receive no motion of innovation, nor alter or change any law whereby the religion or Church of England standeth established at this day.'[10]

That the Queen refused further reform was bad enough for the Protestants: that she expected the absurdities of 1559 to be observed was even worse. The Protestant clergy found that Elizabeth persisted in her determination to make them look like Catholic priests, and she promoted campaigns to enforce conformity in dress. In January 1565 the Queen wrote to Archbishop Parker, stressing the need for 'unity, quietness and concord, as well amongst the public ministers having charge under us as in the multitude of the people by us and them ruled',[11] and ordering the enforcement of clerical uniformity in ceremony and doctrine. Parker and his bishops recognised the difficulty of imposing the full rules of 1559, and instead tried to ensure that ministers at least wore the surplice for communion (expecting copes only in cathedrals and colleges). In consequence of this concession, Elizabeth refused to sanction the 'Advertisements' on dress in 1566, and left the bishops to deprive a few resisters on their own authority. A further intervention by the Queen in 1566 forced bishops into more determined action: at a meeting with Parker and colleagues in March, she ordered Bishop Grindal to proceed against nonconformists in London. Grindal held a meeting of his clergy, paraded a clerical mannequin before them, and suspended from office the thirty-seven ministers who refused the prescribed dress.

In the mid-1580s there were further clashes over vestments and, especially, ceremonies in church. John Whitgift was probably deliberately chosen by Elizabeth as Archbishop of Canterbury, as a man who would enforce the controverted rituals. At his St Paul's Cathedral sermon on Accession Day 1583, Whitgift announced his attack on nonconformists. In a campaign which had the Queen's explicit support, he forced ministers to subscribe to articles which promised liturgical obedience, and suspended those who refused. This determination brought the Archbishop into conflict with Protestant privy councillors, some of whom apparently organised protests against Whitgift's policy in the Parliament of 1584–85. There was a bitter struggle within the regime, which forced Elizabeth to try to impose agreement among her advisors. In a carefully balanced statement to a meeting of bishops and councillors in 1585, the Queen defused some Protestant criticism by complaining of episcopal complacency; she then ordered the bishops to proceed against nonconformists, threatened to dismiss councillors who prompted parliamentary agitation, and sent a message to the Commons prohibiting further proceedings on religion.

It is not obvious why Elizabeth got herself into such difficulties over the surplice and a few controversial ceremonies. Perhaps she preferred some ritual in religion, though in 1558–59 she had given clear indications to the contrary. She certainly disliked disobedience to her laws, and she disliked invasion of what she saw as her prerogative in religion. Perhaps, as William Haugaard has suggested,[12] she was reluctant to weaken her own authority by sanctioning any decline from the liturgical standard set in 1559; it is significant that she refused to give formal approval to the 'Advertisements' of 1566 and the Canons of 1571, which made concessions to Protestant sensibilities. But if her prerogative was the issue, she would have preserved it better by herself amending the rules, rather than by provoking opposition through insistence upon observation of the insufferable. Her determination brought running battles, not only, as Sir John Neale thought, with radicals in the Commons, but with many councillors and bishops too; she offended godly ministers and the godly laity, those to whom she had most obviously appealed at the beginning of the reign. Some significant political explanation seems required, and it is probably to be found in her reluctance to provoke conservative opinion. Elizabeth I was soft on Catholics.

It was a constant complaint of the godly that 'their' queen would not unequivocally commit herself to their cause. They recognised that this was probably because of her concern for conservatives. Sir Francis Knollys told the Commons in 1571:

> what cause there might be to make her Majesty not to run and join with those who seem to be earnest, we are not to search; whether it be for that orderly and in time she hopeth to bring them all with her, or what secret cause or other scrupulosity there may be in princes, it is not for all sorts to know.[13]

Elizabeth could not admit that she was afraid of Catholics, indeed she behaved in ways which made some advisers think she was insufficiently afraid of them. But many of her policies were framed with at least half an eye to English Catholic opinion (and perhaps a glance towards Spain). Elizabeth's liturgical conservatism, her enforcement of clerical conformity, her reluctance to support Protestant rebels abroad, her restraint of Protestant preaching, and her moderation of the persecution of Catholics, all suggest a determination not to drive the Catholics into outright opposition. The same may be true of the burning of two Dutch anabaptists at Smithfield in 1575: the Queen herself signed the warrant, and specified the traditional place of execution, thus emphasising her personal hostility to heresy.

Elizabeth wanted to be queen of the English, not queen of the Protestants, and she tried to associate conservatives with her regime. In 1558 she kept the more moderate (and, it is true, more powerful) of Mary's Catholic councillors in office, Winchester, Arundel, Derby, and Shrewsbury. Sir James Croft was appointed a councillor in 1566, and the Earl of Worcester in 1601; both seem to have been Catholics willing to accept a royal supremacy. In 1579 there were stories that the Queen was considering Catholic nominees for the Council, to bolster support for her marriage to Alençon. There was a Catholic circle at Court in 1581–82, with the Earl of Oxford, Lord Henry Howard, Francis Southwell, and Charles Arundel, though they formed a somewhat disreputable group. Elizabeth visited her Catholic nobles on her summer progress: her six-day stay with Lord Montagu in 1591 signalled her recognition of his unshakeable loyalty, and brought his wife to tears. She tried to comprehend Catholics within the nation, and when they were executed she insisted that it was for their disloyalty to the nation and its queen. Elizabeth was almost proud of her loyal Catholic subjects. When travelling on progress in 1568, Elizabeth heard an elderly bystander call out 'Vivat Regina'; she beamed, and told her companion, the Spanish Ambassador, 'This good old man is a clergyman of the old religion.'[14]

Elizabeth has been credited with a deliberate policy of toleration towards Catholics, to draw them gradually into conformity to the Church of England. Certainly there was a rhetoric of even-handedness against Protestant and Catholic deviation. Lord Keeper Bacon declared at the end of the 1559 Parliament that the laws should be enforced upon 'as well those that be too swift as those that be too slow, those, I say, that go before the law or beyond the law, as those that will not follow'. Elizabeth herself made the same point to Archbishop Parker in 1571: no one should be 'suffered to decline either on the left or on the right hand from the direct line limited by authority of our said laws'.[15] Although Protestants were horrified to be presented as a danger equal to the papists, Elizabeth told Parliament in 1585 that she would neither 'animate Romanists' nor 'tolerate new-fangledness'. There was, too, a rhetoric of toleration of opinions. A proclamation in 1570 promised no investigation of the beliefs of those whose conduct was 'not manifestly repugnant and obstinate to the laws of the realm', and the Lord Keeper told judges that Elizabeth wished nobody 'molested by any inquisition or examination of their consciences in causes of religion' provided they did not flout the law.[16]

Francis Bacon's gloss on this declared policy is well known 'Her Majesty, not liking to make windows into men's hearts and secret thoughts, except the abundance of them did overflow into overt express acts and affirmations, tempered her law so as it restraineth only manifest disobedience in impugning and impeaching advisedly and ambitiously her Majesty's supreme power, and maintaining foreign jurisdiction.' There is some justice in his claim that Elizabeth protected the consciences of Catholics. When a 1563 statute prescribed execution for a second refusal of the supremacy oath, the Queen ordered her archbishop to ensure that no one was asked to take the oath twice. In 1571, a Bill to punish absence from communion passed the Commons and the Lords, with the support of bishops and councillors, but the Queen vetoed it – and she blocked the proposal when it was repeated again in 1572, 1576 and 1581. But Elizabeth's tolerance was extremely limited. She claimed, as in 1591, that Catholics were executed only for treason, not for 'matter of religion'[17] – but if she believed that, it was because she allowed herself to be deceived by officials who framed Catholics, and because the definition of treason had been extended to include actions which Catholics could hardly avoid. Men and women might differ from Elizabeth in religion, provided they did nothing about it and kept their opinions to themselves. It was not a policy to permit the survival of inoffensive Catholicism, but a policy to stifle the old religion so that it died in a generation.

Queen Elizabeth defended her military intervention in the Netherlands in 1585 as principled protection of the Dutch from an inquisition, but this was a propaganda smokescreen – she was pursuing English national interests as she saw them. She had claimed not to be forcing the consciences of the English, but she restrained herself for policy, not principle. She was tolerant when intolerance was dangerous, and intolerant when tolerance was dangerous. In the 1560s and 1570s, when the Queen could expect that English Catholicism would die out if it was not provoked to militant resistance, consciences were not forced; even the external act of recusancy was only punished during political scares, as in the aftermath of the Revolt of the Northern Earls and the publication of the papal bull of deposition. Limited toleration of Catholics made good political sense: repression would be administratively difficult, especially with so many conservatives among the justices and clergy, and possibly counter-productive. So Elizabeth made tolerant virtue out of political necessity. But, later, the balance of advantage changed.

With the inflow of Catholic seminary-priests from 1574, and the arrival of the Jesuits in 1580, Catholic resistance was hardening; with a new supply of priests, the old religion was not going to die out – it would have to be murdered. Elizabeth adjusted slowly to the new circumstances – she was always reluctant to change a policy which had worked. She was probably responsible for the reduction of penalties against recusants proposed in a 1581 Bill, and in 1582 Leicester wailed that 'Nothing in this world grieveth me more than to see her Majesty believes this increase of papists in her realm can be no danger to her.'[18] But then she gave in: a proclamation of 1582 declared all seminary priests and Jesuits to be traitors, so that status became a crime, and this definition was given statutory force in 1585. From 1583, the Council entrusted detection of recusants to specific recusancy commissions, rather than the ordinary processes of law enforcement, and pressure upon even apolitical Catholics increased. The rhetoric of the free conscience was maintained, but Catholics were fined, imprisoned, and even executed for what had been winked at before. Until 1582, Elizabeth had been afraid to persecute Catholics: thereafter, she was afraid not to.

But at least for the first half of her reign, Elizabeth had tried to avoid giving needless offence to Catholics. It is this which explains her conflicts with the godly Protestants, as she sought to contain those aspects of Protestantism which might alienate conservatives. Her clash with Archbishop Grindal over the prophesyings should be seen in this light, for on preaching, as on other issues, Elizabeth's attempts to conciliate Catholics offended good Protestants. Prophesyings were regular local meetings at which ministers expounded biblical texts for comment by their leaders; they were in-service training sessions to produce a more effective preaching ministry, and, since laypeople were often present, they were a means of evangelisation. The prophesyings emphasised the Protestantism of the Church of England, sought to make it a missionary Church, and, as JPs were often present, they seemed to associate the state with the missionary enterprise. All these aspects must have worried a queen nervous of Catholic opinion, and in 1574 Elizabeth ordered Bishop Sandys to suppress the London prophesyings. Sandys protested that the meetings were well established and useful, and procrastinated. When Archbishop Parker passed on the same prohibition to the diocese of Norwich, Bishop Parkhurst solicited the help of privy councillors, but he had to begin action against the meetings. In 1575, Elizabeth ordered the Bishop of Lincoln to suppress prophesyings in his diocese, but he too temporised, sought support from local JPs, and acted only reluctantly. In 1576, on progress through the Midlands, Elizabeth heard of the popular prophesying at Southam, and ordered the Bishop of Lichfield to put it down.

So far, the royal campaign against prophesyings had been piecemeal, as particular meetings had come to the Queen's attention. But in 1576 she instructed Archbishop Grindal to suppress all exercises and to restrict the number of licensed preachers to three or four in each diocese: she was determined to reduce the evangelistic efforts of the Church of England. Grindal was twice given direct verbal orders by the Queen herself, but he would not obey. First, he circularised his diocesans, to get full endorsement of the prophesyings from ten of the fifteen replies, and then he wrote to the Queen refusing to carry out her orders. Grindal produced a determined defence of the necessity of preaching, and virtually told Elizabeth to look after the state and leave religion to the bishops. The supreme governor of the Church was furious: Grindal was suspended from office, and in May 1577 Elizabeth herself ordered the bishops to suppress the prophesyings (though, significantly, she now dropped the demand for a reduction in preaching, probably through lack of support from her Council; Grindal's disobedience had at least narrowed the issue to the prophesyings). There then followed tortuous manœuvres, in which the Queen intermittently tried to force a confrontation with her Archbishop, and leading councillors tried to protect Grindal from her wrath and work out a compromise. For six years, until Grindal's death in 1583, the Church had no active Archbishop of Canterbury.

Why did Elizabeth proceed so far, and produce the scandal of a suspended archbishop? The Privy Council blamed 'the great divisions and sects that had grown, and were like to increase, by reason of these exercises' (prophesyings), undermining unity in doctrine and liturgy. But this explanation was advanced because the Council wished to confine the issue to the prophesyings, and to achieve a settlement by suppression of the most rowdy meetings or the exclusion of the laity. Elizabeth's objection seems to have been to the increase of Protestant preaching in the Church of England, which was offensive to conservative conformists and often divisive in parishes. In March 1576, she had been presented with a parliamentary petition on religious reform, which had bewailed the shortage of preaching, 'the only ordinary means of salvation of souls and the only good means to teach your Majesty's subjects to know their true obedience'.[19] Elizabeth had promised reform, either through Convocation or through her own direct action, and Convocation had introduced new rules on the recruitment of clergy.' But the Queen had no intention of increasing preaching: rather, as her clash with Grindal showed, she wished to reduce it.

At a meeting with her bishops and councillors in 1585, Elizabeth had criticised the bishops for allowing variety in preaching and ritual. When Lord Burghley tried to twist her comments into an attack on bishops for ordaining unlearned ministers, Archbishop Whitgift replied that it was impossible to produce educated ministers for England's 13,000 churches. 'Jesus, thirteen thousand!' cried the Queen, 'It is not to be looked for ... My meaning is not you should make choice of learned ministers only, for they are not to be found, but of honest, sober and wise men, and such as can read the scriptures and homilies well unto the people.'[20] 'Read the scriptures and homilies well' – that was what Elizabeth wanted, and it was a far cry from the demand of the godly, councillors, bishops, ministers, and people, for an educated, preaching, pro-testantising ministry.

Elizabeth ascended the throne as the Protestants' Queen, but she soon came into conflict with them. Over the making of the Prayer Book, her refusal to amend it, her enforcement of conformity, her caution in the repression of Catholics, and her restriction of preaching, she clashed with Protestant leaders and Protestant opinion. Her reign can thus appear to have been, and was described by Neale as, a long-running battle with 'puritans', as she struggled to contain the dynamic forces of radical Protestantism.[21] But 'puritans' were a problem mainly because Elizabeth had gone so far to conciliate Catholics. By her early concessions and her later insistence upon them, Elizabeth contained the problem of conservatism, but at the cost of creating a problem of 'radicalism'. But it was an odd form of radicalism, which was espoused by the leading members of the Privy Council and the majority of the bishops. Elizabeth had shifted the centre of ecclesiastical gravity, and in doing so had pushed her own religious advisers and officials into an opposition role. Until she was able to appoint a generation of bishops who accepted the Church of England produced in 1559, and who had matured within it, the Queen's defence of her 'settlement' put her at loggerheads with her bishops and many of her councillors. Everyone was out of step except Elizabeth.

Despite her own personal Protestantism, Elizabeth's fear of Catholics led her to treat religion as a matter of political expediency. In a heroically foolish sermon in February 1570, Edward Dering told her to her face that she was betraying the faith by her narrowly secular interests. He listed the defects of the Church which prevented an effective evangelical effort, and turned to the Queen – 'and yet you, in the meanwhile that all these whoredoms are committed, you at whose hands God will require it, you sit still and are careless. Let men do as they list. It toucheth not belike your commonwealth, and therefore you are so well contented to let all alone.' Elizabeth's political priorities put her bishops, and especially the first generation of them, in an impossible position. The Queen imposed prescriptions of ceremony and clerical dress which most of them disliked, but she refused to give them public support and expected them to incur the opprobrium of enforcement. She ordered them to strike down nonconformists, but her own councillors impeded them and protected the disobedient. She expected them to be firm disciplinarians and despised them for their failures, but she undermined their status and weakened their power by filching their property. Archbishop Parker complained in 1575 that 'Her Majesty told me that I had supreme government ecclesiastical, but what is it to govern encumbered with such subtlety?'[22]

The Queen gave her bishops a difficult and somewhat distasteful job to do, and then denied them the means to do it effectively. The endowments of bishoprics, which might have supported the prestige of the episcopate and financed more effective administration, were milked for political purposes. The official attitude towards episcopal property became clear at the beginning of the reign. The 1559 Act of Exchange empowered the Queen to substitute impropriated tithes for episcopal lands during vacancies of sees, and it was probably designed to make a quick killing for the Crown after the deprivations of Marian bishops. The vigorous opposition of the Protestant bishops-elect seems to have limited the impact of the Act, and exchanges were enforced against only eleven sees: losses were marginal rather than disastrous. But a subsidiary provision of the Act caused much more damage. Leases of episcopal property were limited to twenty years' duration, unless they were made to the Crown; this led to Elizabeth forcing bishops to give her long leases, which she then transferred to councillors, courtiers, and nobles as political rewards.

Initially, Elizabeth's use of this ploy was modest: between 1559 and 1573, only four long leases were taken by the Queen and passed on, two to William Cecil and two to members of her Privy Chamber. But between 1574 and 1603 at least 57 leases were extorted, for lengths of 40-120 years. Such leases were made a condition of episcopal appointment. In 1584, Raleigh was able to ensure than Godwin got the see of Bath and Wells only in return for a 99-year lease of Wiveliscombe. After Scambler moved to Norwich, in 1588 he gave an 80-year lease of 61 manors, which went to Sir Thomas Heneage. There was little point in protesting: Hutton almost lost his chance of the see of York when, in 1594, he queried the morality of the Queen's demands – Robert Cecil warned him that 'These niceties will hardly be admitted where such a prince vouchsafes to entreat.' When Bilson got Winchester, he had to give leases worth 2,000 marks to Sir Francis Carew: Elizabeth wrote firmly to him in 1596: 'We require therefore a speedy lease in reversion to him, such as shall reward his long service and be least hurtful to the bishopric.' But against greedy courtiers, her second condition was not often observed. In 1592 Elizabeth extracted a lease of Sherborne from the Bishop of Salisbury for Raleigh, but after some ruthless bullying Raleigh got the next bishop to cede ownership in 1599. No wonder Harington remarked that courtiers were more accustomed to 'prey on the Church than in the church'.[23]

Elizabeth bullied her bishops, milked their revenues, and sapped their institutional strength. Her control of appointments gave her the whip-hand over ambitious clergy. When Richard Fletcher acquired the bishopric of Bristol in 1589, he had to surrender some of the property of an already ill-endowed see. Thereafter he managed to make himself one of Elizabeth's favourite clerics by his sermons and his flattery: Harington reported that 'he knew what would please the queen, and would adventure on that, though it offended others'. But in 1595 he had to pay up like the rest. When he was told that his translation from Worcester to London was conditional upon a ninety-nine-year lease to Sir Edward Denny, he protested at 'the scandal which such conditions of coming to our dignities ecclesiastical bring with it'. But he did badly want to be Bishop of London, and a fortnight later he wrote a cringing apology, promised the lease, and praised 'her Highness's most princely care for the preservation of the Church endowments'![24] Such hypocrisy, and the £2,000 in 'gratifications' he paid out to courtiers named by Elizabeth, got him back into the Queen's favour – temporarily. Perhaps to try to recoup his losses, Fletcher married a rich London widow; the wits said they were well suited, since he was 'Dr F' and she was 'Mrs Letcher'. Elizabeth was furious, especially as it was the Bishop's second marriage: to acquire one wife was unfortunate, but a second was carelessness. Fletcher was excluded from Court and, for a time, suspended from his bishopric; he died soon after, it was said, of the royal wrath and a surfeit of tobacco.

Only one bishop was really secure in Elizabeth's affections. She called John Whitgift, Archbishop of Canterbury from 1583 to 1604, her 'little black husband', and the Archbishop of York noted she did 'always bear and show a special good affection towards him'.[25] She backed Whitgift against the Council in 1584 when there were attempts to baulk his drive for conformity, and in 1586 she made him a councillor himself. He was summoned to her deathbed in 1603, and Elizabeth died clasping his hand tightly. But there were limits to the freedom of action Whitgift was allowed. In 1595 he tried to solve a theological dispute in Cambridge by imposing nine articles on predestination as a statement of orthodoxy, but the Queen had no intention of permitting further divisive definition. Elizabeth forced Whitgift to withdraw the articles, and, apparently, threatened him with a *praemunire* prosecution for encroaching upon her sovereignty. She allowed him to lecture her on the need to preserve the property of the Church, but she did not permit his censures to impede her pilfering.

Elizabeth herself profited directly from her right to the revenues of vacant bishoprics – and some sees were kept vacant for lucratively long periods. The Queen left Gloucester and Salisbury without bishops for five years, Chichester for seven years, Bristol for fourteen, and Ely for nineteen – and the bankrupt Earl of Oxford was supported by a pension from Elizabeth out of her Ely revenues. The see of Oxford was vacant from 1568 to 1589, and from 1592 to 1603 – and when a bishop was appointed in 1589, he had to alienate estates to the Crown which were passed to the Earl of Essex. Even in the second half of her reign, when the Queen had an episcopate more to her liking and more eager to do her bidding, she abused her authority as supreme governor. The property of the Church was subordinated to the financial needs of the Crown and the patronage demands of courtiers, while its religion was subordinated to the Queen's political calculations. For all her sincere Protestantism, Elizabeth used the Church as a political weapon. Perhaps Elizabeth was God's instrument, but the Church of England was hers.

. . .

NOTES AND REFERENCES

1. Erickson C 1983 *The First Elizabeth*. Macmillan, p. 181
2. Haugaard W P 1981 Elizabeth Tudor's *Book of Devotions, Sixteenth Century Journal* 12: 103
3. Haugaard W P 1981: 93; Neale J F 1953 *Elizabeth I and her Parliaments, 1559–1581*. Cape, p. 365; Neale J E 1957 *Elizabeth I and her Parliaments, 1584–1601*. Cape, p. 128
4. *Calendar of State Papers Foreign, 1558–59*, p. 101
5. Hartley T E (ed.) 1981 *Proceedings in the Parliaments of Elizabeth I, 1558–1581*. Leicester, pp. 379, 507
6. Neale J E 1953 p. 37
7. Jones N L 1982 *Faith by Statute: parliament and the settlement of religion, 1559*. Royal Historical Society, summarised in Jones N L 1984 Elizabeth's first year, in Haigh C A (ed.) 1984 *The Reign of Elizabeth I*. Macmillan
8. Neale J E 1953 pp. 51–84
9. Sandys E 1842 *Sermons* Ayre J (ed.). Parker Society, p. 43; Hartley T E (ed.) 1981 p. 216; *Calendar of State Papers Spanish, 1558–67*, pp. 636–7
10. Neale J E 1957 pp. 75, 74
11. Parker M 1853 *Correspondence* Bruce J, Perowne T T (eds). Parker Society, p. 224
12. Haugaard W P 1968 *Elizabeth and the English Reformation*. Cambridge, pp. 216–17
13. Hartley T E (ed.) 1981 p. 220
14. *Calendar of State Papers Spanish, 1568–69*, pp. 50–1
15. Hartley T E (ed.) 1981 p. 51; Cardwell E 1844 *Documentary Annals* (2 vols). Oxford, vol. 1 p. 368

16. Neale J E 1957 p. 100; Read C 1955 *Mr Secretary Cecil and Queen Elizabeth*, Cape, p. 466; MacCaffrey W T 1981 *Queen Elizabeth and the Making of Policy*. Princeton, p. 125

17. Haugaard W P 1968 pp. 329–30, 327

18. Neale J E 1957 p. 13

19. Grindal E 1843 *Remains* Nicholson W (ed.). Parker Society, p. 471; Hartley T E (ed.) 1981 p. 446

20. Neale J E 1957 p. 71

21. The struggle provides the unifying theme of Neale J E 1953, 1957

22. Collinson P 1983 *Godly People*. Hambledon, p. 305; Parker M 1853 p. 479

23. Hill C 1971 *The Economic Problems of the Church*. Panther edn, p. 17; Williams N 1967 *Elizabeth, Queen of England*. Weidenfeld & Nicolson, p. 91; Harington J 1804 *Nugae Antiquae* (2 vols), Park T (ed.). Vernon & Hood, vol. 2, p. 42

24. Collinson P 1982 *The Religion of Protestants*. Oxford, p. 27; Stone L 1965 *The Crisis of the Aristocracy, 1558–1641*. Oxford, p. 407

25. Collinson P 1982 p. 6

Chapter 3

THE QUEEN AND THE NOBILITY

Elizabeth I was a bully, and, like most bullies, she harassed the weak while deferring to the strong. She could coerce and humiliate her episcopate, but her peerage had to be treated with greater circumspection. The Queen might slap the face of the Earl of Essex after a particular provocation, but he was her creation, her plaything, and, despite all his efforts, he had no independent power base. With the hereditary magnates of England, however, it was different: they had to be enticed with fair words and bought with favours, for Elizabeth needed them. There were two reasons for this. One was that, by convention, the nobles were the family of the monarch: letters from the Queen to earls began with an affectionate 'Good Cousin', and the nobility formed her natural entourage. The monarchy shone brightest when it reflected the glow of the attendant peerage, and the dignity of the Queen was enhanced by the dignity of her nobles. The second reason was more prosaic and more important: the peers had power, power the Queen feared and power she had to harness.

In East Anglia the power of the Duke of Norfolk was awesome. He had a great palace at Norwich, for entertaining and impressing, an administrative headquarters at Kenninghall, and bases at Framlingham, Castle Rising, Thetford, and Castle Acre. He held an independent franchise of four hundreds and fourteen other manors, and claimed loyalty and service from tenants on consolidated landholdings in Norfolk and Suffolk, where good relations had been fostered by benevolent estate management. The Duke was the centre of a great patronage network, and county families had long traditions of service to the Howards. He ruled the Norfolk commission of the peace, with half the JPs of the 1560s appointed through his patronage, and he controlled parliamentary elections; in Norfolk he named MPs for Castle Rising, King's Lynn, Great Yarmouth, Norwich, and Thetford, and he even chose the two knights of the shire returned at a by-election in 1566. In East Anglia, Elizabeth had to rule through Thomas Howard or she had to break him, so great was his inherited authority.

The Duke of Norfolk was unique: no other magnate had his particular combination of great wealth, vast and compact estates, a liberty, a loyal tenantry, electoral influence, and military strength. But there were other nobles whose power, though less, could not be ignored – the Percy Earls of Northumberland in the far North-east, the Earls of Westmorland and Cumberland in the North-west, the Earls of Derby in Lancashire and Cheshire, the Earls of Shrewsbury in the north Midlands, the Earls of Pembroke in Wiltshire, the Earls of Bedford in Cornwall, the Earls of Arundel in Sussex, and other peers with a more localised influence. In so far as England was a 'federation of counties', it was a federation ruled by regional magnates – and a magnate's local power might be great enough to give him leverage at the centre too. For nobles had come to be essential intermediaries, a county's representative at Court and the Court's representative at county level. They could not be ignored.

In the reign of Elizabeth the leading role of the magnate in county government became institutionalised in the lord lieutenancy, which gave command of the local militia and titular headship of local administration. From the Crown's point of view, the office harnessed local power in the royal interest; it 'borrowed' a local influence which the Crown itself did not have. From the noble's point of view, the lieutenancy conferred a title which validated local supremacy and created an administrative mechanism through which that supremacy could be exercised. In some counties the office was a bauble to be dangled in front of nobles competing in their loyalty to the Queen; in others there was no choice, and if the lieutenancy was to be effective it had to go to the dominating families. There were virtually hereditary lieutenancies in some counties: the Stanleys in Lancashire and Cheshire, the Talbots in Derbyshire, the Hastingses in Leicestershire and Rutland, the Greys in Bedfordshire, the Howards in Surrey, the Herberts in Somerset and Wiltshire, and the Brydges in Gloucestershire. When, in 1595, William Brydges, Lord Chandos, heard a rumour that he might lose the Gloucester lieutenancy, he protested that this would be a disgrace, since his family had always held the post. These lieutenancies, and the limited circulation of many others, show how much the Crown depended on particular noble families.

The electoral patronage of the nobility also shows their local power and the Crown's reliance upon it. Nobles often controlled elections, and Crown management of the Commons required good relations with patrons. All the known Elizabethan MPs for Wilton were nominees of the Earls of Pembroke, who also controlled borough elections at Old Sarum, Downton, and Cardiff. Above all, Pembroke was the power-broker for Wiltshire county elections, and warned a would-be candidate in 1572 that

> I had granted my good will, and these were my considerations, that is, I would have all gentlemen to have their due reserved unto them, which is, from time to time, as parliaments fall out, to be chosen, now some and then some, as they are fit, to the end that they may be experimented [given experience] in the affairs and state of their country.

About one-third of borough MPs were returned through the influence of some great man, often as a result of downright bullying. The Earl of Leicester told Denbigh in 1572 that if they refused his nominee 'be ye well assured never to look for any friendship or favour at my hand in any of your affairs hereafter':[1] the townsmen wisely sent the Earl a blank return into which he entered the name of his candidate. Larger towns might resist, and when Leicester asked Gloucester for a blank return he was refused, but, in the main, nobles got their way. The Earl of Essex collected borough patronage as others might collect paintings: in 1593, half the Welsh boroughs returned Essex followers to Parliament.

Counties were more difficult to dominate, though smaller ones might succumb. Roger North sat as senior knight for Cambridgeshire in 1559 and 1563, he succeeded as Lord North in 1564, and was Lord Lieutenant, controlling elections, from 1569 to 1600: from 1584 all the county members were his sons or his deputy lieutenants. In Leicestershire elections, members of the Hastings family took nine of the twenty Elizabethan seats and got both of the county seats in 1584, 1586, and 1597: at the

Leicester borough election in 1601 George Belgrave got himself elected by appearing in Hastings livery and claiming the Earl of Huntingdon's endorsement. As an election approached, a noble would declare his will. In 1584, the Earl of Sussex wrote to Lord Mordaunt for his support for Thomas Radcliffe in Bedfordshire: 'This shall be to require your good lordship that he may have the voices of yours and such of yours as your lordship can make.' In 1597, Lord Charles Howard told Sir William More that his own son would stand for Surrey, 'Wherewith I have thought good to acquaint you, being one of my especiallest friends, that you may give way and furtherance unto the same.'[2]

A lord lieutenant could exercise his own influence, use the slogan of loyalty to the Queen, and claim to be doing so in the Crown's interest. In 1601 the Earl of Hertford wrote to John Thynne in support of his two Wiltshire candidates:

I do desire not only your voices but, for the better performance of the good of the queen, I do also require you to move such as are your friends and may give voices in this election to be at Wilton on Tuesday next being Michaelmas day, to yield their best help for the finishing of this business; praying you to express that I wish to such as you require to be there, assuring you both of my kind acceptance of your good endeavours, and of my thankfulness towards any that shall do any thing for my sake in this, which I esteem to be beneficial to the whole shire.[3]

Self-interest, county interest, and royal interest, all were to be served by persuading Thynne's followers to vote for Hertford's candidates. So nobles held local office, influenced parliamentary elections, and sat in the House of Lords; they had social prestige, landed wealth, and manpower. In peace, they ruled counties; as war approached, they raised forces; in war, they commanded armies and fleets. In short, they had power. Elizabeth needed such men to give effect to her rule: without them she was an angry but ineffective voice screeching abuse in the Privy Chamber. But she had to ensure that the power of the nobility was used in her interest, and she had to control them.

One feature of the peerage which she could control was its size. At Elizabeth's accession there were fifty-seven peers; at her death there were fifty-five. She had not even fully compensated for the fourteen failures in the male line and six attainders of traitors; she had certainly not compensated for the increase in population and the expansion of the gentry. The Queen had a highly conservative attitude towards noble status. Six titles were restored to families which had lost them, and two titles were allowed to pass through women. There were only ten new creations in forty-four years, and these went to her own relatives and those of existing peers: the only really 'new' man was William Cecil, Lord Burghley. Elizabeth quite deliberately restricted the size of the peerage. In 1588–89, Burghley planned a revitalization of the group, and the Queen approved a list of five promotions and seven new creations drawn from a short list of fourteen leading contenders – but she changed her mind, and nothing came of the project. In 1598 Essex pestered for a title for his ally Sir Robert Sidney; the Queen retorted 'But ... what shall I do with all these that pretend to titles? I could be willing to call him and one or two more, but to call many I will not. And I am importuned by many of their friends to do it.' Whatever the pressure, Elizabeth's determination held, and she would not have any other prince's creations either: she was furious when Sir Thomas Arundel returned to England in 1596 with the title of Count of the Holy Roman Empire, and she refused to recognise it. The Queen herself was to be the only fount of honour: as she told Sir Nicholas Clifford when he acquired a French decoration, 'My dogs wear my collars!'[4]

Elizabeth and her advisers kept a careful watch on existing peers. She expected her nobles to spend some of their time at Court, where she could keep an eye on them. About two-thirds of peers were in some sense courtiers in the early and middle years of the reign, although the proportion seems to have declined in the 1590s – then Elizabeth made her intentions clear, and in 1596 ordered Essex to send back half a dozen young nobles who had rushed off with him to the relief of Calais. Burghley was a walking filing cabinet on the English aristocracy: 'What nobleman or gentleman, and their dwellings, matches and pedigrees did he not know?' wrote a servant.[5] There were murals in his house at Theobalds with the genealogy and heraldry of leading families, and he had maps of the residences of the main families in each county, so that he could always work out their links and alliances. This interest came partly from his antiquarianism and snobbery, but it was also a question of essential political intelligence.

Queen Elizabeth restricted the number of nobles, and she kept them under surveillance. But she did not, unless forced to by plotting or rebellion, seek to destroy magnates or to undermine their power – except in the sensitive and dangerous area of the far North, where border office and garrison commands gave considerable extra power. In 1559 Cecil asked his old ally, Sir Ralph Sadler, to 'send me word by cipher what your opinion is of the changing of the wardens of the East, West and Middle Borders, for it is here seen as the time requireth very necessary'.[6] More reliable men were needed, and Sadler replied with suggestions. Thereafter, the Earl of Northumberland lost the East and Middle Marches, which his predecessors had almost always held; the East March went to an old soldier, Lord Grey, and later to a trustworthy Protestant southerner, the Earl of Bedford. The Middle March went to a local enemy of the Percies, Sir John Forster, who could be relied on to bolster his own power at the expense of Northumberland's. Lord Dacre, Warden of the West March, seems to have been kept at Court, and when he died in 1563 his family lost the post. After the death of Shrewsbury, the lord presidency of the North went to a succession of reliable outsiders – the Earl of Rutland, Archbishop Young, the Earl of Sussex, and, most trusted of all, Elizabeth's cousin, the Earl of Huntingdon, from 1572.

The Tudors had always faced a dilemma on the northern border. Should they entrust office to powerful local lords, who would be effective governors, or should they use more controllable men, who might lack regional authority? Elizabeth, unlike her father, opted decisively for the second approach, and the North was ruled not by its major magnates but by safe southerners and ambitious lesser northerners. In 1569 the Warden of the East March and Governor of Berwick was the Queen's cousin Lord Hunsdon, assisted by Sir William Drury from Buckinghamshire; the Percies' rival Forster was Warden of the Middle March; the obedient second-ranker Lord Scrope was Warden of the West March; and the Council in the North was headed by Sussex and the experienced administrator Sir Thomas Gargrave. The Queen may have chosen wisely: when rebellion irrupted in 1569, the government of the North remained intact and overcame the rising, in sharp contrast with 1536 when rebellion was led by the northerner-dominated government of the province. But the 1569 Revolt was partly a product of her exclusions from favour: office was a means of keeping the great loyal, and those who lost office might abandon loyalty.

The Queen was certainly – and rightly – nervous of disaffection in the North, and sought to weaken potential opponents. But then northern nobles found that their opposition to the Crown's religious policies was compounded by personal grievances, and the Earl of Northumberland's lead-mine was seized by the Queen on a legal technicality. When the Catholic Guise faction took control of Paris and massacred French Protestants at Vassy in 1562, Elizabeth was afraid for the stability of her own realm: she sent a party of her most reliable southern nobles, including four of her own relations, on a hunting expedition into Yorkshire, to forestall any violent action by Catholic magnates. By 1565 Mary Queen of Scots was confident that the earls of Cumberland, Derby, Northumberland, Shrewsbury, and Westmorland could be won over to support her claim to the English throne, for they were all 'of the old religion'.[7] In fact, Mary was becoming a key figure for the future of the English nobility, especially after her flight to England in 1568.

Once in custody in England, Mary became the focus of two groups of conspirators among English nobles. In the North, Northumberland, Westmorland, and Leonard Dacre plotted to free Mary by force, so that she could be used as a figurehead to extract religious concessions from Elizabeth. With Mary recognised as heir, the plotters would be secure in future favour, or, if they were impatient, Elizabeth could be deposed and Mary made queen, perhaps with Spanish support. At Court, there was a coalition of anti-Cecil nobles, Norfolk, Arundel, and Lumley, with Winchester and Pembroke on the fringe, who hoped to force Elizabeth to allow Norfolk to marry Mary. This was partly a means of securing the English succession by bringing Mary under control and making her more acceptable to Elizabeth, and partly a means of forcing Cecil out of office, changing foreign policy and opening the regime to more noble influence. The Earl of Leicester supported what he knew of the plans of the Court group, hoping that if Mary was safely married to an English duke he could then have Elizabeth for himself.

But the conspiracies began to fall apart when the Dacre inheritance came up for grabs. Leonard Dacre and Norfolk fell out, as rival contenders, and Norfolk sought a *rapprochement* with Cecil who, as Master of the Wards, could influence the outcome of the case. Leicester lost his nerve, feigned illness to call Elizabeth to his bedside, and told her of the marriage plans. Norfolk's allies went to ground, and the Duke fled to East Anglia in fear of the Queen's wrath. Elizabeth summoned him back to Court and, after some hesitation, he submitted and wrote to his brother-in-law Westmorland that the northerners should not revolt or 'it should cost him his head'. Norfolk's sister, the Countess of Westmorland, was scornful – 'What a simple man the duke is, to begin a matter and not to go through with it.'8 Elizabeth had come close to facing the probably lethal combination of a coup on her Council, a Howard rising in East Anglia, and a Catholic rebellion in the North with Mary Queen of Scots as a legitimating figurehead. Elizabeth was saved, not by the strength of her own position but by the belated loyalty of Leicester and the cowardice of Norfolk.

But the worst had not yet passed. Norfolk was sent to the Tower, and Arundel, Lumley, and Pembroke were put under house arrest, but the Earls of Northumberland and Westmorland were free and Lord President Sussex dared not move against them until the North was quieter and the weather worse. The two northern earls knew they were compromised: they had been plotting for months, and their intentions were widely recognised. Northumberland sent a message to the Spanish ambassador that he would have to rebel or 'yield my head to the block, or else be forced to flee and forsake the realm, for I know the Queen's Majesty is so highly displeased at me and others that I know we shall not be able to bear it nor answer it'.9 Which course he adopted would depend largely upon Elizabeth. Sussex was optimistic about the outcome and counselled caution, but Elizabeth was thoroughly frightened and trusted no one. She suspected that Sussex, an old political ally of Norfolk, was shielding Northumberland and Westmorland, or worse; she instructed him to report more fully on his actions, and to order Northumberland and Westmorland to Court. When Sussex called Westmorland before him, Westmorland replied, 'I durst not come where my enemies are without bringing such force to protect me as might be misliked.'10

Elizabeth had blundered: she forced the earls to choose between flight and rebellion, when rebellion was still (just) a realistic option. They chose rebellion, because of the Catholic enthusiasm of their followers and the scorn of the Countess of Westmorland – 'We and our country were shamed for ever, that now in the end we should seek holes to creep into!'[11] So the earls rebelled, more in sorrow than in anger: men who had been planning rebellion for weeks, even months, were forced into an unplanned rising. But it was still a dangerous rising, which could use powerful slogans. The revolt was presented in traditional terms, as the revenge of the old nobility against upstart evil counsellors. Their proclamation at Ripon on 16 November declared that

> Forasmuch as divers evil-disposed persons about the Queen's Majesty have, by their subtle and crafty dealing to advance themselves, overcome in this our realm the true and Catholic religion towards God, and by the same abused the queen, disordered the realm and now lastly seek and procure the destruction of the nobility, we therefore have gathered ourselves together to resist by force.

The appeal was quite successful in Durham and north Yorkshire, given the time of year: five or six thousand rebels flocked to the old banners of St Cuthbert and the Five Wounds of Christ, and in many parishes the Bible and Book of Common Prayer were desecrated and altars restored. The earls raised the rabble – but they needed the support of their fellow nobles: their proclamation of 28 November was dispatched to brother peers, claiming their rising was in the name of the 'high and mighty prince Thomas, Duke of Norfolk', Arundel, Pembroke, and 'divers others of the ancient nobility of the realm', and stressing the need to clarify the succession.[12] Theirs was a respectable, responsible, aristocratic rebellion.

The revolt has often been seen as the last fling of the feudal nobility, its failure and futility demonstrating the decline of noble power: this is misleading. The rebellion was strikingly non-feudal: nine-tenths of the known rebels were *not* tenants of the leaders (which is not surprising, as the rising took place away from Neville and Percy heartlands), and there was much more of a popular movement than has been supposed. Nor was the rebellion incompetent, for its leaders pursued a coherent strategy. The earls struck south with a small, fast-moving force to free Mary Queen of Scots from Tutbury, and then when she was moved to the unassailable Coventry they returned north to consolidate their strength and await Spanish assistance. They seem to have intended to hold out through the winter, and to stage a larger, Spanish-backed march south in the spring, expecting, as northern rebels always did, that the South would rise in support. But the Queen's commanders were more determined, and successful, than expected: they recruited without much difficulty, and marched north despite the winter. On 15 December, the earls fled into Scotland, and, except for a bloody clash in February 1570 between Hunsdon's army and the Dacre tenantry, the rising was over. But the price had still to be paid.

When Cecil heard that the earls had fled, he wrote that 'The Queen's Majesty hath had a notable trial of her whole realm and subjects in this time, wherein she hath had service readily of all sorts, without respect of religion.'[13] He was relieved that the rising had not spread across the kingdom, but it was no time for gloating. The interlocking conspiracies of 1569 had been a major threat to Elizabeth's regime, and it would have been a very different 'Elizabethan England' if they had come to fruition. The rising which took place had been extremely dangerous, and if Elizabeth's government had made a few small errors (such as delay in moving Mary) there could have been a disaster. Elizabeth had been very lucky – if only because Leonard Dacre was in London when the rebellion began, and the Cumbrian rising happened three months too late. The rest of the northern nobility had waited on the sidelines. Derby had pledged his loyalty to the Queen when called by the earls, but he had done nothing directly against them; the Earl of Cumberland was nowhere to be seen, and Lords Mounteagle and Wharton were also inconspicuous. The northern aristocracy had contemplated desertion, and almost done it.

The royal forces which southern nobles led against the rebels posed their own threat to political security. The southern troops under Clinton and Warwick became a rampaging army of occupation, with the soldiers seizing goods and the commanders claiming the forfeited lands of the rebels. Sussex protested, but in vain, and he saw that determined opposition to the spoliation would only bring trouble: 'If I weighed not the quiet of my good Queen more than any other matter, I would have stopped them from crowing upon my dunghill or carrying off one halfpenny out of my rule.'[14] From the spoil of the North, southern nobles became richer and, themselves, more dangerous. The Court plotters of 1569 were also a threat. Norfolk remained alienated and ambitious: he continued scheming with Mary Queen of Scots, as did Arundel and Lumley, and he entered into a plot with a Florentine fixer named Ridolfi. Norfolk agreed to raise rebellion in England, if the Duke of Alva would send Spanish troops from the Netherlands, but the interception of letters led to the unravelling of the plot in the summer of 1571. Despite Elizabeth's reluctance, Norfolk had to be executed. The plots of 1569-71, and the rising of 1569, had shown that the exclusion of magnates from favour could lead to disaffection and rebellion. Elizabeth's usual tactic towards the nobility – conciliation rather than confrontation – was much safer: Cecil told her in 1580, 'Gratify your nobility and principal persons of the realm, to bind them fast to you.'[15]

Queen Elizabeth did not generally behave as if she distrusted her nobles, but as if she depended upon them. When in 1596 she called back the young aristocrats who were setting off for Calais with Essex, it was not because she suspected them but because she wanted them at Court, to fulfil their duty by attendance on her. Elizabeth had almost a family relationship with her nobles. She provided them with London houses from among royal properties: Hunsdon had Somerset House; Pembroke, Barnard's Castle; the Charterhouse went in turn to Lord North, the Duke of Norfolk, and the Earl of Rutland; and Essex had Durham House. The relationship of queen and aristocracy was celebrated each year by an exchange of New Year's gifts: the Queen got £700-£1,200 in gold from nobles, bishops, and courtiers, and gave out 4,000-5,500 ounces of silver-gilt plate in return. In January 1562, she exchanged presents with the Duke of Norfolk, 13 marquises and earls, a viscount, 13 duchesses and countesses, 2 viscountesses, 20 lords and 30 ladies, as well as bishops and courtiers. It is true that the exchange became a bureaucratic routine rather than a personal giving, but the system did emphasise the close relationship between Crown and peerage.

Elizabeth acted as godmother to the children of her nobles: in 1560-61, she was godmother to the children of Lords Berkeley, Cobham, Montagu, Mountjoy, and Sheffield, and the christenings took place in the Chapel Royal. She interfered in the personal affairs of her nobles, as if she was head of the peerage family: when the Earl of Lincoln refused to honour his son's marriage contract, Elizabeth intervened in 1597 to force the Earl to provide a suitable home for the young couple. She visited her magnates on summer progress: as a house-guest of her hosts, Elizabeth created opportunities for ostentatious displays of hospitality on their part and of gratitude on hers. Sometimes, as on her visit to the Earl of Hertford at Elvetham in 1591, the favour of her company could demonstrate political rehabilitation: an old grudge had been forgotten, and a personal relationship re-established. The Queen was adept at the personal touch. She added her own postscript to the official letter of thanks to Hunsdon after his success in the North in 1570: 'I doubt much, my Harry, whether that the victory were given me more joyed me, or that you were by God appointed the instrument of my glory, and I assure you for my country's good the first might suffice, but for my heart's contentation the second more pleased me.' She wrote to Lord Willoughby, commander in France in 1589, 'My good Peregrine, I bless God that your old prosperous success followed your valiant acts, and joy not a little that safety accompanieth your luck. Your loving sovereign, Eliz. R.'[16]

Ceremonial functions pandered to the self-importance of nobles. They were sent abroad as special ambassadors for great occasions, and the honour was important enough to be recorded in the pages of Camden's history of the reign. Montagu (a useful Catholic) went to Spain in 1560, Sussex to the Emperor in 1567, Buckhurst to France in 1571, Worcester to France in 1573, North to France again in 1574, and so on. It is true that the privilege was expensive, but it inflated the dignity of nobles to appear as the personal representatives of the Queen. Dignity, indeed, was crucial. When Sir Philip Sidney answered back to the Earl of Oxford in a tennis-court argument in 1579, Elizabeth reminded him of 'the difference in degree between earls and gentlemen, the respect inferiors owed to their superiors, and the necessity in princes to maintain their own creations, as degrees descending between the people's licentiousness and the anointed sovereignty of crowns'.[17] The dignity of nobles was not to be affronted, even by Sidney, paragon of courtly virtues and pattern of the gentleman.

Elizabeth flattered and favoured her nobility for two reasons: she was afraid of their power, and she needed their power. She involved them in her government, she shared her problems with them, she associated them with her decisions, and, in emergencies, she turned to them for protection. Nobles were the Queen's natural counsellors, with conventional references to 'the lords of the Council' and 'the lords and others of the Council'. When Elizabeth first met the councillors she had inherited from Mary, she told them: 'I shall desire you all, my lords (chiefly you of the nobility, everyone in his degree and power) to be assistant to me'; 'the ancient nobility', she reminded them, 'ought in honour to have the more natural care for the maintaining of my estate and this commonwealth'.[18] She retained the magnate councillors, Arundel, Clinton, Derby, Pembroke, Shrewsbury, and added Bedford and Northampton. Later she brought on Norfolk, Sussex, and Warwick, and Hunsdon, Howard, Buckhurst, Cobham, and North; Derby and Shrewsbury succeeded their fathers, and Essex got his place in 1593. It was typical of Elizabeth's attitude towards nobility that more peers became councillors than councillors became peers. It is true that the magnate element on the Council declined in the 1590s, but the Essex Revolt reminded the Queen of their importance and Shrewsbury and Worcester were recruited in 1601.

Nobles might provide counsel even when not of the Council. In 1568 the Queen summoned the Earls of Huntingdon, Northumberland, Shrewsbury, Sussex, and Westmorland to consult with the Privy Council on what should be done with Mary Queen of Scots, because, as Cecil put it, 'the weightiness of this matter is such as none the like hath come in consideration during her Majesty's reign'.[19] There were certain things which could not decently be done without the presence of nobles. Trying a duke for his life was one of them: when Norfolk came to trial in 1572, Shrewsbury presided as Lord Steward, and almost half the peerage sat with him; virtually all the earls were included, and only those who were too ill, too young, or themselves in custody were absent. Although Mary Queen of Scots was tried with rather less publicity in 1586, the commissioners for the occasion included Lord Burghley and eight earls, as well as judges and officials. The association of nobles in such matters of high politics implicated them in controversial decisions, and gave the weight of aristocratic approval to royal policies.

At times of political crisis, Elizabeth needed the power and the prestige of her nobles – and she had to ensure their loyalty by involving them in her actions. The Revolt of 1569 was led by disloyal peers, but it was put down by loyal ones: Hunsdon and Sussex had recruited troops in the North; Clinton and Warwick raised their armies in the Midlands; and Bedford was sent to secure the West Country against the threat of Spanish invasion. In the turbulent aftermath of the revolt, parliamentary elections had to be carefully managed. In 1571 and 1572, when loyal Houses of Commons were particularly necessary, the Council wrote to nobles to ask them to manage county and borough elections, to ensure a 'good choice of knights and burgesses'.[20] The Earl of Bedford was asked to supervise Buckinghamshire; Cobham and Archbishop Parker, Kent; Howard, Surrey; Leicester, Berkshire; Bindon and Sir William Paulet, Dorset; and Pembroke, Wiltshire. Bedford also looked after the western counties, and in 1572 he apparently influenced the return of half of the borough members in Cornwall, Devon, and Dorset. The electoral patronage and local prestige of nobles was an important asset to a regime whose direct electoral influence was really confined to the Duchy of Lancaster boroughs.

In 1584, after the Throckmorton Plot against Elizabeth and the assassination of William of Orange in the Netherlands, the Privy Council organised a Protestant vigilante force under the leadership of the nobility. Recruitment to the 'Bond of Association' was organised through lords lieutenant and other leading nobles: the Earl of Huntingdon looked after Yorkshire, with the assistance of Lord Darcy in the south of the county; Lord Scrope supervised Cumberland and Westmorland, the Earl of Derby managed Lancashire and Cheshire, and Lord Cobham looked after Kent. It is significant that, at what seemed a moment of crisis, the Council worked through the individual influence of peers rather than the formal administration of the state. The same was partly true of the real crisis in 1588, the Armada year. A corps of shock troops of 1,600 horse and 1,500 foot was drawn directly from the tenants of magnates, and three-quarters of the army recruited to protect Elizabeth came from the private followings of the nobility. In 1599, when there was another invasion scare, the Council summoned nobles to Court to protect the Queen with as many horsemen as they could bring. When the chips were down, Elizabeth's reliance upon her aristocracy became clear.

It is often supposed that the Tudor monarchy deliberately trimmed aristocratic power. There is certainly some evidence of official suspicion of mighty subjects. Lord Buckhurst, a privy councillor, told the Earl of Shrewsbury in 1592 that 'Your lordship must remember that in the policy of this commonwealth we are not over ready to add increase of power and countenance to such great personages as you are.' This was a mild threat to warn a powerful magnate involved in a bitter local feud, but an attack on noble power was not 'the policy of this commonwealth'. Excluding the necessary consequences of deliberate disloyalty, only in the North in 1559 did Elizabeth determinedly remove nobles from positions of authority – and then Northumberland had his offices taken away in the context of Elizabeth's war in support of Scottish Protestant rebels against a French Catholic army and a Scottish Catholic queen. The dismissal of Northumberland is an almost unique exception, not an example of a trend. In truth, 'the policy of this commonwealth' was the maintenance of aristocratic power: Sir Robert Naunton (who had been a servant of Essex) wrote later of Elizabeth that 'it was part of her natural propension to grace and support ancient nobility', and she was 'ever inclinable to favour the nobility'.[21]

The Treatise of Treasons, a Catholic propaganda tract of 1572, followed the proclamations of the northern earls in claiming that Elizabeth's ministers pursued an anti-noble policy. The Treatise specifically accused Cecil of hounding Norfolk to his death, and of harbouring a more general determination to break the old nobility. But Francis Bacon and Cecil's anonymous servant-biographer both saw him as a defender of the status of nobility and the interests of particular nobles. As Master of the Wards, Cecil made himself guardian to eight noble wards, including the Earls of Oxford, Surrey, Essex, and Southampton, and two Earls of Rutland: although he married his own daughter to Oxford, he does not appear to have sought profit from these arrangements – rather, he fulfilled what he saw as a national duty, and a role which would bring fame to his own family. He attempted to maintain the patrimony of young nobles, and to educate them in his own household as the next generation of England's leaders. Elizabeth, too, followed a policy which sought to preserve the wealth and prestige of the English aristocracy.

Elizabeth supported, indeed subsidised, the nobility in a variety of ways. The peerage was massively under-taxed, and it came to be almost a mark of disfavour to be realistically taxed. The average subsidy assessments of nobles fell from £921 in

1534 to £487 in 1571 and £311 in 1601; fifteen nobles had been assessed at over £1,000 in 1534, but only nine in 1571 and one in 1601 – despite a fivefold inflation in the sixteenth century. In real terms, Lawrence Stone suggests,[22] the 1601 assessment of the peerage was only 38 per cent of that of 1558. Furthermore, some peers were not even expected to pay their under-assessed subsidies, and arrears of taxation were allowed to accumulate over many years. An inquiry in 1610 found that the Earls of Oxford owed subsidies from 1559; the Earls of Huntingdon owed £422 back to 1581; the Earls of Shrewsbury owed £1,853 back to 1585; and the Earls of Derby owed £1,338 since 1589. It may be that these anomalies were the product of bureaucratic inefficiency rather than deliberate royal benevolence, but the result was the same – the nobility was granted a measure of tax exemption.

Favoured nobles were also allowed to pile up debts in other forms. In 1585 the Earl of Bedford still owed £200 for a wardship he had bought sixteen years before; in 1587 Arundel owed £1,800 for a wardship purchased twenty years earlier; and at his death in 1595 the Earl of Huntingdon owed £8,000 in unpaid Crown rents. Crown officials were permitted to run up huge debts, apparently by living off the revenues they controlled. The Marquis of Winchester eventually owed £34,000 after holding the offices of Lord Treasurer and Master of the Wards. Sussex owed £11,000 after he had been Keeper of the Royal Forests in the South and Lord President of the Council in the North; Warwick owed £7,000 as Master of the Ordnance; and Leicester came to owe £35,000 from a variety of Crown offices. Some of the debts may have arisen from the costs of royal service, but much was the result of disguised borrowing from the royal coffers. When Hunsdon died in 1596, he owed fee-farm rent on Hunsdon Manor granted in 1559, he had paid no subsidy since 1563, and he had not paid for a wardship granted in 1586. Perhaps these debts gave the Queen a weapon to tame her peerage; nobles had to avoid giving offence to the Queen, lest their debts should be called in. But the favoured nobles gained much from the arrangement: they lived out of Elizabeth's till.

The Queen preserved the pretensions of nobles. Elizabethan nominations to the Order of the Garter were almost exclusively of nobles, whereas Henry VIII had recruited nearly half of his Garter knights from the gentry. Despite her well-known parsimony, Elizabeth gave pensions to impecunious peers to save them from the shame of public poverty. Hard-pressed aristocratic widows – the Countesses of Kent and Kildare, Ladies Burgh and Hunsdon – were paid annuities. Those nobles who had no landed estates appropriate to their standing might be supported by the Queen: Lord Howard of Effingham and the landless Lord Henry Howard were each given £200 a year, and the Earl of Oxford – penniless as well as worthless – got £1,000 a year. At death, too, the dignity of nobility might be protected: Elizabeth sometimes paid for funerals, especially those of her own relations – she financed the burials of the Marchioness of Northampton in 1565, Lady Knollys in 1569, the Countess of Lennox in 1577, and Lord Hunsdon in 1596 (though, despite his long years of service in the North, she had refused to pay for Huntingdon in 1595). Lord Burghley had sometimes intervened to force the families of deceased nobles to pay up for fitting funerals – an ignoble end should not deface a noble life.

Elizabeth deliberately maintained the social status of the nobility. As she told Philip Sidney when he dared to argue with the Earl of Oxford, she proposed to protect the dignity of peers. She was unwilling to see nobles disgraced, as her reluctance to allow the execution of Norfolk suggests. The Duke was tried on 16 January 1572, but he was not executed until 2 June; twice a planned execution was cancelled on the Queen's order, and the crowds disappointed. Burghley told Walsingham that 'Sometime when she speaketh of her danger, she concludeth that justice should be done; another time she speaketh of his nearness of blood, of his superiority of honour, etc., she stayeth.'[23] The execution of a duke would erode the dignity of the nobility and weaken conceptions of hierarchy. But the dignity of nobles was less important to Elizabeth than the dignity of royalty, and Norfolk was ultimately sacrificed to quieten the parliamentary clamour for proceedings against Mary Queen of Scots. Norfolk went to the block, but Elizabeth and Cecil showed no determination to hound accomplices to death: Arundel, Lumley, and others had been involved in mutterings and plottings from 1569, but after short periods of detention they were allowed to retire from politics.

When possible, Elizabeth treated her offending peers leniently. Professor Stone has noted[24] that the Queen did little to check the aristocratic gang warfare which disturbed the capital. Disruptions such as the 1582–83 feud between Oxford and the courtier Sir Thomas Knyvett went unpunished, as if nobles could get away with murder as well as treason. Noblemen were detained in the Tower for conduct which would have taken other men to the block – Lord Henry Howard, Henry, Earl of Northumberland, and Philip, Earl of Arundel, were Elizabeth's involuntary guests, though the two earls died in custody. With the necessary exception of the leader, the aristocratic participants in the 1601 Essex Revolt avoided the executions visited upon the smaller fry. Southampton, Rutland, Mounteagle, and Sandys were extremely lucky not to go to the block, and Bedford, Sussex, and Cromwell could certainly have been destroyed if the Queen had been willing. Even Essex himself was, in reputation, protected: the Crown's case was that his ambition had made him susceptible to the unscrupulous plottings of his ignoble adviser, Henry Coffe, and he was not, in himself, wicked – indeed, how could a man of nobility be wicked?

Elizabeth was protective of the dignity of her nobility. Her refusal to expand the peerage except by the promotion of those with noble blood probably enhanced noble status by giving it scarcity value. Her policy of conservation was certainly designed to increase the prestige of existing peers, not to restrict the influence of the nobility of England. Indeed, the nobles were hardly restricted at all: to a quite surprising degree, Elizabeth allowed them to flex their political muscles and compete for office and influence in disruptive ways. Dangerous men were treated as boyish scamps and scallywags, chided by a spinster aunt who rather admired their daring escapades. Elizabeth was indulgent towards them, and she could afford to be: she knew that they needed her as much as she needed them. It seems likely that economic change was eroding the financial independence of the nobility, and forcing them to look to the profits of office and of political favour to subsidise the aristocratic life-style. So the maiden aunt came to provide a proportion of the boys' pocket-money – in consequence, she could rely upon them to visit her regularly and do her errands.

* * *

NOTES AND REFERENCES

1. Hasler P W (ed.) 1981 *The House of Commons, 1558–1603* (3 vols). History of Parliament Trust, vol. 1 pp. 49, 267

2. Hasler P W (ed.) 1981 vol. 1 pp. 41–2, 112
3. Hasler P W (ed.) 1981 vol. 1 p. 268
4. Collins A (ed.) 1746 *Letters and Memorials of State* (2 vols) vol. 2 p. 87; Hasler P W (ed.) 1981 vol. 1 p. 617
5. Peck F 1732 *Desiderata Curiosa* (2 vols) vol. 1 p. 52
6. Read C 1955 *Mr Secretary Cecil and Queen Elizabeth.* Cape, p. 154
7. Stone L 1965 *The Crisis of the Aristocracy, 1558–1641.* Oxford, p. 251
8. Williams N 1964 *Thomas Howard, Fourth Duke of Norfolk.* Barrie & Rockliff, p. 165
9. MacCaffrey W T 1968 *The Shaping of the Elizabethan Regime*, Princeton, p. 333
10. MacCaffrey W T 1968 p. 335
11. Sharpe C (ed.) 1840 *Memorials of the Rebellion of 1569.* Bowyer Nichols, p. 199
12. MacCaffrey W T 1968 p. 341
13. MacCaffrey W T 1968 p. 352
14. Read C 1955 p. 463
15. Murdin W (ed.) 1759 *A Collection of State Papers ... Left by William Cecill.* Bowyer, p. 340
16. Johnson P 1974 *Elizabeth I: a study in power and intellect.* Weidenfeld & Nicolson, pp. 177, 332
17. Greville F 1652 *The Life of the Renowned Sir Philip Sidney*, p. 79
18. Harington J 1804 *Nugae Antiquae* (2 vols) Park T (ed.). Vernon & Hood, vol. 1 p. 67
19. Read C 1955 p. 411
20. Hasler P W (ed.) 1981 vol. 1 p. 252
21. Stone L 1965 p. 237; Naunton R 1641 *Fragmenta regalia, or observations on the late Queen Elizabeth, her times and favorits*, pp. 28, 33
22. Stone L 1965 p. 496 and n
23. Read C 1960 *Lord Burghley and Queen Elizabeth.* Cape, p. 47
24. Stone L 1965 pp. 233–7

Chapter 4

THE QUEEN AND THE COUNCIL

The nobility of England formed Elizabeth's family, and she was, more or less, stuck with them. She could remove her recalcitrant nobles by trial and execution, but this was an extreme course she resorted to most reluctantly. She could alter the composition of the peerage slightly, by admitting new cousins to the charmed family circle, but she seems to have thought her relations sufficiently numerous. Except by such marginal changes, the Queen could not choose her family – but she could choose her friends, her closest councillors. Elizabeth's recruitment of privy councillors was not, however, an entirely free choice: they needed to be men who would give good advice, but also men who could exercise effective authority. The Queen could recruit her own friends, but they had to be powerful as well as reliable, tough as well as trustworthy, competent as well as compatible. The composition of the Council had to recognise the distribution of power in society, for a Council of political weaklings was useless. But a Council should not be taken over by the great men of the kingdom, or government could become a weapon of a magnate faction and the interests of the Crown would be ignored. Great aristocrats were needed, but they had to be balanced by elements more dependent on, or more devoted to, the Queen.

About half of the members of Elizabeth's Privy Council were nobles, but, as the reign wore on, the magnate group declined in number and the Queen recruited more of her trusted courtiers. The Privy Council appointed at the beginning of the reign had 20 members, but the Marians Heath and Cheney were soon lost. Of the remaining 18, 9 were nobles, 6 of them with major regional influence. Elizabeth had compromised with the mighty, and had tried to keep the territorial magnates associated with her regime – but she had balanced them with her own relations and Household officials, as well as former members of Edward VI's government. By 1570, there were 19 privy councillors, including 6 magnates and 5 other nobles, but there was a growing proportion of experienced administrators. In 1586, the Council again had 19 members, including 11 nobles – but only Derby and Shrewsbury were established magnates. Shrewsbury had been appointed in recognition of his position as custodian of Mary Queen of Scots, and only Derby was there because he could not be ignored. Five of the nobles of 1586 were the Queen's own friends and relations, and she now had a Council of hand-picked officials rather than men whose power forced them upon her. By 1597, the process of replacing regional magnates by reliable officers had gone further: the Council had only 11 members, and though 6 were nobles none were territorial magnates and 4 were Elizabethan creations. The late Elizabethan Council was very much a compact group of officials, and Elizabeth seems to have decided that she could manage without the advice of magnates.

The proceedings of the Council were dominated by the reliable official element. Elizabeth's Privy Council usually met twice a week, at Greenwich, Hampton Court, or Westminster, so regular attendance was a considerable burden. The provincial magnates were mainly absentee members, ruling their regions, leaving a relatively small attendance of officers – the Lord Treasurer, Lord Chamberlain, Lord Admiral, Secretary, the Treasurer and the Comptroller of the Household, and the Earl of Leicester. In the 1570s, the average attendance at each meeting was between seven and ten, and the magnates attended only on special occasions or when a full turn-out was summoned for a major decision. So day-to-day government was by a small clique – and it was a clique of relations. At the start of the reign, Elizabeth had stuffed her Council and Household with her Boleyn and Howard relatives, and the insiders of the regime were already intermarried or soon became so. Of twenty-five privy councillors between 1568 and 1582, eighteen were related to each other and the Queen: Leicester and Warwick were brothers; Henry Sidney was their brother-in-law and also brother-in-law to Sussex; Walsingham and Mildmay were brothers-in-law; Cecil and Bacon married Cooke sisters; and other councillors married each other's daughters – Leicester married Knollys's, Norfolk Arundel's, Pembroke Northampton's and Warwick Bedford's.

Elizabeth's early Privy Council was wide-ranging in its membership and representative of different interests and opinions. But, with the decline of the old magnate element, the exclusion of religious conservatives, and the intermarriage of members, it became a small and restrictively recruited body. Late in the reign, sons succeeded their fathers in conciliar rank – Buckhurst, Cecil, Hunsdon, and Knollys followed fathers, and Essex his stepfather. The ruling group was narrow – and narrowing – and important elements in politics were under-represented. Many of the most powerful men in England were excluded from the Council, and perhaps embittered by their neglect. The Essex Revolt in 1601 may have forced Elizabeth to recognise the folly of such restrictions, and she immediately appointed the Earls of Shrewsbury and Worcester to the Council. But for much of the reign, from 1572 to 1601, Elizabeth's Council was dangerously narrow and weak in its membership.

The ruling group of relations shared a common political outlook, which determined their interpretation of events. They were committed Protestants who believed that a Catholic league led by Rome was planning the extirpation of heresy. Every meeting of prominent Catholics was evidence that a conspiracy was afoot: William Cecil wrote in 1563 that 'The devices and determinations of the Cardinal of Lorraine, conceived in a congregation of Antichrist's soldiers, being professedly gathered to destroy the gospel of Christ, can never be truly thought nor with reason maintained to be good, by us that ought to promote Christ's kingdom and pull down Antichrist!'[1] After Mary Queen of Scots had met the Duke of Alva at Bayonne in 1565, and Alva's Spanish army had moved to the Netherlands in 1567, international Protestantism seemed to be at risk and confessional solidarity was essential. In July 1568 Cecil sent his encouragement to French Protestants: 'I pray you put them in comfort, that if extremity should happen they must not be left. For it is so universal a cause as none of the religion can separate themselves one from the other. We must all pray together, stand fast together.' Sir Nicholas Throckmorton, one of Leicester's advisers on foreign affairs, asked Cecil the key question two months later: 'Now when the general design is to exterminate all nations dissenting with them in religion (as it is most apparent and probable), what shall become of us when the like professors with us shall be utterly destroyed in Flanders and

France?'² To those who shared this conspiratorial analysis, the answer was clear: the Catholic league must be combated by a Protestant league, and England must support Protestant rebels against Catholic rulers.

But Elizabeth I saw things differently, and she was most unwilling to blackleg on fellow members of the monarchs' trade union. She had declared in 1565 that she would never support any rebellious subject's disobedience to a prince, for God would punish her if she did. The Queen had a legitimist view of politics, and saw international affairs in terms of relations between monarchs: the idea of an ideological alliance of subjects against rulers struck at her fundamental political conceptions and instincts. There was thus an obvious potential for conflict between a pragmatic Elizabeth and a Protestant group which grew in influence through the 1560s and dominated her Council by 1572. The Queen's relationship with her Council came to centre upon the 'forward' party's attempts to push her into ideological alliance with foreign Protestants: councillors attempted to manipulate the Queen, and sought to pursue a policy which she hated. Cecil told England's ambassador in France in 1567 that 'Her Majesty much dislikes of the prince of Conde and the Admiral, wherein all is done that can be by the Council to cover the same. As I think, the principal is that her Majesty, being a prince, is doubtful of giving comfort to subjects. Nevertheless, you shall do well as occasion shall serve to comfort them'³: the Queen objects to our policy, but you are to follow it anyway!

Privy councillors claimed it was their duty to give Elizabeth even unpalatable advice. In a row over marriage plans in 1566, Pembroke had told the Queen that her councillors 'were only doing what was fitting for the good of the country, and advising her what was best for her, and if she did not think fit to adopt the advice, it was still their duty to offer it'. Cecil's view was much the same:

I do hold and will always this course in such matters as I differ in opinion from her Majesty: as long as I may be allowed to give advice, I will not change my opinion by affirming the contrary, for that were to offend God, to whom I am sworn first; but as a servant I will obey her Majesty's commandment, and no wise contrary the same, presuming that, she being God's chief minister here, it

shall be God's will to have her commandments obeyed,
after that I have performed my duty as a counsellor, and
shall in my heart wish her commandments such good
success as I am sure she intendeth.[4]

The duty of a conscientious counsellor was clear: he should give
honest advice, whatever the Queen's view; and implement the
Queen's decision, whatever his own view. But in fact Cecil and
others allowed themselves more freedom of action. They did not
simply offer advice, but tried to force the Queen to take it; they
did not simply obey commands, but might pursue a covert and
contrary policy.

The Secretary was particularly well placed to manipulate
Elizabeth, since he could manage the flow of information to
her. In 1560, Secretary Cecil had been furious when a report
went directly to the Queen: he expected to be the intermediary
for official correspondence, and he was certainly the main
recipient. In June 1568, Francis Knollys wrote to Cecil the
thirteenth letter sent since he had taken over the custody of Mary
Queen of Scots at Bolton Castle; two had gone to the Queen, one
to the whole Council, and ten to Cecil himself. So the Secretary
could influence the Queen by his selection of information, and
by his presentation. In 1592 Robert Beale wrote a treatise on
how to be a successful secretary of state, based on the practice of
Sir Francis Walsingham, and management of the Queen was a
prominent issue. The Secretary should discover the Queen's
mood before going in to see her; he should not raise important
issues when she was angry; he should chat informally to distract
her while she signed official documents; and he should keep on
good terms with her favourites in the Privy Chamber. In 1597,
the French ambassador saw such manipulation in action,
especially when money was involved: 'In her own nature she is
very avaricious, and when some expense is necessary her
councillors must deceive her before embarking her on it little by
little.' Of course, Elizabeth saw through some of it: 'I perceive
they dealt with me like physicians who, ministering a drug,
make it more acceptable by giving it a good aromatical savour,
or when they give pills do gild them all over.'[5]

In fact, manipulation went much further than sugaring the
political pill. Cecil would massage information to support a
proposed course of action, and then he would lean on Elizabeth
to get her to follow it. In 1559, he tried hard to pressurise her to

intervene in Scotland in support of Protestant rebels. He drafted his memorandum in a way designed to overcome Elizabeth's reluctance to assist subjects against their prince, and claimed she had overlordship of Scotland. He then recruited English ambassadors abroad to press on the Queen the necessity for intervention, and to doctor their reports accordingly. But when the policy was formally put to the Queen by her Council, she rejected it – until Cecil threatened to resign, and she gave in. The Secretary's tactics were repeated in 1560, when he effectively prevented Elizabeth from marrying Robert Dudley. By spreading the story that Elizabeth and Dudley were plotting to poison Amy Dudley, he ensured that, when Amy did die (probably of cancer), the Queen and Lord Robert dared not risk confirming their guilt by marriage – and Cecil used the Spanish ambassador to warn Elizabeth that he would resign if she married Dudley.

The use of English ambassadors abroad was a favourite means of Cecilian manipulation. In 1562, the 'forward' councillors were pushing Elizabeth to give military support to French Protestants and join an international Protestant league. Cecil worked indirectly through Christopher Mundt, ambassador in Germany. He instructed Mundt to persuade German Protestant princes to send an emissary to Elizabeth, to suggest a conference and an alliance. Mundt himself was to warn the Queen that the defeat of the French Protestants had to be prevented: he was to tell Elizabeth that 'if she do not now attempt the furtherance of the Gospel in France, and the keeping asunder of France and Spain, her peril will be the next of any prince of Christendom'. It is clear that Cecil would decide upon a policy, and then seek to force Elizabeth to adopt it. His private assessment of the marriage and succession issues in 1566 concluded that 'The mean betwixt these is to determine effectually to marry, and, if it succeed not, then proceed to discussion of the right of the succession':[6] Cecil then worked through Parliament to try to make Elizabeth adopt one course or the other.

Other councillors, too, tried to pressurise the Queen – though not always successfully. In 1576, an agent of the Earl of Leicester persuaded the Dutch rebels to ask Elizabeth to send an English army, commanded by Leicester, to assist them against Spain. But when the Dutch obediently made their request, Elizabeth refused, leaving the Earl looking foolish and unable to fulfil his promise to William of Orange: 'I have almost neither face nor countenance to write to the prince, his expectation being so greatly deceived.' But Elizabeth's councillors continued to press for military aid to the Dutch, and Leicester, Burghley, and Walsingham plotted how they could secure her agreement. Their persistent advice prompted royal rages, but the Queen's anger changed nothing. Burghley told Walsingham in 1578 that 'we all must dutifully bear with her Majesty's offence for the time, not despairing but, howsoever she misliketh matters at one time, yet at another time she will alter her sharpness, especially when she is persuaded that we all mean truly for her and her surety, though she sometimes will not so understand'[7] – that is, if we all keep at her she'll come round in the end! Privy councillors saw royal objection not as a final refusal but as a problem to be circumvented.

Secretary Walsingham, like Cecil before him, told the Queen's correspondents exactly what to write to her. In 1581 he thought that Huntingdon's reports on the loyalty of northern England would make Elizabeth careless of the threat from Catholics – so he asked the Earl to include more pessimistic assessments, for 'I do wish in this case her Majesty still to doubt the worst'.[8] In 1581 Walsingham had wanted the risk from Catholics exaggerated; later he wanted the risk from Spain played down. Early in 1586, Walsingham tried to minimise the chance of an immediate Spanish armada, to counter Elizabeth's reluctance to spend money on Leicester's army in the Netherlands. But the Queen herself discovered, from a Scottish sea captain, that Philip II was gathering a fleet at Lisbon, had a furious row with Walsingham, and threw her slipper in his face. But, flying slippers notwithstanding, councillors continued to try to force Elizabeth's hand. In 1586; the Council was pushing her to call a Parliament for use in disposing of Mary Queen of Scots: 'We stick upon parliament, which her Majesty misliketh, but we do all persist', Burghley reported.[9] Indeed, it seems to have been manipulation of Elizabeth which finally brought Mary to the block. In January 1587, Walsingham apparently faked the 'Stafford Plot' to blow up Elizabeth by gunpowder under her bed. The 'plot' was a ruse to convince Elizabeth that she was in danger so long as Mary lived, and to neutralise the French ambassador, who might have pleaded successfully for Mary's life, by implicating him in the affair. When Mary was safely dead, Walsingham apologised to the ambassador, and assured him that of course the government had never really suspected him of involvement!

Elizabeth trusted Burghley more than any other man; she certainly loved Dudley and for a time wanted to marry him; and she had a high regard for Walsingham's diplomatic and managerial skills – but she spent twenty years resisting the policies they tried to thrust upon her. After the expensive disaster of the 'Newhaven Adventure' (for which Leicester had been most responsible) in 1562–63, and the trade embargo (and collapse of customs revenue) which followed Cecil's seizure of a Spanish loan in 1569, Elizabeth learned caution. She became suspicious of a forward foreign policy, suspicious of her councillors' advice, and reluctant to take clear and determined decisions. Rather than be deceived and hurried by her Council, Queen Elizabeth vacillated and procrastinated. In 1569, Francis Knollys told her that 'It is not possible for your Majesty's councillors to govern your estate unless you shall resolutely follow their opinion in weighty affairs'[10] – but Elizabeth was resolute only in her irresolution, and she drove advisers to distraction by her caution and indecision.

In 1573, Burghley drafted a paper on 'Certain matters wherein the Queen her Majesty's forbearing and delays hath produced not only inconveniences and increases of expenses, but also dangers'; in a section on Scotland, he argued that 'the charges are greater by prolonging and mincing, and the profit less than if her Majesty would have roundly and openly proceeded'. Walsingham, too, wanted, but could not get, decisive action. He told Elizabeth in January 1575, 'For the love of God, Madam, let not the cure of your diseased estate hang any longer in deliberation!' Her procrastination exhausted Secretary Smith, who bewailed his lot in 1575:

> This irresolution doth weary and kill her ministers, destroy her actions and overcome all good designs and counsels – no letters touching Ireland, although read and allowed by her Majesty, yet can I get signed, I wait whilst I neither have eyes to see nor legs to stand upon. [Smith was now 62, and feeling his age!] And yet these delays grieve me more, and will not let me sleep in the night.[11]

Thomas Smith was not cut out for high politics! Francis Walsingham was, but he too was exasperated. He told Elizabeth frankly in 1581, 'Sometimes, when your Majesty doth behold in what doubtful terms you stand with foreign princes, then you do wish with great affection that opportunities offered had not been overslipped. But when they are offered to you (if they are accompanied with charges) they are altogether neglected.'[12]

Officials used stratagems to counteract the Queen's caution and vacillation. In 1590, Elizabeth postponed the signing of warrants to take up privy seal loans from her richer subjects, until she could be convinced they were essential. While pressure was applied to the Queen, the Clerk of the Signet told Burghley 'I do mean to engross the warrant this day, to be ready at any sudden calling for it, for I think her Majesty will sign at length' – and as soon as she did sign, he would send it off before she changed her mind.[13] Much the same tactic had been used with the warrant for Mary's execution in 1587, though Secretary Davison's hasty dispatch of the warrant had put him in the Tower. Elizabeth revoked her decision to allow Mary's execution, but too late, and Davison became her scapegoat – but her servants never quite trusted her again. Robert Beale warned in 1592 that a secretary of state should always get written confirmation of instructions from the Queen, so that if she changed her mind she could not deny her previous orders.

In time, Elizabeth's indecisiveness became a joke around the Court. In February 1594, the Court's move to Windsor was repeatedly postponed by royal orders. When a carter summoned to transport the Queen's wardrobe stuff was sent away for the third time, he called out, 'Now I see the queen is a woman, as well as my wife!'[14] Elizabeth overheard the cry, and sent the carter money to go away and keep quiet: it did her no good to be seen as a 'mere woman'. But her vacillation was more than just female nervousness and indecision – if such a thing exists: it was serious politics. When Elizabeth was so often under pressure to take decisive (and expensive) action on the basis of information selected for her by others, it became a matter of policy to say 'no' – and, if 'yes' was said, to countermand the order. Rather than embark upon an uncertain activist policy, the Queen preferred to do nothing; rather than take an irrevocable wrong decision, she preferred to take no decision at all.

While privy councillors sought to force the Queen to commit herself to a course of action, Elizabeth determinedly kept her options open. In 1572–73, she confused everyone, including her own diplomats, by pursuing a double policy on marriage negotiations with France. She wrote to Walsingham in Paris in

July 1572 that the offer of Alençon as husband should be refused on grounds of age difference: four days later, she wrote that this difficulty might be overcome if she could see the Duke for herself. Walsingham was then instructed to show both letters to King Charles IX – as Burghley commented to Walsingham, 'I see your negotiation shall be full of perplexities.' Nine months later, Walsingham reported on the progress of his talks, but added 'whether this marriage be sincerely meant or no, is a hard point to judge where dissimulation taketh so deep root'.[15] Elizabeth prolonged negotiations until the balance of advantage became clearer, and maintained good relations with the French royal family without actually having to marry one of them.

Her strategy was much the same in the next round of Alençon negotiations, in 1579–81. After two years of further talks, Walsingham still did not know what Elizabeth intended to do, and found her procrastination dangerous. He told her in September 1581 that

> If your Majesty mean it, remember that by the delay your Highness useth therein you lose the benefit of time, which (if years be considered) is not the least to be weighed. If you mean it not, then assure yourself it is one of the worst remedies you can use (howsoever your Majesty conceiveth it, that it may serve your turn).[16]

Walsingham had no confidence in Elizabeth's convoluted marital diplomacy, and pressed for a decision one way or another. Elizabeth, however, wished to drag out the Alençon affair for as long as possible, for it was far from clear what she should do. There were two broad reasons for an Alençon match: it would prevent France and Spain combining to invade England, and it might give some influence over French policy towards the Netherlands Revolt. But there were two broad reasons against such a marriage: the Queen's own aversion to matrimony, and the objections of her Protestant subjects to marriage with a Catholic. For most of the interminable diplomatic courtship, these considerations balanced each other and Elizabeth did nothing. But for a time in 1579 she pursued a marriage policy with determination, and it appears that her reluctance had temporarily abated.

Elizabeth had played the courtship game many times, but in 1579 she seems to have played for real. At the age of 46, the

Alençon proposal was probably her last chance, and he was the best offer she had had. She was twenty years older than he, and he was disfigured by smallpox, but she called him 'her Frog', kissed him in public, and behaved like a lovesick teenager. The Earl of Leicester's marriage to Lettice Knollys may have had something to do with it. But still the Queen was uncertain, torn between the diplomatic and personal advantages of the marriage and the clear public hostility towards it. A campaign of sermons began in March 1579, and reached a crescendo in the autumn – when John Stubbs published *The discovery of a gaping gulf, wherein England is like to be swallowed by another French marriage, if the Lord forbid not the banns by letting her Majesty see the sin and punishment thereof.* The book argued that the match would threaten reformed religion and English independence, and suggested that Alençon was personally depraved and Elizabeth too old to have a child.

The Queen was outraged. She issued a proclamation banning the book, and Stubbs and his publisher were sentenced to have their right hands chopped off with a cleaver. The carrying out of the punishment, on 3 November 1579, was a public relations disaster for Elizabeth, for the evident patriotism of the victims contrasted with the Queen's intention to marry a foreigner. Stubbs asked the crowd, 'Pray for me, now my calamity is at hand', and after his right hand had been severed he took off his hat with his left and cried out 'God save the Queen!' After the publisher had suffered, he told a shocked and silent crowd: 'I have left there a true Englishman's hand.'[17] These public horrors coincided with, and were influenced by, Privy Council debates on the marriage proposal. It is likely that Stubbs was briefed on what to put in his book by Leicester and Walsingham, who almost certainly orchestrated the sermon campaign and the new portraits of the Queen on the theme of virginity. Councillors opposed to the match may also have influenced the tone of dismay in Spencer's *Shepherd's Calendar* (December 1579). Through October and early November, the Council discussed the marriage. The majority of councillors were opposed, but believed that the Queen wanted it, so on 7 October the Council told Elizabeth that they would recommend neither for nor against.

Elizabeth was furious. What she had wanted was encouragement, and an assurance that the Council would stand by her against the public outcry. Now she did not know what to do. She contemplated bringing four Catholics on to the Council to build up support for the match. On 10 November she told the Council that she would marry Alençon, but two days later she again asked for their advice. On 20 November she appointed a committee to agree marriage terms with Alençon's agent, but on the 24th, as the agent left for France, she asked for a two-month delay while she tried to persuade her subjects to accept the alliance. On the Council, only Sussex whole-heartedly supported the match; Burghley thought it would be better than no marriage at all, and Hunsdon would go along with his royal cousin's wishes. The opponents, led by Leicester, pulled out all the stops. They refused to endorse the Queen's plan; they whipped up public opinion by preaching and the press; Sir Philip Sydney, Leicester's nephew, reminded Elizabeth of her duty to the Gospel and her obligation to English Protestants; Bishop Cox composed a treatise against the marriage; and there were lampoons and broadsheets in the streets of London. Elizabeth gave in, and told Alençon that her people would not consent to the marriage. In fact, it had been dished by the Privy Council.

But still Elizabeth wished to keep her diplomatic options open, and still she was uncertain. As she confided to Burghley in 1581,

> My Lord, here I am between Scylla and Charybdis. Alençon has agreed to all the terms I sent him, and he is asking me to tell him when I wish him to come and marry me. If I do not marry him, I do not know whether he will remain friendly with me, and if I do I shall not be able to govern the country with the freedom and security I have hitherto enjoyed.

So she swung indecisively between plans for a French alliance and plans for a French marriage, testing Walsingham's patience to the end:

> When her Majesty is pressed to marry, then she seemeth to affect a league, and when a league is yielded to, then she liketh better of a marriage. And when thereupon she is moved to assent to marriage, then she hath recourse to the league; when the motion for the league or any request is made for money, then her Majesty returneth to marriage.[18]

Emotionally, at least, Elizabeth had cooled to the marriage, but negotiations continued in hope of diplomatic advantage – especially to use Alençon against Spain in the Netherlands. Privy councillors, however, could never quite be sure: perhaps she would try to marry. On 17 November 1581, Elizabeth and Alençon exchanged rings and announced their betrothal. The Queen had apparently concluded that Alençon would not leave England unless she promised to marry him, if only to save his face. But Leicester and Hatton played safe, and got the ladies of the Privy Chamber to weep and wail about the horrors of marriage, to scare Elizabeth off just in case she had been serious.

The Alençon marriage project effectively died late in 1581, though it took another three months to bundle the Duke out of the country. Alençon himself died in 1584, when Elizabeth was 51 and past hope of childbearing: she wept, went into mourning, and called herself his 'widow'. For a while, in 1579, she had meant to marry him: she had his miniature bound into her book of private prayers, and she was at least in love with the idea of love. But her plans were blocked by the forward Protestant party on the Council, who used Protestant opinion as a weapon to coerce the Queen. Leicester stopped an Alençon marriage in 1579, just as Cecil had stopped a Dudley marriage in 1560–61. The more Protestant councillors did not want the Netherlands problem solved by marriage to a tame French prince; they wanted it solved by direct English intervention in the Protestant cause.

Elizabeth's longest tussle with her Council was over English military action in the Netherlands. The issue dominated her relations with councillors from 1576, when Leicester first proposed the dispatch of force, to 1585, when Elizabeth finally gave in. The Protestant leaders on the Council – Leicester, Walsingham, Knollys, Mildmay, and, more cautiously, Burghley – shared a common view of foreign policy. They believed that France and Spain had conspired with the Pope to extirpate Protestantism, and every move they made was seen as a step in their grand design. To Walsingham, the Catholic states were implacable enemies, and there was no point in seeking agreement with them – as he wrote in 1578, 'if any think they may work her Majesty's surety by procuring a reconciliation between her Highness and them, as I know some have been carried away with such conceits, they will be found to be authors of very dangerous and unsound counsel, building surety on a reconciled enemy'.[19] No safety could be found in the agreements Elizabeth sought with France and Spain: only their defeat, by a Protestant alliance, would do – and Protestant allies had to be protected.

Elizabeth had refused official English military intervention to assist Dutch Protestants (though, typically, she had allowed English volunteers to fight), and she had lent the Dutch only enough money to stop them being defeated. But by 1585 her policy was falling to pieces. Alençon, who had helped the Dutch rebels, was dead, and the French card could no longer be played. William the Silent, who had led the Dutch, had been murdered, Antwerp had fallen to Spanish troops, and the French Catholic League had allied with the King of Spain. England's protective shields, the Dutch and French Protestants, seemed about to buckle. The Privy Council agreed in principle to send troops to the Netherlands in October 1584, despite resistance from Burghley. But Elizabeth could not be brought to a deal with the Dutch until August 1585, and not until mid-December did she allow her army commander, Leicester, to leave from Harwich. Finally, after years of pressure, the Protestant zealots on the Council had got their way: they had used their agents as ambassadors, so they could control the flow of information to the Queen; they had dealt secretly with foreign Protestant leaders, and advised them on how best to approach Elizabeth; and they had kept up a constant barrage of aggressive advice to the Queen and criticism of her caution.

It is worth examining how it was that Elizabeth was able to resist Council pressure for so long, and how she managed to keep her own policy going despite majority opposition. It is not enough to say that she was the Queen and would get her way, for she was forced to act against her will on some occasions. She needed to be able to distance herself from her leading councillors, to identify and resist their manipulation, to secure other sources of advice and information, and to force them to do her will. In short, if councillors tried to manage Elizabeth, she had to manage them. Sometimes she tried to do this by joining in their deliberations. She had attended almost every Council meeting for the first month or so of her reign, but thereafter she was present only rarely and for special purposes. On 17 July 1562, she attended a specially summoned meeting to discuss preparations for war with France – perhaps because Robert Dudley, a leading proponent of war, was not yet a councillor, and the Queen herself pressed his war policy against some

Council opposition. On 12 October 1566, she attended a meeting, to try to prevent councillors using Parliament to push her into marriage or clarification of the succession. In May 1568, Elizabeth called and attended two crisis meetings on what to do about the flight of Mary Queen of Scots into England, probably so that she could defuse Council hostility to Mary.

Elizabeth had to meet her Council as a whole several times in the dangerous days of 1569–70. She was present at a session on 29 April 1570, for discussion of the related problems of Mary, Scotland, the English Catholics, and the threat from France and Spain. She apparently told councillors 'that she herself was free from any determined resolution, and that she would first hear their advice and thereupon make choice of what she should think meetest for her honour'.[20] The idea of Elizabeth asking for advice and listening to it calmly is a strange one, and there is not much sign that she did so again. In fact, all her enquiry revealed was division in the Privy Council, between those (led by Cecil and Bacon) who favoured an aggressive policy of persecution of Catholics at home and alliance with Protestants abroad, and those (led by Arundel and, for the moment, Leicester) who proposed an accommodation with Mary and France, and possibly with English Catholics too. Elizabeth herself preferred the second strategy, it seems, and certainly she was soon touting herself as a potential bride for a French prince: she probably attended the Council meeting to bolster the minority position.

In the early part of the reign, the Queen summoned her Council to her for very special debates, and she did so mainly when her own view was held by a minority who needed her support. It made sound political sense to participate in discussions, and prevent her Council agreeing to give her formal advice which she would have to reject. Later, Elizabeth achieved the same end by insulating herself from her Council, especially over contentious problems such as Netherlands policy. In 1578, Leicester complained that 'Our conference with her Majesty is both seldom and slender', and she maintained her political distance. In April 1586 Leicester, as army commander in the Netherlands, complained that the Privy Council rarely wrote to him. Walsingham replied on the Council's behalf: 'They answer, as it is truth, that her Majesty, retaining the whole direction of the causes of that country to herself and such advice as she receiveth underhand, they know not what to write or to advise.'[21] Elizabeth was refusing to deal with her Council as a body, and discussed policy only with individuals or small groups.

Elizabeth always preferred to face her ministers singly or in twos and threes. Late in her reign (and probably much earlier, too) she would meet chosen advisers individually, make notes on their opinions, and then call them together as a small group to go over a problem together: she would interrupt and cross-question, using her notes to try to catch councillors out. The Queen often worked through an inner ring of advisers, and (especially in her early years) they were not always members of the Council. In the spring of 1559, the Spanish ambassador thought that Elizabeth was using Cecil, Bacon, Parry, and Robert Dudley to run the country. Dudley was not yet a privy councillor, and at that time Elizabeth was also consulting Lord Paget – though she had removed him from the Council at her accession. This suggests that the Queen could not quite have the councillors she wanted: her own ambiguous relationship with Dudley and the unpopularity of Paget among Protestants would have tainted the appearance of the new regime.

Perhaps Elizabeth did not have a free hand in her choice of councillors, but she could decide whom to consult and whom to trust. In the autumn of 1559, when Cecil was pressing for military intervention in Scotland, the Queen's consultations were restricted: Cecil reported, 'In these matters, her Majesty maketh privy but few, the earl of Pembroke, the Admiral, the Treasurer and few others.'[22] Elizabeth's caution was justified, for when the agreed policy was put to the whole Council there was much opposition – but Cecil and his allies had their way. The inner ring of government in the early 1560s comprised Cecil, Bacon, and Dudley, with the addition of Pembroke and Clinton for military matters and Winchester for finance. But the stability of the central group was disrupted by acute factionalism from 1565, though orderly co-operation was again possible after 1572. Thereafter, Burghley, Leicester, and Walsingham formed the core until 1589, with Hatton rising rapidly in influence and the Queen herself often consulting Sussex. It is interesting that Elizabeth did not recruit her very closest advisers from among those who shared her views: she argued for years with Burghley over what to do with Mary Stuart, and with Leicester and Walsingham over the Netherlands. Hatton on domestic matters and Sussex on foreign policy were in some measure antidotes to the militant Protestant line.

The Queen sought to maintain a balance of opinions among her advisers and on the Privy Council. She sometimes appointed councillors in contrasting pairs: Dudley and Norfolk in October 1562; Sadler and Croft in October 1566; Wilson and Hunsdon in November 1577 – each time with a godly Protestant countered by a more cautious or conservative member. But by the mid-1580s, especially with the death of Sussex in 1583, the tone of the Council was decidedly Protestant, and the Queen was being pressed to intervene in the Netherlands and execute Mary. She gave in on both issues, but she tried to give herself more room for manœuvre by appointing the less militant Buckhurst, Cobham, and Whitgift early in 1586. The intriguing position of Sir James Croft seems particularly illuminating. Despite his earlier career, under Elizabeth he was conservative, pro-Spanish, and, by the 1580s, so much in debt that he was selling state secrets to the Spanish ambassador. But he was a useful agent of Elizabeth's policy towards Spain, for she never entirely committed herself to a military strategy. In 1585, while Leicester was leading (or, more accurately, following) his army to the Netherlands, Croft had an agent negotiating with Parma, the Spanish Governor. In 1588, while the Armada was on its way from Spain, Croft was treating directly with Parma in the Netherlands – though Croft spoke only English, and misunderstood the terms Parma offered. Croft was left looking a fool, but Walsingham had regarded him as a major, and dangerous, influence on the Queen.

Elizabeth tried to insulate herself against political pressures by avoiding meetings with the whole Council. She consulted her councillors individually, and she took the views of informed men outside the Council. She often had long, and sometimes private, talks with foreign ambassadors, to ensure that she had other sources of information and ideas. She tried to protect herself from unpalatable advice by promoting divisions of opinion among councillors, and by making them compete for her rewards. Elizabeth's granting and refusing of favour bred competition between councillors, and made it harder for them to band together to manipulate the Queen. Walsingham and Burghley fell out early in 1585, when Burghley seemed to be hindering Walsingham's suit to the Queen for a farm of the customs: the importance of the struggle is suggested by its outcome, for when Walsingham got the lease he made £3,500 a year profit on it. In 1586, Leicester and Walsingham, usually political allies, were in hot dispute, for Leicester suspected that his claim for Crown leases had been undermined by the Secretary: 'I see all men have friends but myself', he wrote bitterly. 'I see most false suggestions help other men, and my upright, true dealing cannot protect me. Nay, my worldly protector faileth me.'[23] Even the triumvirate upon whom Elizabeth most relied were split by such conflicts – and it was all to the Queen's advantage.

Elizabeth's angry outbursts and occasional violence reminded her ministers that her favour was conditional. She would rage that her councillors would be 'shorter by the head', or that she would 'set them by the feet' in stocks. Norfolk and Essex were executed; Davison and Croft went to prison; Arundel and Pembroke suffered house arrest. The Queen threw her slipper at Walsingham, slapped Essex's face, and ranted at Leicester times without number. She had a richly deserved reputation as an evil-tempered woman, and her wrath towards errant councillors, contrived or not, was a dissuasion from disagreement. She was furious with Bacon in 1564 for his covert support of the Grey claim to the succession: he narrowly escaped removal from office, and he was barred from Court for six months. Burghley, Leicester, and Walsingham all found it safer to stay away from Court at times, and in 1579 both Leicester and Walsingham were excluded from the Queen's presence (and therefore her patronage) for a couple of months over their opposition to the Alençon match. Those who had built their fortunes on the Queen's favour had to be sure not to lose it, and this risk imposed limits to the freedom of councillors.

Elizabeth sought to make her councillors afraid, but she did not rule them by fear alone. When Burghley was sick, she would send him her own physician, visit him at home, and feed him soup. When Leicester feared her wrath, he would retire to his sickbed – knowing that she would rush to his side in anxious sympathy. Elizabeth's fury made councillors fear her, but by her attentiveness she also made them love her. The Queen's anger raged fiercely, but it soon passed: as Leicester wrote to Burghley in 1573, 'God be thanked, her blasts be not the storms of other princes, though they be very sharp sometimes to those she loves best. Every man must render to her their due, and the most bounden the most of all.'[24]

NOTES AND REFERENCES

1. Thorp M R 1984 Catholic conspiracy in early Elizabethan foreign policy, *Sixteenth Century Journal* 15: 433
2. Read C 1955 *Mr Secretary Cecil and Queen Elizabeth.* Cape, p. 419; Haynes S (ed.) 1740 *A Collection of State Papers ... left by William Cecill.* Bowyer, p. 471
3. Read C 1955 p. 394
4. *Calendar of State Papers Spanish, 1558–67*, p. 591; Wright T 1838 *Queen Elizabeth and her times* (2 vols). Colburn, vol. 2 p. 452
5. De Maisse A H 1931 *A Journal of All That Was Accomplished by Monsieur de Maisse.* Nonsuch, p. 3; Smith L B 1975 *Elizabeth Tudor: portrait of a queen.* Hutchinson, p. 215
6. Thorp M R 1984: 438; Read C 1955 p. 357
7. Wilson D 1981 *Sweet Robin: a biography of Robert Dudley, earl of Leicester.* Hamilton, p. 239; Read C 1960 *Lord Burghley and Queen Elizabeth.* Cape, p. 195
8. Pulman M B 1971 *The Elizabethan Privy Council in the Fifteen-Seventies.* California, p. 241
9. Read C 1960 p. 361
10. Smith L B 1975 p. 210
11. Read C 1925 *Mr Secretary Walsingham and the Policy of Queen Elizabeth* (3 vols). Oxford, vol. 2 pp. 128n–9n; Read C 1960 p. 145
12. Read C 1925 vol. 2 p. 87
13. Johnson P 1974 *Elizabeth I: a study in power and intellect.* Weidenfeld & Nicolson, p. 339
14. Harrison G B (ed.) 1938 *The Elizabethan Journals, 1591–1603* (3 vols). Routledge & Kegan Paul, vol. 1 p. 284
15. Read C 1925 vol. 1 pp. 208–9, 256
16. Read C 1925 vol. 2 p. 87
17. Harington J 1804 *Nugae Antiquae* (2 vols). Park T (ed.). Vernon & Hood, vol. 1 pp. 157–8; Camden W 1675 *The History of the Most Renowned and Victorious Princess Elizabeth*, p. 270
18. Read C 1960 p. 226; Read C 1925 vol. 2 p. 75
19. Read C 1925 vol. 1 p. 417
20. Read C 1960 p. 21

21. Williams P H 1979 *The Tudor Regime*. Oxford, p. 32;   Read C 1960 p. 329
22. Read C 1955 p. 156
23. Read C 1925 vol. 3 p. 166
24. Wilson D 1981 p. 216

Chapter 5

THE QUEEN AND THE COURT

Elizabeth I was a show-off, and she dressed to kill. She appeared before her courtiers in elegant gowns of black satin or purple velvet, slashed with silks and brocades and encrusted with gold and pearls; she wore richly jewelled pendants, rings, and bracelets; she carried embroidered gloves and decorated fans. Her Wardrobe inventory of 1600 lists, in addition to her formal Coronation, Parliament, Garter, and Mourning robes, 99 robes, 102 French gowns, 67 round gowns, 100 loose gowns, 126 kirtles, 96 cloaks and 26 fans – including 'one fan of white feathers, with a handle of gold, having two snakes winding about it, garnished with a ball of diamonds in the end and a crown on each side with a pair of wings garnished with diamonds' (though six diamonds were missing!). The Queen dressed to impress, and she expected to be admired – even by foreigners. In 1564 she engaged the Scottish ambassador in a tricky diplomatic exchange, questioning him on the comparative beauty of herself and Mary Queen of Scots. She got crosser and crosser, as Melville skilfully defended his own queen's looks without disparaging Elizabeth, until, she thought, she caught him out – when he admitted that Mary was taller, Elizabeth retorted jubilantly, 'Then she is too high! I myself am neither too high nor too low!'[1] Her approach was much the same in 1597, when she was 64: the new French ambassador was confused when the Queen received him in her dressing-gown and kept pulling it open, until he realised that he was supposed to peep admiringly down her front.

To her own courtiers and to foreign dignitaries, Elizabeth showed herself off both as a queen and as a woman. She played both parts, and she played them for all she was worth. Edmund Spenser, in *The Faerie Queene* recognised the duality, and

86

portrayed her as Gloriana, 'a most royal queen and empress', and as Belphoebe, 'a most virtuous and beautiful lady'. The ritual and celebrations of the Court were built around a cult of Elizabeth in the two roles: she was both *above* the Court, as a sovereign claiming the fealty of her knights, and *of* the Court, as the virgin lady for whose honour the knights fought at the tilt. The Court served as a splendid palace for the display of majesty, but also as a more intimate forum for romantic play-acting and political seduction. For Elizabeth attempted to control her councillors and her magnates by drawing them into a web of personal, even emotional, relationships with her, in which she was by turns queen and coquette. She expected her politicians to be courtiers, so that she politicised the Court and made politics courtly: as Sir John Davies noted,

> All funerals, nuptials and like public sights,
> All parliaments of peace and warlike fights,
> All learned arts and every great affair
> A lively shape of dancing seems to bear.[2]

The rituals of Court life and the intimate relationships which developed there were used as techniques of political manipulation. When Elizabeth played upon the virginals for her councillors, she was playing politics as surely as when she presided at the Council board.

Sir Christopher Hatton, courtier, dancer and Lord Chancellor, would say that 'The Queen did fish for men's souls, and had so sweet a bait that no-one could escape her network.'[3] Her fishpond was the Court, and there she fished for the political loyalty of her major subjects. Probably two-thirds of the nobility were at least part-time courtiers early in Elizabeth's reign, and though the proportion fell later it was not by very much. In addition, fifty or sixty leading gentry, mainly from southern England, were resident courtiers, and there were many other occasional callers. Roughly one in five of the political heavyweights of England were thus under the regular influence of the Queen, subject to her tantrums and her temptings – but they were also well placed to exercise influence themselves. Elizabeth had deliberately politicised her Court, by making courtiers into politicians (such as Dudley, Hatton, and Essex) and politicians into courtiers (such as William Cecil, Francis Knollys, and James Croft). This made politics a full-time business, subject to the personal relationships of the Court:

courtiers who captured the Queen's affection could wield political influence without holding political office.

In 1570, William Cecil warned the courtier Thomas Heneage against meddling in politics, but without success. Heneage claimed that he never 'gave her Majesty advice in a corner against the determination of her Council, or ever opened my mouth to her Majesty in matter concerning the public estate or government, *except* it pleased her to ask mine opinion'. That was the catch, for the Queen could consult whomever she wished: the Council claimed a monopoly of political advice to the Queen, but could not enforce it. Robert Dudley was a major political force from the beginning of the reign, and was more than anyone else responsible for the 'Newhaven Adventure' – though he was not admitted to the Council until October 1562. The interference of Lord Paget was much resented by councillors, who protested to Elizabeth in February 1562 that 'it was but a folly for them to debate things if she followed other's counsel'. The Earl of Sussex was central to the political battles of 1565–66, pressing hard in favour of a Habsburg marriage – but he was appointed to the Council only in December 1570, when his defeat of the northern rebels had given him an irrefutable claim. Walter Raleigh established a considerable personal influence over Elizabeth, and was said to be 'a kind of oracle':[4] he led a group of younger courtiers in an agitation against Leicester in 1587, and in the 1590s he advised the Queen on foreign and colonial policy – but he was never a councillor. Just as Elizabeth kept Sussex from the Council to avoid provoking Leicester, so she excluded Raleigh to calm Essex. But she could consult any courtier who took her fancy.

Every courtier was a potential politician, for the life of the Court created non-stop opportunities for private lobbying and personal relationships which could be pressed into political service. It was widely recognised that the Court was the essential centre of political activity and source of power and patronage. But those not at Court were politically crippled, lacking direct access to the sovereign. When, in the early 1590s, the Earl of Shrewsbury was engaged in a power struggle in Nottingham-shire with the Stanhope family, he was at a real disadvantage because his rivals were courtiers. Lord Buckhurst warned him

> that the continual presence of these two brethren in Court, with the near place they hold to her Majesty, and that

which is above all the rest, the especial favour which her
Majesty doth bear unto them, will always prevail with so
great advantage against you as it will not be possible for
you or your friends to carry this cause in that course of
good success which peradventure you hope for.[5]

In 1593 the Stanhopes won and Shrewsbury was humiliated,
showing that Court influence would beat provincial power.

It was therefore a major tactical coup to have a rival posted
away from Court by the Queen. Robert Dudley seems to have
been behind the nomination of the Duke of Norfolk as general
of the army for Scotland in 1559, to remove an opponent of his
marriage plans from Court. Sir Christopher Hatton got Sir
John Perrot appointed Lord Deputy in Ireland in 1584, to prise
him away from Elizabeth, whose half-brother he claimed to be.
In 1599 it was probably Robert Cecil who ensured that Essex
would be made Lord Lieutenant in Ireland; foolishly, Essex
wanted the job – wisely, Cecil made sure he got it. In the
enforced absence of a rival, a courtier's own position could be
strengthened. In 1586, while Leicester was in the Netherlands,
Burghley got his own allies Buckhurst, Cobham, and Whitgift
on to the Council; in 1596, Burghley had Robert Cecil made
Secretary while Essex was away sacking Cadiz; and in 1597 Cecil
also gained the chancellorship of the Duchy of Lancaster while
Essex was on the Azores expedition. Essex should have listened
to the advice he had been given: 'Let nothing draw thee from the
Court; sit in every council.'[6]

Presence at Court was crucial to political success, because the
Court was the clearing-house for royal patronage and the
distribution of patronage was a key to political power. Lesser
men attached themselves to courtiers who might secure them
offices or grants, and the great channelled rewards to those
whose support was worth having. A courtier's following in his
locality was dependent upon ability to provide patronage, and
that was dependent on the favour of the Queen – so the
distribution of political power could be determined by the
Queen's affections. Fluctuations in royal favour were of vital
importance to suitors, and Court agents and gossip-writers
passed news of the fortunes of leading courtiers. In May 1573,
Gilbert Talbot reported to the Earl of Shrewsbury that Leicester
was high in favour, Sussex declining, Oxford rising fast, and
Hatton at risk from a challenge by Edward Dyer. 'At all these

love matters my Lord Treasurer winketh, and will not meddle any way', Talbot wrote[7] – but Burghley had his own special relationship with Elizabeth, and her trust gave him massive influence over patronage.

Lord Burghley received 60–100 letters a day from suitors and clients, and the management of royal favour was a major task. He organised his private office into two sections, one to deal with foreign affairs and the other, under Michael Hicks, to handle patronage. As Lord Treasurer and Master of the Wards, Burghley controlled the biggest reward-giving institutions, and he sought to supervise other areas of royal patronage. He had told Sir Ralph Sadler that 'As fish are gotten with baits, so are offices with seeking'[8] – and he wanted the seeking to be done through him. In 1581 Burghley was furious with Thomas Wilkes, Clerk of the Council, for putting a suit to the Queen via Walsingham rather than through him. Burghley's vigorous activity was partly to prevent Leicester achieving a monopoly of influence, for since the Earl always stood highest in Elizabeth's affections he was potentially the most effective patron.

Leicester, like Burghley, was constantly besieged by suitors anxious to make use of his standing with the Queen. George Gilpin wrote for assistance in the speedy execution of a land grant: 'Seeing the great affairs whereat your Honour is continually travailed, I have been afraid to trouble you with my humble suit, but now am of pure necessity constrained most humbly to beseech your Honour to stand my good lord to further this my suit, whereof I have here enclosed a brief note unto the queen's majesty.'[9] Leicester was a highly successful patron in some areas, especially the Church: he had patronised at least six of the first Elizabethan bishops, four later bishops, six deans, and any number of heads of Oxford and Cambridge colleges. In addition, he almost controlled the diplomatic service, and most appointments to the Netherlands were made from among his followers. In military posts, too, Leicester's influence was clear, especially for the 'Dudley' expeditions of 1562 and 1585. But his parliamentary patronage seems surprisingly restricted: as high steward of a number of boroughs, he advanced their petitions at Court, but his suggestions of MPs were often resisted and he made no systematic attempt to collect nominations.

Below the level of the great, lesser men pursued their own interests and used their contacts to advantage. A host of sinecures, wardships, leases, and licences went to second-rank courtiers, and the band of gentlemen pensioners was notably successful. Brian Ansley was a gentleman pensioner from 1564 to 1603: his position at Court enabled him to gain licences to import steel and to export cony skins, and the office of warden of the Fleet prison, which he leased for £100 a year. Lancelot Bostock, gentleman pensioner between 1564 and 1588, acquired a grant of fines under the Pluralities Act and the constableship of Flint Castle in 1572, the constableship of Holt Castle in 1585, and lands in Ireland in 1587. Simon Bowyer was a gentleman usher of the Privy Chamber, little more than a glorified doorman, from 1569 to 1597: he gained the captaincy of a castle in Hampshire, worth £100 a year, and a patent to inquire into offences against the wool statutes (which gave huge opportunities for blackmail and receipt of bribes). Not all Court careers were profitable, however. Robert Markham and Sir William Cornwallis were both ruined by expensive failure: Cornwallis claimed to have spent £20,000 trying to establish himself at Court, but, after twenty-seven years of effort, all he had by 1597 was the role of stand-in groom porter, and his plea for the reversion of the post was refused.

What kept these men trying was the example of the real successes, those who most effectively caught Elizabeth's attention. Christopher Hatton joined the Court in 1564, and by the early 1570s was a recognised favourite. But in 1575 he was £10,000 in debt and had no established office. He was hoping for an annuity from the Queen, but she had hinted that if he asked he would not get one: he told Burghley that 'The annuity I dare not speak of, because it seemeth to me by her Highness that it should be delivered me before I looked for it.'[10] But then Hatton's luck turned. In 1575 Elizabeth granted him an annuity of £400, the Dean and Chapter of Peterborough were forced to give him favourable leases, and the Bishop of Ely had to hand over his London house. In 1577 he became Vice-chamberlain of the Household, and in 1578 he got the office which established his fortune – as Receiver of First Fruits and Tenths, he was able to live out of Elizabeth's till, and by his death in 1591 he had run up debts to his department of £42,000. He became Lord Chancellor in 1587 – jealous Court wits called him 'the dancing chancellor' – and he speculated in the discovery of concealed Crown lands, the wine trade, and taxes on foreign merchants. Hatton's influence on the Queen made him a major patronage-broker, and his servant Samuel Cox managed patronage for him as Hicks managed it for Burghley.

But while some made spectacular profits, others fretted at their neglect. The Duke of Norfolk complained in 1565 that 'her Highness hardly thinks anything well-bestowed upon me, be it never so small'. In 1570 Sussex remarked crossly that he was 'kept but for a broom, and when I have done my office to be thrown out of the door'.[11] Perhaps it was not simply the money they wanted, but the signs of royal favour which gave prestige and therefore power. In 1582, when Sir Henry Sidney was asked to return to Ireland as Lord Deputy, he requested some reward, 'that it may be known and made apparent to the world that her Majesty hath had gracious consideration of his service past, and for his better encouragement thereafter'. This may have been a convenient cover, since Sidney's demands do not suggest he sought a token reward – he asked for an English peerage, an Irish peerage, and a large grant of land. Elizabeth refused, perhaps thinking, as she had twenty years earlier, that 'no prince's revenues are able to satisfy the insatiable cupidity of men'.[12] But this 'insatiable cupidity', the constant search of courtiers for greater rewards, gave the Queen a formidable political weapon – for it made her courtiers and her politicians grovel for her favour. It put the Queen's own affections at the centre of the political system, forced political leaders to approach her as adoring supplicants, and enabled her to turn political relationships into a promiscuous series of romantic interludes.

While Elizabeth as Gloriana was portrayed as a formalised icon of idealised authority, Elizabeth as Belphoebe was chatting up the boys. The Queen sought to establish personal relationships in her Court in a relaxed and intimate fashion, in which all attention was upon her as a woman – and therefore upon her as monarch too. No matter how informal she became, no courtier (except perhaps for Essex) quite dared ignore her higher role. Edward Dyer advised Hatton, who was courting Elizabeth in 1572, 'Consider with whom you have to deal, and what we be towards her who, though she do descend very much in her sex as a woman, yet we may not forget her place and the nature of it as our sovereign.'[13] This duality made it possible for Elizabeth to use personal friendships, even feigned loves, as political strings to manipulate her servants. She treated her courtier-politicians as if they were her intimate friends, and had nicknames for those closest to her: Burghley was 'Sir Spirit', Walsingham 'The Moor', Raleigh 'Water', Leicester 'Eyes', and Hatton 'Lids'. Leicester and Hatton would sign their letters to her with symbols representing their pet names, and it is an indication of the seriousness of the second Alençon courtship that he was her 'Frog' and his agent Simier her 'Monkey'.

The life of the Court was a routine of secularised rituals for an earthly goddess, interspersed with intimate attentions to an adored woman. As she did with her nobles, Elizabeth exchanged New Year's gifts with her councillors, household officials, courtiers, ladies of the Chamber and grooms of the Chamber. Although the exchange had become bureaucratised on the Queen's side, it was meant to symbolise close relationships. Many of the gifts to Elizabeth were personalised expressions of devotion from those seeking her favour. In 1578 Hatton gave

a fair jewel of gold, being a cross of diamonds fully garnished with small diamonds and a fair pearl pendant, the queen's picture on the back side; and more, a jewel of gold, wherein is a dog leading a man over a bridge, the body fully garnished with small diamonds and rubies, and three small pearls pendant, the back side certain verses written.[14]

In return for these carefully chosen tokens, he received 400 ounces of gilt plate, four times the weight given to any other courtier.

Elizabeth invited, indeed she insisted upon, the most extreme praise, expecting her courtiers to tell her obvious lies. She forced them into the role of worshippers at her shrine, and made obeisance to her alleged qualities fundamental to Court rhetoric. Edward Dyer told Christopher Hatton in October 1572 that he would best retain the Queen's favour, against the challenge of the Earl of Oxford, by flattery: 'Never seem deeply to condemn her frailties, but rather joyfully to commend such things as should be in her, as though they were in her indeed.' Hatton followed this advice, and became a fulsome flatterer. In June 1573, he wrote to Elizabeth from Antwerp:

This is the twelfth day since I saw the brightness of that sun that giveth light unto my sense and soul. I wax an amazed creature. Give me leave, Madam, to remove myself out of this irksome shadow, so far as my imagination with these good means may lead me towards you, and let me thus salute you: Live forever, most excellent creature, and love some man, to show yourself thankful for God his high labour in you.[15]

The most improbable declarations of eternal devotion were expected, and the Earl of Essex – and his secretaries – excelled in the style. A letter from Essex to Elizabeth in 1591 promised

The two windows of your Privy Chamber shall be the poles of my sphere, where, as long as your Majesty will please to have me, I am fixed and unmovable. When your Majesty thinks that heaven too good for me, I will not fall like a star, but be consumed like a vapour by the sun that draws me up to such a height. While your Majesty gives me leave to say I love you, my fortune is as my affection, unmatchable. If ever you deny me that liberty, you may end my life, but never shake my constancy, for were the sweetness of your nature turned into the greatest bitterness that could be, it is not in your power, as great a queen as you are, to make me love you less.

When Walter Raleigh was excluded from the royal presence for getting Elizabeth Throckmorton pregnant, he sent to Robert Cecil a letter obviously meant to be shown to the Queen:

I that was wont to behold her riding like Alexander, hunting like Diana, walking like Venus, the gentle wind blowing her fair hair about her pure cheeks like a nymph, sometime sitting in the shade like a goddess, sometime singing like an angel, sometime playing like Orpheus; behold! the sorrow of this world once amiss hath bereaved me of all.[16]

This was in 1592, when Elizabeth was in her sixtieth year, with neither fair hair nor pure cheeks!

But age had not lessened the Queen's demand for flattery. The French ambassador reported in 1597 that she would call herself old and foolish, or decry her own intelligence, to prompt others to praise her gifts. The pageantry of the Court was also focused upon the Queen's qualities, making elaborate metaphorical statements of her glory. In the late 1570s, the 17 November Accession Day tilts, which had been simply boisterous Court sports, were turned into formalised public spectacles in which nobles and courtiers dressed as valiant knights and jousted for the favour of an idealised Virgin Queen. On festive occasions the whole Court was involved in ritualised role-playing. In 1579, during the Alençon courtship, an elaborate allegory of the wooing was mounted at Court. Two groups of knights, representing Desire and Despair, jousted over the Queen's virginity, while a pageant showed the Fortress of Perfect Beauty, representing Elizabeth, besieged with cannon shooting perfumed water and sweets, and attackers threw flowers at the walls of the impregnable castle. Virtue defended the castle, and successfully resisted the assaults of Desire.

Such pageants were partly public propaganda, but they were also mass indoctrinations of the participants. The rhetoric and ritual of devotion were more than a woman's fancy or a gallant style; they formed a framework for political relations and a constant reinforcement of loyal attitudes. From 1586, it became the fashion among courtiers to sport miniatures or jewelled cameos of the Queen, as badges of devotion – almost an owner's brand-mark. Francis Drake, Hatton, Heneage, and Walsingham had their portraits painted wearing such medallions, and even the ageing Burghley was portrayed with a cameo of the Queen in his hat. Elizabeth was arrogant, but she was not a fool: she knew she was extolled with shallow gestures and flattering lies – but she wanted it done because it elevated her above all others and enforced extreme deference upon those with whom she worked. Courtiers and politicians were drawn into play-acting conspiracies to deceive themselves and the world: they acted out exaggerated versions of what reality was supposed to be, and in doing so came to believe some of it.

Elizabeth's projection of herself as the desired object of all her courtiers, and the devoted lover of some, put the ladies of the Court in a difficult and vulnerable position. They lived in a sexually charged environment, but they were not allowed to challenge the Queen. When Elizabeth heard false rumours that Lettice Dudley was to join her husband Leicester in the Netherlands and establish a viceregal household, she raged that 'she would have no more courts under her obeisance but her own'. It was partly to subdue any rival attractions that Elizabeth tried to exert a rigid sexual discipline upon the Court, and especially over the unmarried Maids of Honour – and, of course, it did the reputation of the Virgin Queen no good if the

Maids kept getting pregnant! In 1581 Ann Vavasour and the Earl of Oxford were both sent to the Tower after Ann gave birth in the Maids' Chamber. In 1591 a courtier went to prison for what was euphemistically described as 'Mistress Southwell's lameness in her leg',[17] and one of the Dudleys was banished from Court for kissing a Maid. In 1592, Walter Raleigh and Elizabeth Throckmorton went to the Tower for her pregnancy, though they had married when it became known. In 1598, the Earl of Southampton fled to Paris when the Queen discovered his affair with Elizabeth Vernon, and they were both sent to the Tower when he returned to marry her. The Earl of Pembroke was imprisoned in 1601 when he admitted paternity of Mary Fitton's stillborn child, and he was later barred from the Court when he refused marriage.

Elizabeth found Court marriages only slightly less annoying than sex without marriage: she tried to prevent the Maids and Court ladies marrying, and was angry if they did so without her approval. In 1585 Frances Howard asked the Queen if she could marry the Earl of Hertford, but was forbidden; when the couple went ahead and married anyway, Elizabeth was furious. When Mary Shelton sought to marry, Elizabeth beat her and broke her finger. When Mary Arundell asked for permission, Elizabeth promised to secure her father's consent – but when the Queen obtained the father's letter of approval, she taunted the girl and told her, 'I vow thou shalt never get it into thy possession, so go to thy business!'[18] In 1594, Bridget Manners knew the Queen would refuse permission if she was asked, so she ran away from the Court and married Robert Tyrwhit; the two were summoned to London, Bridget was put under house arrest, and Robert got out of prison only when his health failed. Elizabeth was cross about most Court marriages – those of Leicester, Sir Philip Sidney, Sir Thomas Perrot, Robert Carey, and John Wingfield, as well as Hertford, Southampton, Raleigh, and Tyrwhit.

Perhaps sexual jealousy was the main reason for her opposition, for it is notable that the cases of trouble generally occurred after her own failure to marry Alençon (and after Leicester's marriage to Lettice Knollys). Perhaps it was the bitterness of an ageing woman at the attractions of the young: she had, after all, in her late thirties, set up a Dutch alchemist in a secret laboratory in Somerset House to find the elixir of youth! But even at her most emotional, Elizabeth was at least partly political. She wanted to be surrounded by celibate bachelor admirers – though of those close to her only Hatton made the expected sacrifice. She hoped to ensure that she was the centre of attention – and therefore of authority. But, above all, she wished to prevent the women about her becoming the pawns of male politicians and place-seekers. She wished to preserve her women's principal loyalty for herself, and she wished to keep them out of politics. Soon after Elizabeth's accession, she had called together the women of the Chamber and ordered them 'never to speak to her on business affairs'.[19] The Queen was to be the only petticoat politician.

It is usually supposed by historians that Elizabeth succeeded in creating an apolitical Privy Chamber, and there is some evidence to support this view. Rowland Vaughan, nephew of Blanche Parry of the Privy Chamber, remembered that 'in Queen Elizabeth's days my Lady of Warwick, Mistress Blanche and my Lady Scudamore in little lay matters would steal opportunity to serve their friends' turns ... because none of these (near and dear ladies) durst intermeddle so far in matters of commonwealth'. The women interfered in patronage, though not in politics. But Vaughan, and other later commentators such as Robert Naunton, had been prejudiced by their experience of the Jacobean Court, and they wrote of Elizabeth's Court as they would have liked it to have been. Contemporary Elizabethan opinion was different. In 1578 a foreign observer of the Court reported that the Queen discussed political secrets with her ladies, so that it was necessary to cultivate them to discover what was going on. Walter Raleigh thought the women could ruin a politician; they were, he said, 'like witches', 'capable of doing great harm but no good'.[20]

Certainly Elizabeth used her ladies as sources of political gossip. In 1569 she heard of the plot to marry Mary Queen of Scots to Norfolk from 'some babbling women', as Leicester complained.[21] In 1586, Elizabeth picked up some of the truth about Leicester's conduct in the Netherlands from the Court ladies – though the same source was presumably responsible for the false story that his wife was crossing to set up a Court. It is also clear that the women could be used to provide essential information on the Queen's thoughts, and even to influence her views. Two ladies of the Chamber suffered house arrest in 1562, for aiding the King of Sweden's suit for Elizabeth's hand. In 1564, Cecil's knowledge of the candidates to be the English representative at the Emperor's funeral came from the women of the Chamber. In 1569 it was probably Cecil who organised the whispering campaign against Norfolk, and in 1572 Francis Carew used his influence with the ladies to persuade Elizabeth not to make him ambassador to Scotland. In 1581, after the Queen had announced that she would marry Alençon, Hatton and Leicester got the ladies to weep and wail through the night about the horrors of marriage, to frighten her off. By the time Robert Beale wrote his advice on how to be a principal secretary, in 1592, the significance of the Privy Chamber in political life was well established: the Secretary had to work with his friends in the Chamber.

The role of the ladies of the Chamber in the distribution of patronage was especially clear. In 1566, when Leicester was in mild disfavour, he was advised to pursue a request for lands through Blanche Parry. In 1592, the Countess of Warwick put a suit to the Queen for John Dee, the astrologer, and Ladies Warwick and Huntingdon were active patrons in the late 1590s. Sir Robert Sidney used Lady Scudamore as an intermediary for his claim to become Warden of the Cinque Ports in 1597 – but even her backing could not counteract the disadvantage of over-energetic support from the Earl of Essex. The campaign to rehabilitate Essex in 1599 depended upon female influence: it was reported that 'what is wrought for his good is done by the ladies that have access to the queen'. The importance of Court ladies was widely recognised: in the 1590s, several books were dedicated to the women of the Privy Chamber in the hope that they would seek rewards for the authors. In 1601, Joan Thynne told her husband rather shortly that, if he could not get a knighthood through the influence of Court politicians, he had better make use of his friendships with the ladies! So in politics and in patronage, Elizabeth had to keep her women under control. She sought to make them afraid of the royal wrath, and her natural ill-temper served her well. She was especially prone to anger at table: she stabbed one lady in the hand for clumsiness in serving, and, in 1598, when Lady Margaret Howard missed her cue while serving, she cried 'out with all such ungracious, flouting wenches!'[22]

Queen Elizabeth made her emotions a tool of politics. She attempted political intimidation by her anger, and political seduction by loving words. But in using her emotions to manipulate others, she made her feelings means by which others could manipulate her. Almost any sacrifice was worth while to maintain Elizabeth's good temper. She became such a bad loser at cards that her courtiers had to let her win: Roger, Lord North, paid her £40 a month in 'losses' in the 1590s. The Queen's mood was a crucial fact of political life, and it was the need to know her mood which put the ladies and gentlemen of the Chamber in such an influential position, as Beale's advice acknowledged. John Harington reported in 1598 that one of her gentlemen 'came out of her presence with an ill countenance, and pulled me aside by the girdle, and said in a secret way, "If you have any suit today, I pray you put it aside; the sun doth not shine!" 'Tis this accursed Spanish business, so will not I adventure her Highness's choler, lest she should collar me also.'[23]

Elizabeth's affection was a major political prize: he who had it became a powerful figure, able to influence government decisions and the distribution of rewards. Hence the intense competition for her approval, and the importance of displaying signs of her favour. This could make Elizabeth by turns puppeteer and puppet. In 1566 she seems deliberately to have flirted with Sir Thomas Heneage, to weaken Leicester's influence during the bitter factional conflict between the Dudley and Howard alliances. In 1573 Gilbert Talbot sent detailed news to his father, the Earl of Shrewsbury, of the Queen's feelings for Leicester, Oxford, and Hatton, and reported on a plot (apparently by Burghley and Leicester) to build up Dyer as a rival to Hatton for her affections. In the winter of 1588-89 there was sharp rivalry between Charles Blount and the Earl of Essex, which led to a duel: Elizabeth had sent Blount a golden queen from her chess-set, which he then wore on a ribbon on his arm to show her favour – prompting Essex's jibe that 'Now I perceive that every fool must have a favour!'[24]

Such competitiveness could produce apparently childish behaviour. In 1597 Elizabeth made Lord Admiral Howard of Effingham Earl of Nottingham, which gave him precedence over Essex, and the patent of creation gave him credit with Essex for the attack on Cadiz. Essex stayed away from Court and Parliament, pretended to be ill, challenged Nottingham or any of the Howard kin to a duel, and demanded that the offending words in the patent be changed. He was only quietened when Elizabeth made him Earl Marshal, thus giving him precedence over Nottingham – and then it was Nottingham's turn to sulk and feign illness! There was, however, a serious political point at issue, for Essex's claim to influence policy was based on his alleged military success. The struggle for favour and office is a constant feature of political life, but Elizabeth made competition more intense than was healthy. By making affection and sexuality pronounced features of political relationships, she raised the emotional temperature of the Court to a dangerous level. By forcing politicians to compete for her attention, she put a premium upon exaggerated and extravagant behaviour, which led to over-emotional gestures and childish responses. By seeming to be impressed by show, she made a Court career an expensive investment and reward an essential return. And by narrowing her regime in the 1590s, she frustrated ambitions and produced ever more furious rivalry for the few prizes on offer.

Elizabeth has been praised, by contemporaries and by historians, for creating and balancing factions to maintain political stability. Robert Naunton, who had been a servant of Essex, wrote in the 1630s that 'A principal note of her reign will be that she ruled much by faction and parties, which herself both made, upheld and weakened, as her own great judgement advised.'[25] But the factionalised politics of Elizabethan England seemed more attractive after the experience of the Duke of Buckingham's monopolistic dominance in the 1620s. Much of the praise of Elizabeth's political style came from jaundiced Jacobeans such as Fulke Greville and William Camden, and should be read as disguised commentary on the reign of James. The Queen ought not to be seen as a cool political manipulator, maintaining equilibrium with a sharp eye and a steady hand. In fact, her own political behaviour, and her emotional relationships with some politicians, brought bitter factional rivalries which sometimes threatened disaster.

In the 1560s and the 1590s, there were dangerous factional conflicts which destabilised English politics. The 1565–66 struggle between the Dudley and the Howard alliances created deep divisions within the Court, as two groups strove for royal favour and sought to destroy the credit of their rivals. Leicester tried to convict Sussex of misconduct in Ireland, while Norfolk and Sussex attempted to prove that Leicester had murdered his wife. Elizabeth's obvious partiality for Leicester seemed to make her the Queen of a faction, and the Howard group pressed the advantages of a Habsburg marriage to prevent their rival carrying off the Queen. The leaders of the factions found it unwise to go about without armed escorts, and their retinues were identified by party colours. Leicester's followers wore purple ribbons and Norfolk's wore yellow, and there was a good deal of scuffling about the Court and challenging to combat. Finally, as Leicester and Sussex were about to fight a duel, Elizabeth herself was able to regain control and defuse a tense competitive situation – but for a time civil war had seemed the likely outcome.

The Court conflicts of the 1590s, between the Essex and Cecil groups, were even more disruptive. Every political decision and every official appointment became objects of closely observed factional competition, in which defeat was a serious blow to prestige and power. In 1594, when the post of attorney-general was up, Essex pressed the claims of Francis Bacon, telling Robert Cecil that 'the attorneyship for Francis is that I must have, and in that will I spend all my power, might, authority and annuity, and with tooth and nail defend and procure the same for him against whosoever; and that whosoever getteth this office out of my hand for another, before he have it it shall cost him the coming by'. The political atmosphere was much the same in 1597: 'The Court is now full of who shall have this and that office', Sir Robert Sidney was told.[26] There was no escape from the conflict, and each side demanded total loyalty. Lord Grey complained in 1598 that Essex 'has forced me to declare myself either his only, or friend to Mr Secretary and his enemy; protesting that there could be no neutrality'. The factional struggle affected every decision, and the Court became a political minefield – 'As God help me, it is a very dangerous time here; for, the heads of both factions being here, a man cannot tell how to govern himself towards them', reported Sidney's agent in 1599.[27]

In 1566, Queen Elizabeth had been able to take the heat out of factional conflict, and bring about at least a formal reconciliation between Leicester and Sussex. In 1569, she had been able to detach Leicester from the anti-Cecil alliance, intimidate Norfolk into inertia, and leave the northern earls isolated. But in the 1590s she was unable to compose the bitter struggles. 'The factions never more malicious', Robert Sidney was warned in 1596, but 'she whom it most concerneth doth rather use her wisdom in balancing the weights than in drawing all to one assize.'[28] It is usual to blame the overweening ambitions of the Earl of Essex for the troubles at Court, and it is certainly true that Essex fought every fight to the finish and always expected to win. The monopolistic claims of the Cecils also contributed, as Burghley sought to give his son Robert an unassailable authority to see out Elizabeth's reign and establish the Stuart dynasty. It may also be true that the decline of the aristocracy's real income from land forced them into fiercer competition for patronage, at a time when war expenditure meant a contraction of royal largesse. But the real blame for the problems of Elizabeth's last decade lay with the Queen herself.

As Elizabeth grew old, she came to run a narrowly based regime, composed of old men and the sons of previous councillors, with pluralist office-holding and rewards concentrated in just a few hands. When old advisers died, they were not replaced: by 1597, the Privy Council had only eleven members and none of them were great territorial magnates. Courtiers lost real influence, the provincial nobility was excluded from government, and the next generation of aspiring politicians saw their careers blighted. The French ambassador found the English Court a factious and fractious place in 1597, with widespread discontent. He reported that Elizabeth's government was 'little pleasing to the great men and the nobles, and if by chance she should die it is certain that the English would never again submit to the rule of a woman'.[29] Elizabeth seemed to have thrown in her lot with the Cecils and their friends, who were taking the major offices and the profits that went with them. Government had become the tool of a single and unscrupulous faction.

Not surprisingly, the ambitious and frustrated turned for advancement to the Earl of Essex, a charismatic leader who had some emotional pull on the Queen. Elizabeth had created a system of emotional engagement, in which political leaders had to behave like lovers and lovers became leaders. But after the deaths of Leicester and Hatton, she had separated power from love-play: she flirted with Essex and Raleigh, but made decisions with Buckhurst and Cecil. Although the Queen continued to play emotional politics with the next generation, she failed to reward them; she treated them as her intimates while ignoring their advice. Her affection was now politically worthless. Those who clustered about Essex found their expectations thwarted, for the coat-tails of a favourite no longer took his followers into office. Indeed, as the highly charged relationship between Elizabeth and Essex turned sour, the Earl's backing for a suitor became a kiss of death. After Essex had failed to obtain the attorneyship for Francis Bacon in 1594, he sought him the solictor-general's post in the following year – but he pressed the claim so determinedly that the Queen threatened to give the job to anyone except Bacon.

The Essex party was composed of impoverished nobles and failed courtiers. Essex, Rutland, Sussex, Southampton, and their allies were deeply in debt, and looked anxiously to the Queen for financial salvation. But their claims for patronage were consistently dismissed, and the Essex candidates were invariably beaten by Cecilians. Essex and his allies could not understand why they failed – they blamed their rivals for cheating, fought harder themselves, and did not realise that Elizabeth had changed the rules of the game. The Earl's own position was dependent upon his lease of the customs on sweet wines, which was due for renewal in the autumn of 1600. He wrote in despair to the Queen, that 'This day seven-night, the lease which I hold by your Majesty's beneficence expireth, and that farm is both my chiefest maintenance and mine only means of compounding with the merchants to whom I am indebted.'[30] When Elizabeth refused a new lease, she forced Essex into a desperate ploy. On 8 February 1601, he and his followers staged a last-ditch effort to smash their way to political success, by an attempt to seize control of the Queen and make her their pawn – but they failed to raise London, and their coup was a fiasco.

Elizabeth had brought the Essex rising upon herself. As royal favour contracted, so factional conflict intensified, but Elizabeth refused to spread her trust and her rewards any wider. Ambitious men were made politically impotent, and there was frantic competition for prizes which were not on open offer. The Court which had been the scene of Gloriana's splendour became a sordid and self-seeking playpen for overgrown and ill-tempered children. The Queen herself noticed the change, remarking in August 1601 that 'Now the wit of the fox is everywhere on foot, so as hardly a faithful or virtuous man may be found.' A broadsheet circulating in London at about the same time showed how it appeared to outsiders:

The courtiers craved all,
The queen granted all,

The Parliament passed all,
The Keeper [Egerton] sealed all,
The ladies ruled all,
Monsieur Drybone [venereal disease] spoiled all,
The crafty intelligencer [Cecil] heard all,
The bishops smoothed all,
He that was [Essex] opposed himself against all,
The judges pardoned all –
Therefore, unless your Majesty speedily amend all,
Without the great mercy of God the devil will have all.[31]

It was all very discreditable, but Elizabeth had only herself to blame.

NOTES AND REFERENCES

1. Nichols J 1823 *The Progresses and Public Processions of Queen Elizabeth* (3 vols). Nichols, vol. 3 p. 511;   Melvil J 1683 *The Memoires*, Scott G (ed.), p. 50
2. Loades D M 1986 *The Tudor Court*. Batsford, p. 8
3. Neale J E 1979 *Queen Elizabeth I*. Panther edn, p. 219
4. Haynes S (ed.) 1740 *A Collection of State Papers ... left by William Cecill*. Bowyer, p. 602; Bernard G W (forthcoming) A mid-Tudor chronicle, *Camden Miscellany*; Naunton R 1641 *Fragmenta regalia, or observations on the late Queen Elizabeth, her times and favorits*, p. 31
5. MacCaffrey W T 1960 Talbot and Stanhope: an episode in Elizabethan politics, *Bulletin of the Institute of Historical Research* 33: 79
6. Williams P H 1979 *The Tudor Regime*. Oxford, p. 27
7. Nichols J 1823 vol. 1 p. 329
8. Beckinsale B W 1967 *Burghley: Tudor statesman*. Macmillan, p. 228
9. Wilson D 1981 *Sweet Robin: a biography of Robert Dudley, earl of Leicester*. Hamilton, p. 98
10. Brooks E St J 1946 *Sir Christopher Hatton*. Cape, p. 156
11. Haynes S (ed.) 1740 p. 442;   Pulman M B 1971 *The Elizabethan Privy Council in the Fifteen-Seventies*. California, p. 48

12. Johnson P 1974 *Elizabeth I: a study in power and intellect.* Weidenfeld & Nicolson, p. 157;   Neale J E 1979 p. 114
13. Brooks E St J 1946 p. 86
14. Nichols J 1823 vol. 2 p. 74
15. Brooks E St J 1946 pp. 87, 97
16. Neale J E 1979 pp. 328, 333
17. Bruce J (ed.) 1844 *Correspondence of Robert Dudley, earl of Leycester.* Camden Society, p. 112;   Neale J E 1979 p. 332
18. Stone L 1965 *The Crisis of the Aristocracy, 1558-1641.* Oxford, p. 606
19. Erickson C 1983 *The First Elizabeth.* Macmillan, p. 174
20. Adams S L 1984 Eliza enthroned? The Court and its politics, in Haigh C A (ed.) *The Reign of Elizabeth I.* Macmillan, pp. 73-4;   Erickson C 1983 p. 350
21. Adams S L 1984 p. 73
22. Collins A (ed.) 1746 *Letters and Memorials of State* (2 vols), vol. 2 p. 139;   Harington J 1804 *Nugae Antiquae* (2 vols). Park T (ed.). Vernon & Hood, vol. 1 p. 233
23. Harington J 1804 vol. 1 pp. 175-6
24. Naunton R 1641 p. 34
25. Naunton R 1641 p. 6
26. Harrison G B (ed.) 1938 *The Elizabethan Journals, 1591-1603* (3 vols). Routledge & Kegan Paul, vol. 1 p. 285; Collins A (ed.) 1746 vol. 2 p. 25
27. *Calendar of Salisbury Manuscripts,* vol. 8 p. 269;   Collins A (ed.) 1746 vol. 2 p. 128
28. Collins A (ed.) 1746 vol. 2 p. 8
29. De Maisse A H 1931 *A Journal of All That Was Accomplished by Monsieur de Maisse.* Nonsuch, pp. 11-12
30. Johnson P 1974 p. 403
31. Nichols J 1823 vol. 3 p. 553;   Williams N 1967 *Elizabeth, Queen of England.* Weidenfeld & Nicolson, p. 345

Chapter 6

THE QUEEN AND THE PARLIAMENT

On her throne, Elizabeth was the Virgin Queen; towards the Church she was a mother, with her nobles she was an aunt, to her councillors a nagging wife, and to her courtiers a seductress. But what was the appropriate female role for the Queen in Parliament, when she met her ruling class ranged as Lords and Commons? At the end of the parliamentary session of 1566, she delivered a tetchy speech in which she rebuked them all for meddling in her affairs and disobeying her rules. She concluded:

> Let this my discipline stand you in stead of sorer strokes, never to tempt too far a prince's patience; and let my comfort pluck up your dismayed spirit, and cause you think that, in hope that your following behaviours shall make amends for past actions, you return with your prince's grace; whose care for you, doubt you not to be such as she shall not need a remembrancer for your weal.[1]

In other words, 'I have told you off rather than spanked you, and let that be enough – don't misbehave again! But there's no need to be upset, I shall forgive you if you're good boys from now on – and never forget, Nanny loves you really.' It was, indeed, the authentic voice of the English nanny. Elizabeth adopted a tone of condescending superiority towards her Parliaments, confident that if she explained things often enough and slowly enough, the little boys would understand. For Elizabeth, parliamentarians *were* little boys – sometimes unruly, usually a nuisance, and always a waste of an intelligent woman's time.

Queen Elizabeth did not like Parliaments, and it showed. Her father, brother, and sister had summoned a Parliament twenty-eight times in the thirty years which preceded Elizabeth's accession; by contrast, she called it nine times in her first thirty years and only thirteen times in a reign of forty-five years. Her reluctance to summon meetings was generally recognised and freely admitted. In 1593, Lord Keeper Puckering told both Houses that the Queen was 'most loth to call for the assembly of her people in Parliament' – but that was not a criticism, it was a compliment. Puckering noted that her predecessors had summoned Parliament frequently, but 'she hath done the same but rarely, and only upon most just, weighty and great occasions' – and 'she would yet still forbear, as she hath done, to draw you often together',[2] if she was not forced by circumstance. The Queen saw a Parliament as a regrettable necessity, for which her ministers should apologise.

The behaviour of members suggests that the Queen's lack of enthusiasm was widely shared, and there was a marked reluctance to participate in the real work of the two Houses. Attendances at the House of Commons always declined as a session wore on. In the 1559 Parliament, only 219 MPs, 54 per cent of the total, were present by 24 February, after the House had been in session for a month. Despite an attempt to increase numbers in mid-April by calling the roll of the House, attendance was down to 32 per cent by 24 April and 28 per cent a week later. In the 1563 session, known attendances varied from 64 per cent of the total down to 31 per cent. By 1571 the Commons regulars were so cross with their idle colleagues that they established a daily fine of 4d. each for the poor-box, imposed upon all who missed the opening prayers at 8.30 a.m. This failed to work: in 1581 the roll was called seven times to catch absentees, and a new rate of fines was introduced for absence from a whole session – £20 for county members, and £10 for borough representatives.

It was much the same in the Upper House, with a respectable attendance early in each session, a rapid decline thereafter, and some days with only half a dozen peers in the Chamber. In 1563 the session began with nearly 60 attending, out of a maximum of about 80, but the turn-out fell to 34 at the end. In later sessions the initial attendance fell to about 45, though the end-of-session level remained steady at 30–35 nobles and bishops. Of course, attendance was one thing, real participation another. Only about 10 per cent of MPs are known to have spoken in each Parliament, though this may have doubled in 1601. The long discussion of monopolies in the 1601 session seems to have raised the level of interest. In ten recorded divisions in 1601, the average vote was 47 per cent of MPs, though attendance ranged from 66 per cent of members when a Bill on tillage was considered to 17 per cent for a Bill on bankrupts – from which we may conclude that there were many more landlords than moneylenders in Parliament!

It is therefore difficult to see pressure from the political nation as a major reason for the calling of Parliament. It would not be true to say that nobody cared, but it seems that only a few cared very much. Such ill-attended Parliaments are unlikely to have been occasions of dramatic constitutional conflict between Crown and Commons – whatever was happening in Parliament, most MPs and most peers seem to have thought it was not worth while turning up to join the fun. When Elizabeth met her Parliaments, she did not face the serried ranks of the rising gentry, baying for their constitutional rights; at the end of a session, she faced only the unfortunate few who had nothing better to do. So why did Elizabeth call Parliaments, if neither she nor the nation was eager for them? Puckering explained at the opening of Parliament in 1593. He apologised for the summons, but the threats to national security made one necessary: the risk of invasion by Catholic Spain, and the risk of treason by discontented minorities, had forced the Queen to ask for taxation. Of course, she was as reluctant to ask for money as she had been to ask for a Parliament: 'Her Majesty saith there was never prince more loth to have aught at the hands of her subjects than she is'[3] – but ask she must.

And ask she did. Elizabeth asked twelve of her thirteen sessions of Parliament for supply. The exception, the session of 1572, had been called in a hurry to meet a political crisis, and the second instalment of the subsidy granted in 1571 had not yet been collected. So Elizabeth needed Parliaments because Elizabeth needed taxes – but the taxes had to be justified. In every session but that of 1572, the Queen's spokesmen (and they were spokesmen, not spokespersons) went through the same routine: the Protestant religion was in danger, the defence of the realm was expensive, and the Queen, with the greatest possible regret, had to ask for money. The necessary speech was easy enough at the beginning of the reign. Lord Keeper Bacon in 1559 could blame Mary for the risk of invasion, the insufficiency of revenues and the inadequacy of defence – but

Elizabeth was still reluctant to make demands. She had instructed Bacon to say that 'Were it not for the preservation of yourselves and the surety of the state, her Highness would have sooner adventured her life (which our Lord long preserve) than she would have adventured to trouble her loving subjects with any offensive matter, or that should be burdenous or displeasant unto them.'[4] But needs must.

Thereafter, the plea for money became more difficult. Parliamentarians had to be persuaded that they had a wise and skilful ruler, who had taken every precaution, but who for no fault of her own was now short of money. In 1563 Bacon blamed the essential military expeditions to Scotland and France for the royal penury – and then in 1566 William Cecil had to use the same excuses to justify further demands. By 1571, the plea of legitimate necessity had worn a little thin, and Bacon argued that a subsidy should be granted partly in gratitude for the Queen's achievements – the restoration of the Gospel (though he for one had pressed for a more radical settlement); more than a decade of peace (he slipped over the wars which had justified earlier taxes); and her merciful rule (he forgot the ruthless executions after the 1569 Revolt) – and partly because of pressing financial needs, resulting from the northern rebellion (which had been Elizabeth's fault), military support for Scottish Protestants (peace again!), preparations against invasion (but who had provoked Spain?), and falling customs revenues after the disruption of trade (for which Elizabeth and Cecil were entirely to blame).

Sir Walter Mildmay, Chancellor of the Exchequer, used much the same approach in 1576. First he exaggerated the seriousness of Mary's inheritance from her sister, and then he exaggerated the success of Elizabeth's rule: peace with neighbours, stability at home, general prosperity, 'and that which is the greatest, we enjoy the freedom of our consciences delivered from the bondage of Rome, wherewith we were so lately pressed'.[5] Finally, he had to list the unfortunate accidents and necessities which, despite the soundness of Elizabeth's policies, had led to excess expenditure and the request for a parliamentary subsidy. In reading these speeches, it is almost reassuring to see that ministers have always misled Parliament, and underlings have always lied to save the face of their mistresses and masters. In parliamentary terms at least, the war with Spain from 1585 was an advantage: the need for taxation was obvious, and the Queen's spokesmen no longer had to wriggle with embarrassment when they asked the Commons for money.

Elizabeth wanted taxes, and she wanted them quickly: her ideal Parliament was one which granted her money and went home. Sir John Puckering was open about this, as about so much else, in 1593. The Queen did not intend Parliament to devise new laws, for there were too many already, nor to debate great issues: 'Misspend not your good hours upon new and curious inventions, the which, have they never so glorious a show in the first opening, yet be they but wearisome in the handling and deceivable in the winding up.'[6] The lords and gentry were needed not at Westminster, but in their counties, and the message was clear – shut up, pay up, pack up. But some MPs had other ideas, and other interests. Though there is little evidence of pressure for Parliaments to be called, once they were in session private interests made use of them. There were general Bills promoted by interest groups, such as London livery companies or provincial corporations, seeking to change the law to their own advantage; and there were strictly private Bills, which usually dealt with the property of individuals and tried to sort out uncertainties and disputes. Such business boomed in Elizabeth's reign, to create a legislative log-jam.

So there was a conflict of interests: the Queen wanted short sessions which got government business, especially the Subsidy Bill, through Parliament quickly, but some MPs wanted constituency and private interests considered. Before the opening of the Parliament of 1572, an anonymous government business manager (perhaps Thomas Norton) drafted a paper of advice which faced the problem of getting a short session and government business through: 'If her Majesty's meaning be to have the session short, then it is good to abridge the things that lengthen the session', especially the number of private Bills. But it would be unwise for the Queen to issue a direct order, 'for so would by and by be raised some humorous [ill-tempered] body, some question of the liberty of the House and of restraining their free consultation'.[7] Instead, there should be heavy hints, and reminders of the risk of prolonging a session into the spring and the London plague season – a threat which had been explicitly used in April 1571, and was to be hinted at in June 1572.

But subtle hints did not work, and more direct interference

became necessary. When the 1572 Parliament had been in session for a month and still had not finalised its Bill on Mary Queen of Scots, Elizabeth harassed and chivied the Commons. She sent a message that 'the Queen's Majesty's pleasure is that this House do proceed in that and other weighty causes, laying aside all private matters', and that the Bill on Mary be read twice on consecutive days. In 1581, too, Elizabeth wanted the speedy transaction of parliamentary business: Speaker Popham co-operated by asking MPs not to speak at first readings, and to save time by avoiding 'unnecessary motions or superfluous arguments'.[8] Parliaments caused difficulties, not because they would oppose government business, but because some MPs and peers would pursue their own business. There was therefore a problem of management, not to stifle criticism but to get Bills through a Parliament with 550 members of the two Houses, each with his own interests, his own self-importance, and his own conviction that only he had really understood the case at issue.

One way of managing Parliament was to influence its composition. The membership of the House of Lords was not much interfered with, except in 1559, when Catholic bishops were told to stay away and put in prison; and in 1572, when four anti-Cecil peers were in detention and Norfolk was in his grave. But there was regular, if not very determined, influence on the composition of the Commons. In 1571, the ostensible reason was the need to ensure that MPs really represented their constituencies, not private interests – but after the Revolt of the Northern Earls and the papal bull of deposition, the Council's request for 'discreet, wise and well-disposed'[9] members was clear enough. Instructions to supervise elections were certainly sent to local dignitaries for Berkshire, Buckinghamshire, Dorset, Kent, Surrey, and Wiltshire. The magnates seem to have answered the call by naming their own relations and servants as MPs, and the Council was satisfied enough as the request was repeated in 1572 – when councillors wanted a Parliament which would push Elizabeth into executing the Duke of Norfolk and excluding Mary Queen of Scots from the succession.

In 1584, Parliament was again summoned in a period of crisis, with the assassination of William the Silent, the Throckmorton Plot against Elizabeth, and the fear of Catholic invasion and insurrection. Just as peers were asked to sign up recruits for the Council's own vigilante force in 1584, so they were asked to ensure the return of reliable MPs. Lord Cobham, Warden of the Cinque Ports, was told to see that Members elected 'be not only discreet and sufficient persons, but known to be well-affected in religion and towards the present state of this government'.[10] The Queen herself did not much like the Commons elected in 1584, and at the end of the session she had Lord Chancellor Bromley reprimand them for discussing religious matters when she had expressly forbidden it. But the Council had been pleased, and in 1586 sent around a circular asking constituencies to re-elect the MPs of 1584: usually about 40 per cent of Members were returned to the next Parliament, but in 1586 52 per cent of Members reappeared. The only other general intervention was in 1597, when the Council passed on the Queen's own request that boroughs should elect local men rather than carpet-baggers – but this seems to have been a typical example of Elizabeth's traditionalism, and it had little effect.

It seems likely that official intervention in elections strengthened the influence of powerful patrons rather than the influence of the Queen. A Council order gave Cobham a piece of paper to wave at the electors of Hythe, the Earl of Huntingdon one for Leicester, and the Earl of Warwick for Warwick, to ensure the return of their own friends. And since many of the magnates used to supervise elections were privy councillors or their allies, official intervention increased the influence of individual councillors – which was extended further by their own local power and by the willingness of others to offer them nominations. Burghley's electoral influence was exercised primarily through his political allies (such as Bedford) and his relations (such as Killigrew): he placed about a dozen MPs in each of the first four Elizabethan Parliaments, and as many as twenty-six in 1584 (when the Earl of Bedford apparently gave him a free hand in the West Country).

The most determined conciliar collectors of parliamentary patronage were the Earl of Essex and Robert Cecil, who competed with each other in 1597 – though the Earl was disadvantaged by his absence in the Azores during the run-up to the election. Essex collected borough stewardships, so that he could nominate one or two Members for each town, and Cecil collared the patronage of the Duchy of Lancaster. Essex had named half the Welsh borough MPs in 1593, and had also done well in Staffordshire, but Cecil probably got thirty MPs elected in 1597 and thirty-one in 1601. By then, Robert Cecil's supremacy was obvious and patrons were anxious to please. Viscount Bindon collected nominations for the Dorset boroughs in 1601, and then offered them to Cecil to fill as he wished. At least six of Cecil's secretaries and servants sat in the Commons in 1601. So official pressures and patronage influences did not give the Queen control of Parliament – they gave individual councillors power. It is therefore likely that if Council solidarity was maintained and councillors co-operated together, they would be able to manage the business of the Commons.

Perhaps the Council could control the Commons, but could the Queen control her Council? The problem of Queen Elizabeth's relations with her Parliaments has changed since Sir John Neale wrote about it more than thirty years ago.[11] Then it seemed to be an issue of executive against legislature, the attempt of a beleaguered government to control a rebellious Commons. But when, as in 1586–87 over religion, there was a rebellious group in the Commons, it was brought under control by the councillors and disowned by the majority of MPs. The real difficulties arose when privy councillors permitted, or, through their business managers, organised, Commons agitation to press the Queen to accept policies she disliked – as over marriage and the succession in 1563 and 1566, over religious reform in 1571, over the execution of Norfolk in 1572, over anti-Catholic laws in 1581, and over the execution of Mary in 1586. Elizabeth's problem of controlling her Parliament was thus part of her problem of controlling her Council: just as councillors tried to manipulate information to force policies upon the Queen, so they sought to manipulate Parliament to force policies on her.

Elizabeth's Parliaments were under the influence, if not quite the control, of Elizabeth's councillors. The Council members, and especially Burghley, nominated MPs, planned business in advance, and tried to manage proceedings. Except in 1597, there were always at least five, and often eight, councillors in the Commons, and the rest sat in the Lords. In addition, the Speaker was a Council nominee, and the Council had its own business managers in the Commons. One of the most interesting developments in recent parliamentary historiography has been the recasting of Neale's leaders of the puritan opposition. By careful analysis of their correspondence, their parliamentary drafts, and especially their role in committees and debates, Michael Graves has discovered[12] that Thomas Norton, William Fleetwood, Thomas Dannett, Thomas Digges, Robert Bell, and others were not leaders of an opposition but agents of the Council! They, and a group of aspiring lawyers, managed Commons proceedings in the interests of getting government business through in the time available. These 'men of business' led the Commons into those issues which councillors wanted discussed – which were often the issues Elizabeth wanted *not* to be discussed.

Above all, it was William Cecil, Lord Burghley, who master-minded the work of Parliament – especially from the spring of 1571, when he sat in the Lords himself and tried to manage the Commons through his agents and allies there. He obtained regular reports on Commons proceedings from Fulke Onslow, the Clerk of the Commons, and from Robert Bell, Speaker in 1572 and 1576, and information on the progress of particular Bills from interested agents. He was able to monitor Commons business with frequent lists of the stages of Bills, and he used his influence with councillors and in the Lords to determine the order and speed of business. In the busy session of 1571, he orchestrated a message from the Lords asking the Commons to drop consideration of private Bills to concentrate on official business; he organised a Commons committee to sort Bills into an order of priority, with preference for government Bills; and he arranged for private business to be pushed in the afternoons, leaving the mornings free for the consideration of public Bills.

By Burghley's strategic planning and the tactical manœuvres of the 'men of business', the Council could lead the Commons – especially as the Council so often wished to lead where many MPs wanted to go anyway. This made Parliament a most useful means of applying pressure on the Queen, taking advantage of her oft-expressed desire to rule with the love of her people. In 1563, the campaign to get Elizabeth to marry and/or fix the succession was orchestrated by councillors. The committee which drafted the Commons' petition to the Queen was chaired by Sir Edward Rogers, Comptroller of the Household, and it included all eight privy councillors sitting in the Commons; the draft was steered through the full House by Thomas Norton, one of the 'men of business'. It is true that the initiative in 1563 may have come from the Dudley faction rather than the

Council as a whole, but the aim was certainly to force the Queen's hand. In 1566, Lord Keeper Bacon in the Lords and Secretary Cecil in the Commons organised a joint delegation of both Houses to the Queen on the succession, and it was Cecil who drafted the Commons defence of its proceedings. Again, it was the councillors and their allies who made most of the speeches and got the business done.

On religious matters, reform-minded councillors often worked in collaboration with the bishops. This certainly seems to have been true in 1566, when an order from the Queen to the Lords to abandon consideration of a Bill to give statutory authority to the Thirty-nine Articles prompted a formal request from the bishops for her to allow the Bill through. Elizabeth had her way in 1566, though she had warned the Spanish ambassador that 'such pressure would be brought to bear upon her that she could not refuse her consent'.[13] The 1571 Parliament saw councillors, bishops, and the Commons business managers co-operating to push a number of Bills on religion, especially a Bill to punish those who refused communion in the Church of England. Radical proposals were killed off when the Queen's displeasure became known, but on the Communion Bill Elizabeth was faced with a united demand of the Protestant ruling class, led by her own Council, for harsher action against Catholics. She vetoed the Bill, on one of fewer than ten occasions when she had to veto a major public Bill.

The Parliament of 1572 was probably called as a result of Council pressure on the Queen. No subsidy was asked for, and it was the only Parliament of the reign summoned so late in the parliamentary year and to sit through June. It was called for no purpose of the Queen's; rather, it was to force her to execute Norfolk and at least bar Mary Queen of Scots from the succession. Norfolk had been convicted of treason on 6 January 1572, but Elizabeth would not sanction the execution; twice the warrant for execution was cancelled, and the crowds disappointed. Elizabeth was persuaded to agree to a Parliament (perhaps she calculated that fear of parliamentary attack would make Mary more amenable), and it met on 8 May. The clamour against Norfolk was encouraged in the opening speeches of the Speaker and the Lord Keeper, and the Duke was executed on 2 June, forestalling the Commons' petition for his death which was then being prepared. But there remained the question of

Mary, and again the Council took the lead. A joint Commons committee with the Lords, led by councillors and 'men of business', drafted two Bills, one a petition for Mary's attainder for treason, the other a Bill excluding her from the succession.

One hundred years before Charles II, Elizabeth had *her* 'exclusion crisis', and she faced a more formidable combination of forces. Sir Francis Knollys and Sir James Croft, of the Privy Council, and several of their agents led by Thomas Norton, managed the Commons, while Lord Keeper Bacon and other councillors led the Lords, and Burghley acted as co-ordinator. The bishops produced a long list of theological reasons to justify the execution of Mary, and a committee of lawyers produced legal arguments. All was going well from the Council's point of view – if only the Queen would give in. Burghley noted on 21 May that 'there can be found no more soundness than in the Common House, and no lack appearing in the Higher House; but in the highest person such slowness in the offers of surety and such stay in resolution as it seemeth God is not pleased that the surety shall succeed'.[14] God – and Elizabeth Tudor – remained displeased: the Queen announced that she would not agree to an attainder, and she deflected effort into the 'Exclusion' Bill.

Although the councillors had pursued Mary's attainder with determination, perhaps they had expected that Elizabeth would not execute a fellow prince. But the attainder issue had apparently forced Elizabeth to consider 'exclusion'. The Council and its business managers struggled to get the complicated 'Exclusion' Bill through its stages before the plague season began and the Queen would close the session. They cut corners by packing the Commons committee and hurrying the full House along, and the Bill was pushed through just in time. But it was all for nothing. Burghley wrote in despair to Walsingham:

> Now for our Parliament, I cannot write patiently: all that we laboured for and had with full consent brought to fashion – I mean a law to make the Scottish queen unable and unworthy to wear the crown – was by her Majesty neither assented to nor rejected, but deferred until the feast of All Saints. But what all other wise and good men may think thereof, you may guess.[15]

It had been a classic example of Elizabeth's manœuvring. She had been made to agree to a Parliament, but she did not have to agree to its legislation. Her councillors, led by Burghley, had organised pressure for the execution of Mary. To defuse that campaign, and to avoid an open clash between Council and Parliament on the one hand, and herself, almost alone, on the other, she had seemed to agree to an exclusion from the succession. But finally (because a discredited Mary was more use to her in the succession than out of it), she had (in all but name) vetoed the Bill, and prorogued Parliament.

Despite this defeat, privy councillors continued to apply parliamentary pressure to the Queen, especially in the Parliament of 1586–87. The 1586 session was a milder rerun of 1572, with councillors wanting a Parliament to help Elizabeth accept execution of Mary. There was clearly a struggle over whether a Parliament should be called. Burghley reported in September 1586, 'We stick upon parliament, which her Majesty misliketh, but we all persist to make the burden better borne and the world abroad better satisfied': it was presumably hoped that Elizabeth would be more likely to agree to execution if she could shift the blame on to Parliament. When Parliament met, Hatton, Mildmay, Croft, and Knollys led the Commons, and Lord Chancellor Bromley and Burghley led the Lords, into an attack on Mary, and a joint petition for her execution was presented to the Queen. On 24 November 1586, Elizabeth gave her reply to a deputation from both Houses: it was, as she described it, 'my answer answerless'.[16] The Queen would not commit herself, and parliamentary pleas were insufficient. So Francis Walsingham probably faked the Stafford Plot to frighten Elizabeth into action. This time, the Council got its way, and Mary went to the block at Fotheringay on 8 February 1587 – though Elizabeth insisted on a scapegoat, and Secretary Davison's career was ruined.

A week after the execution, Parliament reopened, and its second session was also used to try to force the Queen's hand – on this occasion, to get her to accept sovereignty over the Low Countries in the interests of a more effective joint campaign against Spain. Once more, privy councillors in the Commons took the lead: Hatton, Mildmay, and Knollys hinted broadly that the Queen should be asked to take sovereignty, and the 'men of business' and courtiers such as Thomas Cecil, Burghley's son, supported the case. A committee, managed by councillors and Speaker Puckering, decided to bribe the Queen, taking advantage of her financial difficulties. Elizabeth was offered an annual grant for as long as the war with Spain lasted, if she would accept sovereignty. The Council and the Commons wished to bind the Queen to fight to free the Low Countries from Spain, but Elizabeth still hoped to force Philip II to reach a settlement with his Dutch subjects. She declined the grant: Elizabeth had sacrificed Mary, but she would not sacrifice her foreign policy.

To Sir John Neale, Queen Elizabeth faced a constant battle with pretentious Parliaments led by puritan militants. This, as Sir Geoffrey Elton has shown,[17] was not true. For most of the time of most of its sessions, Parliament got on with its business, voting the subsidies requested for the Queen, debating and passing public Bills, and dealing with the private Bills needed to sort out the tangles of the land law and conflicts of particular interests. For most of the time there was no need for any but the gentlest management, to ensure that business was completed. But sometimes there was trouble, and, from Elizabeth's point of view, it was even more serious than Neale thought. For the trouble was not usually between Elizabeth's government and her Parliament, it was between Elizabeth herself and her government and Parliament in alliance. Such difficulties arose when the Queen's ordinary techniques of political management had proved inadequate – when she had been unable to break opposition in Council by bullying and dividing; and when she had been unable to defuse opposition through the bribery, political seduction, and emotional blackmail of Court life. When the Queen could not silence her ministers in Council and Court, she had to defeat them in Parliament: her weapons there were her own personality and her own version of her constitutional powers.

Elizabeth's most important tools were her speeches to Parliament, and she took great care in their drafting, delivery, and publication. Although her lord chancellors and keepers spoke in the Queen's name, Elizabeth also made speeches for herself. She was her own speech-writer, and she became a skilled draftswoman: it is noticeable that her speeches became much more clear and direct as she grew more experienced and confident. Except for a kind of 'end-of-term report' in 1576, her addresses were invariably responses to some parliamentary petition or problem, often pressures engineered by councillors. So she usually spoke in a political crisis, when her righteous indignation had to be tempered by tact and seduction. Her surviving drafts show that the early versions of speeches were ragingly angry, but she then toned them down. The first draft of her reply to a parliamentary delegation on the succession issue in 1566 accused its members of treason, but that insult was deleted, and in her drafting Elizabeth struggled to be gracious towards her people. She was especially complimentary and endearing to the Commons: she would rage at peers and bishops, whom she thought should know better than to cross her, but the Commons represented her loving subjects. Though she would threaten her councillors and chastise obstreperous minorities, her addresses to MPs were larded with flattery and promises of devotion to their interests.

Elizabeth often tried to divide the parliamentary phalanx ranged against her, blaming bishops or councillors or puritan militants for misleading the sensible, loyal back-benchers. She would promise moderate reforms, if only the hotheads would be silenced. In 1585 she told councillors and representatives of the clergy, after disputes over religion in the Commons, 'We will not charge the whole House with this disorder, for although there be some intemperate and rash heads in that House, yet there be many wise and discreet men.' She then admitted that minor reforms were needed in the Church, and criticised the inertia of the bishops. The Queen often made promises of reform which she did little to fulfil. She had made vague promises on monopolies in 1597, but in 1601 found herself being tactfully reminded of her word by the Commons. It was clear in 1601 that there was considerable constituency pressure against monopolies, and Elizabeth finally recognised that a real concession was needed. She summoned Speaker Croke, and announced the suspension of offensive monopolies: 'God make us thankful, and send her long to reign amongst us', the Speaker told the Commons.[18]

But the Queen's key tactic was to stand on her considerable dignity, reminding MPs and peers that they were her subjects and she was their queen, chosen by God. She would not be bullied, she told them in 1566: 'I am your anointed queen; I will never be by violence constrained to do anything.' Elizabeth threatened those who complained and those who encouraged them, as in 1585: 'they meddle with matters above their capacity, not appertaining unto them, for the which we will call some of them to an account. And we understand they be countenanced by some of our Council, which we will redress or else uncouncil some of them.'[19] She appealed beyond her Council and the immediate issue to MPs in general and to their loyal constituents. Sometimes, as in 1576 and 1593, her great parliamentary speeches could not be heard by those at the back of the crowd, for whom they were really intended – so she had them copied and circulated. She sent a copy of her 1576 end-of-session speech, of which she seems to have been proud, to her godson, John Harington, and numerous other copies circulated around the Court. Her carefully rehearsed rhetoric was not to be wasted. From 1585, her speeches were deliberately and systematically copied and widely distributed, and were printed in contemporary chronicles and in separate editions.

Elizabeth also sought to reduce parliamentary pressure by limiting the area of debate. She attempted to prevent her councillors using Parliament against her by arguing that some issues were beyond its competence, and could only be decided by the Queen in consultation with her Council. In 1571, in his reply to the Speaker's traditional request for freedom of speech in the Commons, Lord Keeper Bacon reported that the Queen 'said they should do well to meddle with no matters of state, but such as should be propounded unto them, and to occupy themselves in other matters concerning the common wealth'. Elizabeth had formulated a new distinction between 'matters of state', high politics, which Parliament should only discuss if she invited it, and 'matters of commonwealth', those social and economic issues which were the ordinary business of a Parliament. Members were warned off what were now defined as prerogative issues. Lord Chancellor Bromley told the Commons in 1581 'not to deal with her estate, which he showeth to be intended as well touching her prerogative as also in religion'.[20] In practice, Elizabeth attempted on a number of occasions to stifle discussion in Parliament – of the succession in 1566; of religion in 1572, 1576, 1581, 1584, 1585, 1589, and 1593; and of royal finance in 1589, 1597, and 1601.

There was a further distinction upon which Elizabeth insisted. Bacon told MPs in 1559 that the Queen granted them freedom of speech, provided 'they be neither unmindful nor uncareful of their duties, reverence and obedience to their sovereign'. As Sir Walter Mildmay explained in 1576, 'we may not forget to put a difference between liberty of speech and licentious speech, for by the one men deliver their opinions freely but with this caution, that all be spoken pertinently, modestly, reverently and discreetly. The other, contrariwise, uttereth all impertinently, rashly, arrogantly and irreverently, without respect of person, time or place'. Freedom of speech was permitted, but only if it was exercised with discretion – as Puckering put it succinctly in 1593, 'Her Majesty granteth you liberal but not licentious speech; liberty, therefore, but with due limitation.'[21] This restriction on the manner of debate caused much less dispute than did her limitation of the area of discussion, and those who, like Peter Wentworth, went too far were punished by the Commons. But it was an important restraint nevertheless, for it made it virtually impossible for Members to oppose direct royal orders.

The Queen did not always, or even usually, manage to confine parliamentary debate to 'safe' issues. Councillors and their agents led members into areas defined as off limits by Elizabeth, and sought to exert public pressure upon her – especially on the succession, religious reform, Mary Queen of Scots, and foreign policy. But she was able to enforce caution upon all but the most determined, she made her anger an item in any political calculation, and she made her Parliaments wary of her prerogative. As a diarist reported in 1572, 'The message that forbade the bringing of bills of religion into the House seemed much to impugn the liberty of the House, but nothing was said unto it.'[22] In 1601, when MPs were determined to secure some reform of monopolies, there were long debates on how to proceed on a matter which closely touched Elizabeth's sovereign authority. We should not imagine that Parliament sought deliberately to challenge the powers of the monarchy: rather, by invoking her prerogative in novel ways, Elizabeth could limit discussion and avoid confrontation. By tactical manoeuvres, skilful oratory, and occasional concessions, Elizabeth usually prevented her Council-led Parliaments from presenting her with objectionable bills.

And if her techniques of prevention failed, if an objectionable Bill was presented, she could always veto it. But it is a measure of Elizabeth's parliamentary success that she rarely exercised the veto on major issues: she did not need to. In thirteen sessions, about 506 Bills were put to Elizabeth for the royal assent: she agreed to 436, and vetoed about 70 – 14 per cent of the total, and an average of 5 per session. Which were the vetoed Bills? In 1597, an unusually high number of Bills was vetoed, 12 out of 55. They were: a Bill for recording fines in the Court of Common Pleas; a Bill to restrain brewers to employing two coopers each; a Bill to allow alteration of gavelkind customs; a Bill to allow the Spencer family to alienate lands; a Bill to prevent double payment on shop books; a Bill to repress offences committed by stealth; a Bill to regulate baize-making in Essex and Suffolk; a Bill to enable Edmund Mollineux to sell lands to pay his debts; a Bill for the reform of pawnbrokers; a Bill to allow defaulting lessees to hold leases against patentees; a Bill concerning Garret de Malynes and John Hunger, foreign merchants; and a Bill for confirmation of the statutes merchant in Newcastle upon Tyne. Only one of the Bills, on lessees, involved Crown interests, so why should the Spencers, or coopers, or Essex baize-makers, or Garret de Malynes, have suffered the veto?

Almost all the Bills vetoed in the reign of Elizabeth touched the interests of private individuals and groups. It seems that objectors who had failed to stop a Bill in the Commons and Lords might ask the Queen to veto it. In 1585 the bailiffs and burgesses of Conway in north Wales wrote to Burghley to ask him to persuade Elizabeth to veto a Bill to hold the Caernarfonshire quarter sessions at Caernarfon only, instead of at Caernarfon and Conway. The Bill had been promoted by Caernarfon MPs, Conway had no representatives, and the town had to resort to a request for a veto. Burghley presumably co-operated, for Elizabeth vetoed the Bill. In the whole reign, Elizabeth vetoed fewer than 10 Bills because they invaded her prerogative or conflicted with her policy – 10 political vetoes on 506 Bills. On only 10 occasions (and the number may be as low as 5) had her political skills failed her. Only then had she been unable to manipulate her councillors, bribe her courtiers, browbeat her bishops and peers, and entrance her back-benchers: only then did she have to use constitutional force.

When they failed in Council and Court, Elizabeth's ministers turned to Parliament – but they failed to coerce her there too. Elizabeth did not give in over the succession in 1563 and 1566; or over religion in 1566, 1571, and 1584; or over anti-Catholic laws in 1571 (though she compromised in 1581). She did not give in over Mary Queen of Scots in 1572, and if she did in 1587 it was because there was evidence that Mary really had plotted to kill her – and because, after nearly thirty years as queen, she knew she no longer needed the threat of Mary's succession to keep

Englishmen loyal. Elizabeth got her way, because she had mastered the art of ruling over Englishmen: she nannied them. She used the power of her personality, and the fierce personal loyalty she was able to evoke, to dissolve the political alliances which sometimes sought to coerce her. Those who cried out for determined action were made to feel guilty and embarrassed: were they really contesting her commitment to the Protestant religion, or her love for her subjects? Given the effectiveness of the Elizabethan myth-making machine, no man could admit doubt – and the women were not asked.

. . .

NOTES AND REFERENCES

1. Hartley T E (ed.) 1981 *Proceedings in the Parliaments of Elizabeth I, 1558–1581*. Leicester, p. 175
2. Neale J E 1957 *Elizabeth I and Her Parliaments, 1584–1601*. Cape, p. 246
3. Neale J E 1957 p. 247
4. Hartley T E (ed.) 1981 p. 38
5. Hartley T E (ed.) 1981 p. 442
6. Neale J E 1957 p. 248
7. Graves M A R 1983 The management of the Elizabethan House of Commons: the Council's 'men of business', *Parliamentary History* 2: 14; Elton G R 1984 Parliament, in Haigh C A (ed.) *The Reign of Elizabeth I*. Macmillan, p. 91
8. Neale J E 1953 *Elizabeth I and Her Parliaments, 1559–1581*. Cape, p. 281; Elton G R 1986 *The Parliament of England, 1559–1581*. Cambridge, p. 107
9. Parker M 1853 *Correspondence*, Bruce J and Perowne T T (eds). Parker Society, p. 380
10. Neale J E 1976 *The Elizabethan House of Commons*. Fontana edn, p. 278
11. Neale J E 1953, 1957 *passim*
12. Graves M A R 1983: 17–21
13. *Calendar of State Papers Spanish, 1558–67*, p. 604
14. Graves M A R 1983: 27
15. Read C 1960 *Lord Burghley and Queen Elizabeth*. Cape, p. 50
16. Read C 1960 p. 361; Neale J E 1957 p. 129
17. Elton G R 1986 pp. 350–72

18. Neale J E 1957 pp. 69, 385
19. Hartley T E (ed.) 1981 p. 148;   Neale J E 1957 p. 69
20. Hartley T E (ed.) 1981 pp. 199, 526
21. Hartley T E (ed.) 1981 pp. 43, 453;   Neale J E 1957 p. 249
22. Hartley T E (ed.) 1981 p. 331

Chapter 7

THE QUEEN AND THE MILITARY

Elizabeth I had a constant struggle to get men to do what she wanted. She badgered her councillors, she entranced her courtiers, she nannied her parliamentarians, and she almost always got her way – or almost all of her way. She had to sacrifice the Duke of Norfolk in 1572 and the Queen of Scots in 1587, but otherwise she won her political fights and maintained authority over the males around her. But with her military and naval commanders, it was different: she was much less successful. To a degree, this is surprising, for they were subject to the skills and seductions which tamed other men. Her generals and admirals were not separate professional groups: they were her nobles, her councillors, her courtiers, and her MPs, men whom in other capacities she could control. But when they were given military command, when they were sent overseas with the power of the Queen's commission, they forgot their obedience – they even forgot their orders – and they strutted battlefield and poop as independent leaders.

The extreme case was the Earl of Essex, who regarded war as a glorious game and an opportunity for grand display – until, in 1599, the Irish taught him better. When, as English commander in Normandy in 1591, he met the King of France, he was preceded by six pages in orange velvet embroidered with gold; he and his horse wore orange velvet adorned with precious stones; six trumpeters sounded before him, twelve esquires followed him, and sixty well-dressed gentlemen formed his escort. Meanwhile, his soldiers deserted for lack of pay and provisions, and the military aims of his expedition were not achieved. But it was not just Essex. The Queen's commanders, from the beginning of the reign to the end, ignored their instructions and sought their own glory and their own profit. Elizabeth's relations with her military leaders show the limits of her power. It was as if Nanny's authority extended only to the nursery door: once outside, the little boys played their own silly games.

In the spring of 1559, at the Treaty of Cateau-Cambresis, Elizabeth's agents managed to wriggle out of the expensive war with France inherited from Mary's time. But the threat from France remained, and the dominating problem in foreign policy was the presence of a French army in Scotland – where it was propping up the Catholic regime against Protestant rebels. The Spanish ambassador in London, who thought the English were cowardly weaklings, reported haughtily, 'It is incredible the fear these people are in of the French on the Scottish border.'[1] The Privy Council suspected that if the French could overcome the Protestant rebels in Scotland, they would then invade England to put Mary Queen of Scots on the English throne: Mary had, after all, been sporting the English coat of arms. So the objective of Elizabeth's foreign policy was clear: to get the French out of Scotland. The means caused a good deal of debate. William Cecil, backed by the soldiers on the Council, favoured military intervention; Elizabeth, nervous of the cost and unpredictability of war and reluctant to assist Scottish rebels, wished to negotiate the French out. Cecil got his way, by threatening to resign if his policy was not carried out.

The decision to invade Scotland was taken on Christmas Eve 1559 and the mustering of troops began soon after – but the order to cross the border was not given until 29 March. It was to be a typically Elizabethan exercise, begun in hesitation and delay, and carried through to an inglorious end because policy was insufficiently clear and the generals could not be controlled from London. The long-drawn-out siege of the French garrison at Leith was the centre of the campaign, and the failed assault on 7 May 1560 was the key disaster. The broad reasons for the military failure in Scotland were all pointers to future problems. Elizabeth's clear preference for a negotiated solution encouraged over-hasty action by her generals, who wanted a glorious victory before the Queen could tell them the war was over. The chain of command was complicated by the appointment of the Duke of Norfolk as Lord Lieutenant of the North, intermediary between the Council in London and Lord Grey, commanding the army in Scotland. There was little military justification for Norfolk's posting, and it was probably engineered by Robert Dudley, to get an opponent of his proposed marriage to Elizabeth away from Court. So, in the North, the Duke pressed his subordinates for a swift conclusion to the campaign, so he could return to London.

In Scotland, Grey's plan for an assault on Leith required more men than he actually had, and shortage led to failure. Weeks of hanging about on the Border, followed by a siege, had led to high levels of desertion from his army, but captains concealed the erosion of their companies so that they could continue to claim wages for the men who had gone. Grey was supposed to have 9,500 infantry, he drew up a plan of attack which needed 9,000, but he probably had fewer than 5,000. Lastly, the men were asked to do the impossible. Sir James Croft was sent to examine the breach in the walls of Leith which an artillery barrage was supposed to have created; he reported that the French had repaired the wall, and an assault could not succeed. But Grey, the commander, decided to go ahead anyway, probably thinking that his reputation required a quick victory. There was nothing Croft could do: since he had been conspicuously feathering his nest out of the revenues of his command at Berwick, he dared not complain to Norfolk or the Queen in case Grey, in retaliation, exposed his corruption. So the attack went ahead.

As is always the way in armies, the front-line troops paid the price of their commanders' self-interest: the assault on Leith was a fiasco. The resistance of the French was bad enough, but the English were particularly annoyed by the efforts of Scottish prostitutes, who, eager to protect their French clients, threw stones, blocks of wood, and burning coals down on the besiegers. About five hundred English soldiers were killed in the attack, and desertions continued, leaving Grey with too small a force for any further assault. The Queen was furious at the cost of it all, especially the need to send expensive reinforcements. She gave Cecil a hard time: he reported 'I have had such a torment herein with the queen's Majesty as an ague hath not in five fits so much abated'[2] (which might be modernised as 'the queen's been a pain in the neck!'). But, fortunately, the French were also tired of keeping an army in Scotland, and a withdrawal of both forces was negotiated. In that sense the strategic objective of intervention was achieved, despite its tactical failure. But it had been an expensive and illuminating enterprise, which should have taught Elizabeth the perils of military action.

But, two years later, the Queen allowed herself to be persuaded into a similar, though much more disastrous, expedition – an invasion of France to support Huguenot rebels. She was carried away by the enthusiasm of Robert Dudley, who was anxious to prove himself a serious politician after the rumours that he had murdered his wife. Above all, Dudley was struggling to re-establish his Protestant credentials after the embarrassing publicity of his attempt to secure marriage to Elizabeth with Spanish and Catholic backing. So he had thrown himself into the international Protestant cause: he negotiated privately with French Huguenot leaders, he sent his own representatives to France, and he persuaded Elizabeth to support intervention. In the Privy Council debates in 1562, for the only time in her reign, Elizabeth was an advocate of military activism, threatening to take the decisions alone if the Council was afraid to share the responsibility. But it was very much a Dudley show.

It was Robert Dudley who had taken the lead in establishing links with the French Protestants. His brother Ambrose, Earl of Warwick, was appointed commander of the invasion army, despite his limited military experience: the French Protestants were nervous, and hoped Warwick would have experienced advisers. Warwick's military council was stuffed with Protestant zealots and Dudley allies, and the whole enterprise was conceived and carried out by those who wanted an international Protestant league to protect the faith against popery. But Elizabeth had not entirely lost her head to the ideologues. Her own objective seems to have been the regaining of Calais, rather than the defence of righteousness. In the event, however, no objective was achieved, and everything went wrong in France from October 1562 to July 1563. The French Protestants gave Warwick's army Dieppe and Le Havre to defend, but Elizabeth was nervous of the division of her force and the Dieppe garrison was kept too small. Dieppe was soon surrendered to the Catholics, and the English army found itself cooped up in Le Havre.

The French Protestants became increasingly – and rightly – suspicious of Elizabeth's intentions. They had no wish to keep the French Catholic army busy while the English acquired Calais, nor to see the English exchange Le Havre for Calais. The warring French factions made peace, and the small English force faced the French alone. Elizabeth now seems to have abandoned all hope of success: when Warwick asked for reinforcements so that he could break out of Le Havre, she refused; when he asked for money to improve its defences, she refused that too. Then plague struck the garrison. Soon the death-rate reached 100 a day, with twice as many falling sick, and there were not enough men to man the defences. Warwick had to surrender to the French, and take the remnants of his army back to England – where they began a disastrous plague epidemic. Warwick had taken 3,500 men to France, but he returned with hardly more than 1,000. The Le Havre expedition cost Elizabeth £250,000, when her ordinary revenue was about £200,000: she was forced into debt, and her credit collapsed on the Antwerp money market. She had to turn to Parliament for a subsidy, and the tax bands had to be revised downwards to bring the poorer into the tax net. It had all been a chastening experience for the Queen, and the disasters of the 'Newhaven Adventure' made her determined to avoid military entanglements abroad.

When Elizabeth next sent an expedition to the Continent, in 1585, it was in many respects an intriguing repetition of 1562. Again, she sent an army to aid Protestant rebels against their Catholic ruler – Dutch rebels against Philip II. Again the enterprise had been planned, packaged, and sold to the Queen by the Dudley faction, as the defence of the Protestant cause. Again the expedition was commanded by a Dudley with inadequate military experience, Leicester himself – and again it was an expensive failure, in which the main sufferers were the soldiers, who shivered and starved. But in one crucial respect 1585 was different from 1562: Queen Elizabeth had distrusted the project all along, and her doubts contributed much towards its outcome. Except for under-funded expeditions to put down disorders in Ireland, Elizabeth avoided direct military action for twenty-two years after Newhaven. She was pressed by Leicester and his allies from 1576 to sanction military intervention in the Low Countries, but she resisted and tried a number of cheaper expedients. She agreed in the end only when forced by a series of diplomatic disasters.

In June 1584, the death of the Queen's pock-marked old flame, the Duke of Alençon, deprived her of the pawn she had been using to maintain French interest in protecting the Low Countries from Spain. In July, the assassination of William, Prince of Orange, removed what seemed the only uniting force in the disunited Provinces: Parma's military advance accelerated, and a string of Dutch towns surrendered to Spanish arms. In December 1584, the French Catholic League signed a treaty with Philip II at Joinville, so that Elizabeth faced the possibility of Spanish domination of both France and the Low Countries, leaving England dangerously exposed to invasion. So in August 1585 England and the States-General of the United Provinces signed the Treaty of Nonsuch, by which Elizabeth took the Dutch under her protection, and promised to assist them with 6,400 infantry, 1,000 cavalry, and £126,000 a year for their maintenance. But, in an ominous sign, the Queen immediately breached the treaty by sending a secret emissary to the Duke of Parma to tell him of her alliance, and to suggest concessions to the Dutch.

On 24 September 1585, Elizabeth finally agreed to the appointment of Leicester as captain-general of the army for the Netherlands. At once, Leicester sent out 200 letters to his friends and allies, with orders for embarkation – but on 26 September, the Queen ordered him to abandon preparations. Though the disruption proved brief, there were further delays late in October because of the Queen's doubts over costs and the risks of escalation. Leicester's formal commission was issued in mid-November, giving him authority to wage war in the Netherlands at his discretion, but the instructions issued to him in December were more restrictive: 'We do require you that you rather bend your cause to make a defensive than offensive war, and that you seek by all the means you may to avoid the hazard of a battle.'[3] Leicester saw his expedition as the first step in the creation of a league of Protestants to destroy Catholic power; Elizabeth saw it as a means to persuade Philip II to observe the provincial liberties of his Burgundian subjects.

Elizabeth disliked and distrusted Leicester's expedition. She delayed the departure of her general until December 1585, though the first of the troops had gone over to the Netherlands in August. She proved reluctant to stump up the money for preparations, and Leicester had to raise a £25,000 loan from the City on the security of his own estates. She openly told the Court of her distaste for the project, so worrying her Dutch allies and giving confidence to Parma, the Spanish commander. And she continued to negotiate with Parma, leaving Leicester nervous that he would be used as a catspaw and then made to look a fool. Leicester wrote anxiously from the Netherlands for reinforcements and for information on the Queen's intentions, and his agents at Court confirmed his fears. Thomas Vavasour reported in March 1586 that

> I gather by her Majesty that an indifferent peace will not be refused, whereof you are only used for an instrument; for, talking with her Majesty of the necessity to put men into field, to the which I found her ears altogether stopped, especially blaming the charges, 'And what', quoth she, 'if a peace shall come in the meantime?'[4]

Leicester's enterprise in the Netherlands was almost a rerun of the Scottish campaign of 1560. The Queen, who regarded her army as a bargaining counter, wanted her general to keep his forces safe and spend as little as possible; the general, who thought an inactive army would achieve nothing, tried to fight a campaign for which he had too few men and too little money. But there was an added complication. The Earl knew that his position at Court was, in his absence, weak, and he suspected that Burghley, Cobham, and Croft were conspiring against him. Not surprisingly, he was tempted to strengthen himself in the Netherlands, and to embroil Elizabeth more deeply in Dutch affairs. When the States-General offered him the post of Governor-General, he accepted it, despite the Queen's insistence that he should do nothing which implied that she asserted sovereignty or responsibility there. The Dutch sought to bind England irrevocably to their cause, and Leicester thought he could not defeat Parma without a united command. He took the office, though he knew Elizabeth would be furious, and allowed his title to be proclaimed across the Netherlands.

But the Queen was more furious than expected: she thought the Dutch had duped Leicester and that he had duped her. She wrote to him that 'Our express pleasure and commandment is that, all delays and excuses laid apart, you do presently, upon the duty of your allegiance, obey and fulfil whatsoever the bearer hereof shall direct you to do in our name: whereof fail you not, as you will answer the contrary at your uttermost peril!' The bearer, Sir Thomas Heneage, told Leicester he was to make a humiliating public resignation of the governorship. When Heneage reported to the Queen that it was considered unwise to ruin Leicester's authority and offend the Dutch by such a gesture, she replied, 'Do as you are bidden, and leave your considerations for your own affairs!' A month later, Elizabeth was still boiling away; Leicester's brother wrote to him that 'Our mistress's extreme rage doth increase rather than anyway diminish, and giveth out great threatening words against you. Therefore make the best assurance you can for yourself, and trust not her oath, for that her malice is great and unquenchable, in the wisest of their opinions here.'[5]

In the end, after considerable pressure on the Queen from privy councillors, the matter was quietly dropped. Leicester did not have to make a public surrender of the office, but he and everyone else had to forget that he had been given it. There was a compromise, but only after months of bruising political conflict which had prevented him doing anything useful in the Netherlands. Leicester did make minor military gains in the summer campaign of 1586, but he was crippled by his own incompetence as a commander; by poor relations with more experienced deputies and the distrustful Dutch; by the inadequacies of the English recruiting and supply system; and by Elizabeth's unwillingness to spend men and money. The Queen wanted war on the cheap, and refused to recognise that there is no such thing. Leicester never had enough men. Companies were always short, through under-recruitment, death, and desertion, and it was in the interests of captains that they should remain so – the captains claimed the wages of every soldier on the roll, and pocketed the shares of the dead men and deserters. By the time Leicester himself reached the Netherlands, his force had already fallen to half its paper strength: it took three months of complaining to get the Queen to send 2,000 reinforcements, but she failed to provide money for them.

Leicester was given insufficient money for wages, supplies, and equipment, so desertions continued and decisive military action was impossible. In her determination not to spend more than was absolutely essential, Elizabeth did not send enough, and she did not send it regularly – though it is true that her general's financial control was inadequate and his accounting ludicrous. So soldiers went unpaid, and they had to forage from their Dutch 'allies', which soured relations. In the garrison at Deventer, things got so bad that Sir William Stanley and Rowland Yorke handed the town over to Parma, and led off their Irish troops to fight in Spanish service – which further weakened Leicester's position with the States-General. When Leicester was unable to raise the siege of Sluys and the town

surrendered, Elizabeth decided to seek agreement with Parma –
which finally destroyed Leicester's reputation in the
Netherlands. He resigned his command in December 1587, and
returned to England in ignominy, if not quite in disgrace.

An English army remained in the Netherlands until the end
of the reign: it was calculated in 1603 that this had cost
£1,419,596, perhaps six years' ordinary revenue, and it is
difficult to say that anything much was gained. Perhaps the
only real achievement was a negative one: the army in the
Netherlands brought the Spanish Armada down on England's
neck. For whatever the assumptions of English nationalist
historiography, the Armada was not sent to conquer gallant
little England; it was sent to force interfering little England out
of the Netherlands. Philip II's instructions to his commanders
were that once they had defeated Elizabeth's army of defence,
they should demand toleration for English Catholics (a papal
loan meant he had to ask for that) and English withdrawal from
the Netherlands. Philip seems to have been more impressed by
the English contribution to the defence of the United Provinces
than most historians. But the cost of resisting the Armada,
thought to have been £161,000, should be added as an indirect
cost of the Netherlands campaign, to give £1,580,781 in all.
Robert Dudley, Earl of Leicester, had been an extremely
expensive boyfriend.

The defeat of the Spanish Armada in 1588 solved nothing.
There was still a successful Spanish army in the Netherlands,
still Spanish support for French Catholics against the
Huguenots, and still a risk of Spanish invasion: there were
further armadas in 1596 and 1599. In 1591, Sir Roger Williams,
an experienced army commander and self-appointed strategist,
told the Privy Council that there were three ways to bring Spain
to terms: by defeat of the Spanish land army in the Netherlands;
by amphibious operations to harass the coasts of Spain and
Portugal; and by naval sorties into the Atlantic to disrupt the
flow of Spanish silver from Mexico and Peru. This was hardly
an encouraging analysis: the land option would be extremely
expensive; the amphibious option would be difficult to co-
ordinate; and the naval option was too uncertain – silver fleets
could creep by in Atlantic storms, and English fleets could not
be kept at sea for long enough for effective blockade. Each of
these approaches had their advocates in Court and Council, and
the debates contributed to the factional conflicts of the 1590s.

There was a party, led by the Earl of Essex, Lord Willoughby, and Sir Robert Sidney, which espoused the old Leicester programme of a continental land strategy and decisive military commitment in defence of Dutch and French Protestants. The naval lobby, led by Lord Admiral Howard and Sir Walter Raleigh, and backed by the Cecils, advocated a war at sea, arguing that it was cheaper, safer, and more likely to be successful. Elizabeth was attracted by the low-cost option, especially as the prospect of spoils from Spanish ports and ships meant that private investment in expeditions could be invited. The Essex group was much weaker politically, and the Cecil stranglehold on patronage made it difficult for the Earl to advance his allies. So the Queen usually supported the naval lobby, though at times she was forced into land campaigns in France rather than see Spain triumphant there. But the existence of rival strategies, and the sharp division within the Court, meant that military and naval planning was often confused and erratic, and that policies were rarely pursued to a decisive conclusion. Above all, Elizabeth found time after time that once an army or a fleet was dispatched from England she could not control its commanders.

The failure of control at sea was demonstrated in 1589, 1596, and 1597, when the Queen sent out naval expeditions with clear instructions to weaken Spain. But once the fleets were down the Channel, the commanders did much as they wished and Elizabeth's forces were used to further private interests and ambitions. In February 1589, Elizabeth issued unequivocal orders to Sir Francis Drake and Sir John Norris: they were to destroy the remaining Armada ships in the Spanish Biscayan ports, to forestall another attack, and once that had been accomplished (and only then) they were to seize the Azores as a base for further action against the silver fleets. The original plan, in September 1588, had envisaged an attack on Lisbon as well, but this had been dropped when it was realised that the survivors of the Armada had sailed to Santander and San Sebastian rather than Lisbon and Seville. However, the whole enterprise had been planned as a commercial undertaking: the Queen was to provide £20,000, and the commanders and their backers another £40,000 – and the investors expected a return. But Elizabeth's final orders left little scope for profit, and there was no money to be made from sinking Spanish warships.

It seems that the commanders decided in advance that they

were going to Lisbon, whatever the Queen said. This was partly because of the involvement of the Earl of Essex and the 'land lobby' in the enterprise: although he was not formally a commander, Essex had invested heavily in the project, many of his allies participated, and he rushed off to join the expedition despite the Queen's prohibition – sailing straight for Lisbon. The main fleet, under Norris and Drake, sailed to Corunna, where they found only one Armada warship: instead of sailing on, they landed their troops and began looting. The soldiers liberated large quantities of Spanish wine, got thoroughly drunk, and were useless for days. The army wasted two weeks at Corunna, recovering from its collective hangover, and then the fleet sailed south to Lisbon – leaving the Armada ships safely behind them in the Biscayan ports. Little was actually achieved at Lisbon: the commanders had no siege equipment (they were not supposed to be tackling a city!), and, after some ineffectual marching up and down outside the gates, the army had to withdraw.

The force was now much weakened: ships were in disrepair, and sickness and desertions in Spain and Portugal had left few fit sailors and soldiers. While Norris led the main fleet back to England, Drake and a smaller group now set off for the Azores, though the Queen had ordered that they were not to do so unless the warships in Spanish ports had first been destroyed. But Drake's fleet encountered severe gales; many of the ships were damaged, and they too had to head for home. The fleet returned to England, with probably £100,000 spent and 11,000 out of 19,000 men lost – and all for nothing. Elizabeth wrote in fury to Norris and Drake, reminding them that

> before your departure hence you did, at sundry times, so far forth promise us with oaths to assure us and some of our Council that your first and principal action should be to take and distress the king of Spain's navy and ships in ports where they lay; which, if you did not, you affirmed that you were content to be reputed as traitors.[6]

But whatever their orders, and whatever their oaths, they had counted for nothing once the commanders had left Plymouth.

It was very little different in 1596, with the expedition to Cadiz. This was a private enterprise action, largely financed by the joint commanders, Essex and Howard, and there was always the risk that return on investments would take priority over strategic considerations. Furthermore, the enterprise was bedevilled by factionalism and rivalry between the leaders. A large fleet sailed to Cadiz and destroyed a number of Spanish warships and merchantmen, and troops under Essex landed and seized the town. But the commanders could not agree what to do next: Essex and his allies, advocates of land war against Spain, wanted to establish a permanent base at Cadiz, but the naval lobby formed the majority and they wanted to get home with their loot. Cadiz was set on fire, and the fleet sailed away home. The main Spanish fleet in the Tagus was not attacked, and there was no attempt to intercept the merchant fleet from America. The plunder from Cadiz, promised to the Queen, was handed over to their men by Essex and Howard, so that the strategic failure was, from the Crown's point of view, a financial flop as well.

On the Cadiz expedition, Essex at least had had a sense of strategic interest that had gone beyond mere looting: he had proposed that Cadiz be garrisoned as a base, and he had wanted to tackle Spanish shipping. But in 1597, on the 'Islands voyage', he too abandoned good strategy in the hope of easy pickings and a glamorous triumph. As in the previous year, the 1597 exercise was conceived in factionalism: it was thought by some Court observers that the whole project had been designed by Cecil and Raleigh to get Essex away from Court. Essex, however, had no choice but to go: he was in desperate need of money, and, even more, of a dramatic victory to establish his political position. The 1597 voyage was planned as a successful rerun of the 1589 expedition: Essex was to destroy the Spanish fleet in port at Ferrol, and then sail to the Azores to intercept the American treasure fleet. But again it all went wrong. By the time the English fleet reached the Iberian coast, it was thought too disorderly to take on the Spanish fleet, partly because of antagonism between Essex and his second-in-command, Raleigh. The first, and more important, part of the plan was abandoned.

Instead, the fleet sailed on to the Azores. Raleigh got there first, and upstaged his commander by taking a town: Essex threatened to behead him for insubordination. Disorganised by disputes, the English failed to stop Spain's treasure fleet, which sailed safely past, and Essex led his ships back to England with nothing to show for an expensive enterprise. Essex had failed once again to achieve the victory he needed to overcome his weakness at Court. In 1589, 1596, and 1597, Elizabeth had sent off fleets with two crucial objectives, the destruction of the Spanish navy and the capture of the treasure fleet. In 1596 there had been some attempt to weaken the Spanish navy, and in 1597 an abortive effort to catch the treasure fleet. But in essentials the orders had been ignored and commanders sought guaranteed plunder and easy fame. Elizabeth might draw up plans of campaign, but she could not ensure that they were carried out: once at sea, Drake, Norris, Howard, Essex, and Raleigh ignored her instructions.

On land, the generals too went their own way – though as sixteenth-century armies were much less mobile than fleets, the disobedience was less flagrant and the generals at least attacked more or less the right enemy in more or less the right place. But the same problems of political control over military ventures can be seen in action. In 1589, Elizabeth decided that she had to prop up the new Protestant King of France, Henry IV, to prevent a Spanish take-over in France – or, at least, to prevent Philip II seizing the French Channel ports. She agreed to send 4,000 men to Normandy, commanded by Lord Willoughby, for one month. But just before the force embarked at Dover, Henry IV sent a message through the English ambassador that he no longer needed support, and Willoughby was ordered to wait. Willoughby, however, was anxious for personal achievement, and shared the old Leicester vision of a Protestant military league: he ignored the news, and set off anyway without consulting Queen or Council. Walsingham warned him that he could expect minimal financial support: 'I fear that the troops serving under your lordship, for lack of pay shall endure some extremity.'[7] But Willoughby went on.

He led an indecisive ten-week winter campaign, in which his soldiers fought five engagements and marched 400 miles through rain and mud, from Dieppe to the Loire and back to the coast near Caen – while Henry IV rushed about in search of a plan of action. The English troops suffered, as Walsingham had predicted, from shortage of food and clothes, cold, sickness, exhaustion, and the hostility of the French – of the French Catholic enemy, of the French Protestant allies, and of the French peasants who cut the throats of English stragglers and of those foraging for food. At the end of December 1589, the shattered remains of the army were withdrawn in disorder; only half of the original force made it back to England, and many of them died in the south coast ports. Although there is some dispute among historians as to the contribution Willoughby's force made to Henry IV's recovery, it does not appear to have been very much. It seems that the soldiers suffered in no more crucial cause than their commander's ambition.

But by 1591, Henry IV really was in need of English assistance, with a Spanish and French Leaguer army in Brittany and, by the end of the year, another in Normandy. Again there was a threat that Spain would capture the French Channel ports, which, the arrogant English supposed, would immediately lead to an invasion. In May 1591 Elizabeth sent a small army of 3,000 men to Brittany under Sir John Norris, but the campaign was a disaster from the start. The Queen was reluctant to raise (and pay) a wholly new force, so 1,500 of the men were transferred from the Netherlands, weakening the forces there. Some of Norris's men were detached to help defend Dieppe from the Catholic Leaguers, and they were not replaced for a couple of months. There were, as ever, high levels of desertion and of sickness, and supplies were inadequate. The English force wandered aimlessly around Brittany, losing men as it went, until it was down to barely a thousand men: in February 1592, Norris left his men in winter camp, and returned to England to plead for reinforcements. In his absence, his tattered army was almost totally destroyed by Leaguer forces in a battle at Craon in May.

In July 1591, another English force had been sent to France – 4,000 men under the Earl of Essex, to help Henry IV with a siege of Rouen. But it was much the same story in Normandy as in Brittany, with the added ingredient of Essex's impetuosity. Henry IV was busy minding his own business and watching out for an invasion from the Netherlands by Parma, and Essex was left to march around in glory wasting his army's time and his queen's money: 'Where he is, or what he doth, or what he is to do, we are ignorant', wrote Elizabeth in impotent anger[8] – a sentence which just about sums up her relations with her commanders! By the time the siege of Rouen finally began on 31 October, the Essex force was down to probably a thousand men and the Earl was pleading for reinforcements. The siege made slow progress, the reinforcements who were sent melted away, the expected invasion by Parma materialised, and in January 1592 Essex himself gave up and headed for home. In April, Henry IV was forced by Parma to abandon the Rouen siege, and

Elizabeth had nothing to show for almost £300,000 which had been spent in France.

And then there was Ireland, where, for the English, almost everything almost always goes wrong. The campaigns against Tyrone's rebellion provide two classic cases of the Queen's inability to control her generals once they were in the field. In April 1599, Essex was sent to Ireland to command an army of 16,000 foot and 1,300 horse, with firm instructions to attack Tyrone in Ulster. But, once in Ireland, Essex did everything but what he had been told to do. Elizabeth was furious as he squandered her money marching up and down Leinster and Munster: she told the Court it was costing her £1,000 a day to send Essex on a summer progress. Essex was taunted by the Queen in a letter of mid-September for his failure to move into Ulster:

> If sickness in the army be the reason, why was not the action undertaken when the army was in better state? If winter's approach, why were the summer months of July and August lost? If the spring were too soon, and the summer that followed otherwise spent, if the harvest that succeeded were so neglected as nothing hath been done, then surely we must conclude that none of the four quarters of the year will be in season for you![9]

Essex had got himself into an impossible position. He had sought the Irish command for a desperate attempt to gain political influence by military success, and had arrived in Ireland promising, 'By God, I will beat Tyrone in the field!'[10] But there were no easy victories to be had in Ireland. He had spread out his forces garrisoning unimportant forts and towns in Leinster and Munster, leaving himself with too small a field army for an effective campaign against Tyrone. His captains thought that he had no chance of defeating Tyrone or of establishing a bridgehead in Ulster, and advised him to wait. But his failure to attack Tyrone had destroyed what remained of his political credit at Court, and turned the Queen finally against him. He adopted a desperate, and treasonable, course: he agreed a truce with Tyrone, withdrew his army to Dublin, and, despite explicit orders to stay in Ireland, dashed back to Court to try to rebuild his political position. He had wasted £300,000 in five months.

Essex was replaced as Lord Deputy in Ireland by Lord

Mountjoy, a much more reliable soldier – though he too dabbled in treason and considered taking his army to England to restore Essex to power and declare James VI of Scots heir to the throne. But a Spanish landing at Kinsale forced Mountjoy to concentrate on the job in hand: at the end of 1601 he defeated Tyrone's main army, and then forced the Spanish to surrender. But there was still the problem of Tyrone himself: Mountjoy hoped to induce him to submit, but Elizabeth was determined he should be taken and hanged. Eventually, she agreed that Tyrone should have his life, but she laid down impossibly strict terms. Robert Cecil recognised that Mountjoy would have to disobey his orders, and in February 1603 simply asked the Lord Deputy to keep quiet: 'And so hoping, by your next dispatch, you will write that which is fit to be showed her Majesty, and that which is fit for me to know ..., in which kind all honest servants must strain a little when they will serve princes.'[11] Mountjoy made his secret deal with Tyrone, and Elizabeth died before she knew the truth.

So Elizabeth could not control her commanders, from Grey in Scotland in 1560 to Mountjoy in Ireland in 1603, and so her objectives were rarely achieved. Raleigh claimed later that the failures against Spain resulted from Elizabeth's own refusal to give the military a free hand:

> If the late queen would have believed her men of war as she did her scribes, we had in her time beaten that great empire in pieces and made their kings kings of figs and oranges as in old times. But her Majesty did all by halves, and by petty invasions taught the Spaniard how to defend himself, and to see his own weakness.[12]

It was the usual military cry – 'If only the civilians had given us the tools, we could have finished the job'. There was just something in the argument. Elizabeth did keep her generals and admirals on a tight budget of men and money, and her soldiers were often underfed and badly equipped. But the sufferings of the common soldiers were as much because their commanders kept them in the field longer than had been intended, as because the initial allocations were inadequate. There is no reason to suppose that if the Queen had given her commanders more men and money, they would have been used more effectively. The problem lay with the military leaders, not with the government.

It is true that the commanders were asked to do difficult

things, and that failures came partly from influences beyond their control. In the Netherlands and in France, Leicester, Willoughby, Norris, and Essex were leaders of subsidiary forces which depended for success on the co-operation of foreign allies, and Essex was not the only commander to have failed in Ireland. At sea, Drake, Howard, Essex, and Raleigh were hampered by inadequate communications and intelligence, and nervous of hazarding the Queen's ships far from port. But these officers were not dispatched against their military will to pursue the politicians' schemes: they had proposed the ventures, and they had pleaded for command. And once they had got command, they simply went their own way, in flagrant disregard of instructions: they were in charge, and they could do as they liked. Despite the Queen's clear opposition, Essex continued to exercise the prerogative of commanders to give knighthoods in the field – 21 at Rouen in 1591, 68 at Cadiz in 1596, and 81 in Ireland in 1599, while Elizabeth herself made only 10 new knights a year. Perhaps power went to the heads of commanders. when Nanny let the boys out of the nursery, they made the most of their freedom.

Elizabeth's control of her commanders was limited by her attempts to hold down costs. By taking financial partners into her initiatives, she shared her own authority and left her associates freedom of action. English military efforts in the Netherlands were a joint enterprise with the Dutch; those in France were (in theory) partly paid for by Henry IV. This brought problems of conflicting interests and divided loyalties, as well as slow payments. At sea, the Queen went into partnership with her own subjects: in 1589, 1596, and 1597, the commanders had a direct financial stake in operations, and it is not surprising that they concentrated on plundering Spanish towns rather than sinking Spanish warships. When the Queen had privatised warfare, she should not have been surprised that the profit motive ruled. In the last years of the reign, councillors and courtiers were investing heavily in privateering expeditions to the West Indies, the Spanish coast, and the Mediterranean. They saw naval enterprises in much the same light, as opportunities for private gain rather than for national security. Commanders therefore followed their own interests, rather than the Queen's orders.

Problems also arose because there was no general agreement on the strategy to be followed, and the two main approaches, land campaigns and naval strikes, were adopted by different Court factions. It therefore became politically impossible to opt decisively for one strategy, and any expedition was likely to have a high command chosen to balance the factions. As early as the intervention in the Netherlands in 1585, subordinates who did not share Leicester's vision of his purpose were appointed, and he regarded Sir John Norris and Sir Thomas Cecil as little better than spies. Later, of course, it was much worse: commanders pursued tactics for which they had not been equipped, as in 1589; or they could not agree what to do, as in 1596; or their arguments wrecked hopes of doing anything, as in 1597. Forces which were sent out to sink ships in the event concentrated on besieging towns, as the generals had their way over the admirals – and opportunities to establish foreign bases were lost when the admirals insisted on sailing for home. Failure to carry out the Queen's orders was partly a consequence of disputes among strategists and rivalry between commanders.

But all these reasons do not quite explain the repeated and flagrant disregard of royal instructions. It seems clear that commanders concluded that those instructions did not really matter, that the Queen was a woman and war was men's business. In Council, Court, and Parliament, Elizabeth could show her competence; she could beat men at their own game – if necessary by using feminine tactics. But in war she was at the mercy of her generals, who thought they knew better – and she never succeeded in persuading them that they did not. In no other area of activity or policy was there such blatant disobedience to her express orders, such scorn for her authority, such contempt for monarchical dignity. A woman could browbeat politicians and seduce courtiers, but she could not command soldiers. Try as she might, Elizabeth could not quite escape from her sex: as Sir John Oglander put it a generation later, 'there was nothing wanting that could be desired in a prince, but that she was a woman'[13]

· · ·

NOTES AND REFERENCES

1. Read C 1955 *Mr Secretary Cecil and Queen Elizabeth*. Cape, p. 136
2. Read C 1955 p. 171

3. Adams S L 1973 The Protestant cause: religious alliance with the west European Calvinist communities as a political issue in England, 1585–1630. Oxford University D.Phil. thesis, pp. 53–4

4. Bruce J (ed.) 1844 *Correspondence of Robert Dudley, earl of Leycester*. Camden Society, p. 195

5. Bruce J (ed.) 1844 pp. 110, 243, 151

6. Wernham R B 1984 *After the Armada: Elizabethan England and the struggle for western Europe*. Oxford, p. 99

7. Wernham R B 1984 p. 161

8. Neale J E 1979 *Queen Elizabeth I*. Panther edn, p. 327

9. *Calendar of State Papers Ireland, 1599–1600*, p. 152

10. Moody T W, Martin F X, Byrne F J (eds) 1976 *A New History of Ireland*. Oxford, vol. 3 p. 127

11. Goodman G 1839 *The Court of King James the First* (2 vols). Bentley, vol. 2 p. 48

12. Johnson P 1974 *Elizabeth I: a study in power and intellect*. Weidenfeld & Nicolson, p. 325

13. Oglander J 1936 *A Royalist's Notebook*. Bamford F (ed.) Constable, p. 192

Chapter 8

THE QUEEN AND THE PEOPLE

Elizabeth I was a woman in danger: from the beginning of her reign to the end, she faced plots and rumours of plots. Some of the conspiracies posed real threats to her throne and to her life. In 1569, some of the leaders of the Revolt of the Northern Earls planned to remove Elizabeth and make Mary Stuart queen. In 1571, the Florentine banker Roberto Ridolfi hatched an elaborate scheme involving a Spanish invasion from the Netherlands, an English rebellion raised by the Duke of Norfolk, and the deposition of Elizabeth: the Pope, Philip II, and Norfolk were willing enough to help, and Elizabeth was saved only by the reluctance of the Spanish commander in the Netherlands and by Ridolfi's weakness for bragging to everyone what a wonderful plot he was organising. In 1583, Francis Throckmorton was the link man in a conspiracy to synchronise a French Catholic invasion with a rising of English Catholics, to free Mary Queen of Scots and make her queen of England. In 1586 a group of young Catholic fanatics swore to kill Elizabeth, and again planned to make Mary queen with foreign assistance. In 1599, the Essex circle formulated various schemes to seize Elizabeth, to make her the pawn of their faction, and force her to name James VI as heir.

These were real intrigues, even if government agents were sometimes on the fringe of them. In addition, there were smaller schemes, in which unfortunate individuals were probably framed by councillors to put the frighteners on Elizabeth: in 1584, William Parry was said to have intended to stab the Queen with a dagger; in 1587, Stafford and Moody may have conspired to put gunpowder under Elizabeth's bed and blow her up; in 1594 the Portuguese doctor, Roderigo Lopez, was alleged to have planned to poison the Queen; and in 1598 Squire was to have killed her by putting poison on her saddle-pommel. And then there were the far-fetched stories and lunatic plots. In October 1559 there were rumours that Elizabeth and Robert Dudley were going to be poisoned at a banquet given by the Earl of Arundel. In 1562, two relations of the late Cardinal Pole were consulting astrologers about the Queen's future and planning an invasion through Wales. In 1583 the Warwickshire Catholic, John Somerville, told his neighbours he was going to shoot Elizabeth, and set off for London – but he declared his intention to everyone he met on the way and was arrested. There were Protestant madmen too: in 1591 John Hacket decided he was the new Messiah, and announced that Elizabeth had been deposed. He sent his two apostles out into the streets of London, 'and tell them in the city that Christ Jesus is come with his fan in his hand to judge the earth. And if any man ask you where he is, tell them he is at Walker's house, by Broken Wharf.'[1]

With much justification, Elizabeth and her councillors feared for her safety. After all, in 1570 the Pope had declared the Queen excommunicate, and absolved her subjects from obedience to her. In 1584, after Somerville and Throckmorton, and the successful assassination of William of Orange in the Netherlands, the Council organised a Protestant vigilante group, the 'Bond of Association', pledged by oath to protect the Queen's life and, if they failed, to hunt down and murder her killers. The Privy Council drew up an 'Instrument of an Association for the preservation of the Queen's Majesty's royal person', and Secretary Walsingham supervised the distribution of copies to lords lieutenant and reliable magnates across the country. These local leaders then put the oath of membership to the leading gentry, and collected signatures for the Bond. It was a panic measure at a panic time, but the fear of disaster remained strong. In her last years, Elizabeth slept with a rusty old sword by her bed, and she made a bit of a fool of herself stalking around the Privy Chamber with the weapon, stabbing at curtains in case assassins lurked.

Nor was it simply a danger of assassination plots: there was a risk of rebellion. In 1597 Elizabeth told the French ambassador that 'she had to deal with nobles of divers humours, and peoples who, although they made great demonstration of love towards her, nevertheless were fickle and inconstant, and she had to fear everything'. Some of her councillors agreed. One of the arguments used against expensive land wars in the 1590s was that heavier war taxation and military recruitment would lead to widespread popular disorder; Burghley was opposed to war because of 'the nature of the common people of England, inclinable to sedition if they be oppressed with extraordinary payments'.[2] So Elizabeth pursued a propaganda policy designed to maximise popular loyalty to herself – not just because she liked to be cheered (though she certainly did), but because it was politically sensible. If she could attract the intense loyalty of ordinary people, then they might serve as a protection against assassination attempts – they would be on the lookout for critics of the regime, and might turn in any who posed a threat. A loyal nation would be less likely to rebel in hard times, and might more readily pay taxes and serve in royal armies and fleets. So Elizabeth did not only have to present sophisticated and allusive images of female rule to her educated courtiers; she had to present a simpler, more basic message to ordinary people. Somehow, the townspeople and peasants of England had to be made to love her.

Some of Elizabeth's work was done for her. The clergy in their churches read out prayers for the Queen's safety and preached sermons on God's favour towards her; the judges at assizes warned of the need for vigilance against the enemies of the state; the sheriffs read out statutes and proclamations which stressed the need for order and obedience. But these tactics sought an allegiance which was passive and formal: a more fervent and active devotion to the royal person was needed if she was to be really safe. Elizabeth had to show herself to her people, and gain their adoration. In London, it was easy enough: from the beginning of the reign to the end, Elizabeth paraded in splendour through the streets and sailed on the Thames where her people could see her. On St George's Day 1559, a great spectacle was staged on the Thames, in which the Queen's barge was rowed up and down, escorted by a flotilla of boats and observed by large crowds on the banks; there was music and artillery salutes, and, in the evening, a firework display.

Elizabeth was very much a public queen. She always appeared in public for her Accession Day celebrations, which were usually associated with an elaborate procession through London before the splendid jousting in the tilt-yard. Even on 17 November 1602, when she was 69 and there was suspicion of an assassination attempt, she merely changed her route to avoid the danger and appeared much as scheduled. It is clear that the

Queen always made a great impression on her subjects. Bishop Goodman, years after the event, remembered how, as a boy of 5 in 1588, he had seen Elizabeth one night at Whitehall. On news that the Queen was coming, he and his friends had run through the streets, to join the crowd shouting 'God save your Majesty!' as she passed by in torchlight. 'God bless you all, my good people', she had replied,[3] and the crowds were made to feel they really were blessed and they were truly her good people.

Away from London, of course, it was much more difficult for the Queen to establish a rapport with the common people, but her regular summer progresses provided some opportunity. Elizabeth and her Court usually went on a ten-week summer progress: she went every year from 1559 to 1579, except in 1562 before the French War and in 1570 after the Revolt of the Northern Earls. She began her travels again in 1591, perhaps conscious of the growing pressures of war taxation, repeated the exercise in 1592, and went off annually in 1599–1602 in a final burst of energy, daring those who were too old to travel to stay at home. Historians usually think of progresses in the context of Elizabeth's relations with nobility and gentry, but they were also occasions for the Queen to show herself to ordinary people as she crossed the countryside at a sedate pace. The major progresses of the reign usually included a ceremonial visit to one of the great corporate towns: Winchester in 1560, Cambridge in 1563, Coventry in 1565, Oxford in 1566, Warwick in 1572, Bristol in 1574, Worcester in 1575, Norwich in 1578.

Most progresses were major public relations exercises, with careful preparations for maximum impact. The itinerary was drawn up by the Vice-Chamberlain in consultation with the Queen, and arrangements were made in detail by correspondence with the towns and houses Elizabeth would visit. The Queen would prepare herself before setting out, and before her projected visit to Kent in 1577 Burghley studied Lambarde's *Perambulation of Kent* to brief her on local features, so she could give the impression she knew the area well. Progresses were, however, restricted in their geographical scope: the state of the roads and the speed at which the Court could travel precluded very long trips. Elizabeth never went west of Bristol or north of Stafford, and plans to visit York in 1562 and 1575 were cancelled. Except for the great Midlands progresses in 1565, 1572, and 1575, and the westwards progress in 1574, Elizabeth invariably kept to the Home Counties and

East Anglia. But the major progresses were given wider publicity by printed accounts of ceremonies, with personal details of the Queen's own words and responses.

For those outside the South-east, if Elizabeth was to be seen at all it was in pictures, carefully controlled and widely distributed. In 1563 a proclamation was drafted, forbidding further pictures of the Queen until a master portrait had been painted for others to copy. The proclamation was not issued, but there were approved versions of her portrait which were widely copied. The extant pictures of Elizabeth all conform to one or other of half a dozen face patterns, and the pattern from the 'Darnley portrait' of about 1575 remained in use into the 1590s. In a bid for a monopoly, the Painter Stainers' Company petitioned for regulations on royal portraits in 1575 and 1578, and a Book of Ordinances was issued in 1581. Although official controls were loose, they were not ineffective, and there were general patterns in the development of Elizabeth's picture. From 1579, perhaps coming out of the Protestant campaign against the Alençon match, the allegorical style came to dominate picture-making, with symbolic representations of the Queen's qualities and of imperial aspirations. The royal portrait was now a means of propaganda, not of representation.

By the 1580s there was apparently a huge demand for images of the Queen: as well as the wholesale copying of portraits, the lower end of the patriotic market was now being catered for. Just as Elizabeth's courtiers began to wear jewelled cameos of the Queen, so her poorer subjects could acquire base-metal medallions to wear as expressions of loyalty. In the 1580s, too, woodcuts and engravings of Elizabeth became more common in books, and in the next decade many separate printed pictures were produced for sale. But the more widely the royal image was displayed, the more important controls became. There appears to have been some official decision in about 1594 that Elizabeth should be pictured as eternally youthful, presumably to prevent fears for the future. Although the face of the famous 'Ditchley portrait' became a pattern for the rest of the reign, in the copies it was rejuvenated into the softer face of a young woman. In 1596, the Privy Council ordered officials to seek out and destroy all unseemly portraits, which were said to have caused the Queen great offence: the object of the campaign seems to have been the elimination of the image of Elizabeth as an old woman, and engravings which showed her age appear to have been destroyed.

Those of Elizabeth's subjects who could not buy her picture might at least learn simple ballads of loyalty. The ballads were both unofficial propaganda weapons and opportunities for individuals to share by singing in public devotion to the Queen. There were love-songs to Elizabeth, as in the 1559

> Come over the born, Bessy,
> Come over the born, Bessy,
> Sweet Bessy come over to me;
> And I shall thee take,
> And my dear lady make
> Before all other that ever I see.

As the reign wore on, there were ballads in the form of hymns of thanks to God for Elizabeth's rule and her achievements: 'A prayer and also thanks unto God for his great mercy for giving and preserving our noble Queen Elizabeth to reign over us . . . to be sung the 17 day of November 1577', an Accession Day song. There were Accession Day ballads in her later years too: 17 November 1600 saw 'A pleasant ballad of the most blessed and prosperous reign of her Majesty for the space of two and forty years, and now entering her three and fortieth, to the great joy and comfort of all her Majesty's faithful subjects' –

> Ring out your bells!
> What should you do else?
> Strike up your drums for joy;
> The noblest queen
> That ever was seen
> In England doth reign this day.[4]

Despite the poor quality of the verse, this particular ballad seems to have sold well: it was reprinted to celebrate 17 November 1601 and 1602, with only the dates changed.

The authors and printers of ballads seem to have understood their market, and to have known when sales would be good. An emergency always produced a flood of ballads. In 1570, after the Revolt of the Northern Earls and the papal bull of deposition, there was 'A godly ditty or prayer to be sung unto God for the preservation of his Church, our queen and realm, against all traitors, rebels and papistical enemies'. In 1578, when Elizabeth was almost killed in a shooting accident, 'A new ballad declaring the dangerous shooting of the gun at Court' published the shock-horror story. In 1586, after the discovery of the Babington Plot, there was 'A godly ditty to be sung for the preservation of the queen's most excellent Majesty's reign':

> All English hearts rejoice and sing
> That fears the Lord and loves our queen;
> Yield thank to God, our heavenly king,
> Who hitherto her guide hath been.[5]

The English were to be made to feel lucky, for having Elizabeth in the first place, and for God's preservation of their darling. And, of course, each well-publicised crisis showed how God had intervened to sustain their queen, thus illustrating his special favour towards her.

By the 1590s, however, the technique had changed. Until then, the ballads had usually related to real events, and given thanks for the Queen's accession or her continuing safety. But in her last decade, as the war dragged on, taxes grew more burdensome, food prices soared, and living standards fell, the ballad-writers ignored the facts and resorted to the 'big lie'. In the midst of war and growing poverty, the peace and prosperity of the reign were celebrated: 'A joyful new ballad of our queen's going to the parliament, showing her most happy and prosperous reign and the great care she hath for the government of her people, made this year 1593'; 'A triumphant new ballad in honour of the queen's Majesty and her most happy government, who hath reigned in great prosperity thirty-seven years' and 'England's triumph, containing divers of those abundant blessings wherewith this our realm hath been blessed by our most gracious Queen Elizabeth's reign' in 1595.[6] In many ballads, and especially in those published late in the reign, the emphasis was upon Elizabeth's care for her people, her motherly concern for the welfare of all her subjects and for the poor in particular. There was a deliberate attempt to project Elizabeth as the Queen of the poor, as the protectress of all those who carried the burdens of society. It was, of course, government by illusion.

Throughout her reign, Elizabeth had cultivated the common touch, determinedly showing herself willing and able to care for and communicate with her subjects. In her coronation procession of 1559, she tried to establish an intimate relationship with ordinary people, and the official published account of the occasion stressed the ways in which she showed her concern:

What hope the poor and needy may look for at her Grace's hand, she, as in all her journey continually, so in hearkening to the poor children of Christ's Hospital with eyes cast up into heaven, [she] did fully declare that neither the wealthier estate could stand without consideration had to the poverty, neither the poverty be duly considered unless they were remembered, as commended to us by God's own mouth.

In her procession, she stopped her carriage whenever a poor person tried to give her flowers or some other small gift, and listened to the petitions of the poor as she went on her way. When Elizabeth was presented by the recorder of London with a purse of 1,000 gold marks, she promised to care for her people:

And whereas your request is that I should continue your good lady and queen, be ye ensured that I will be as good unto you as ever queen was to be people. No will in me can lack, neither do I trust shall there lack any power. And persuade yourselves, that for the safety and quietness of you all I will not spare, if need be, to spend my blood. God thank you all![7]

It was all heady stuff – and the people believed it. Perhaps Elizabeth did too.

The Queen's approach was much the same on progress, when she deliberately sought the affection of her subjects in public and well-publicised gestures. The Spanish ambassador, who travelled with her on the progress through Berkshire in 1568, reported that the Queen ordered her carriage into the thickest parts of the crowds, and stood up to wave and thank them for their welcome: 'She was received with great acclamations and signs of joy, as is customary in this country; whereat she was extremely pleased and told me so, giving me to understand how beloved she was by her subjects.' Elizabeth informed the ambassador that 'she attributed it all to God's miraculous goodness',[8] but in fact the enthusiasm was the product of her own hard work and that of her propagandists. In 1572, on progress through Oxfordshire, Elizabeth sheltered from the rain in a barn; there, an old woman told her that the copyhold on the family's small farm was about to run out, so the Queen got her Council to write to the landlord asking him to extend the tenancy. The story soon spread – with help from the Council.

The Queen tried to make the people she met feel special, as if their particular qualities had brought them to her attention. Her hosts at the manor-houses she visited on progress, and the mayors and recorders of the towns she passed, would be treated to some small gesture of affection, to make them glow with pride – some compensation, no doubt, for the expenditure necessary to receive the royal guest appropriately. She behaved, too, as if every town she visited was her favourite in all England, and she would turn on the tears as she rode out through town gates – it was so at Worcester in 1575, and at Norwich in 1578 she told the mayor, 'I have laid up in my breast such good will as I shall never forget Norwich'. 'Farewell, Norwich!' she cried out in tears, as she passed out of the city[9] – she was, after all, one of the best weepers in the business, and she was not one to let a talent go to waste.

Elizabeth sought to display her care for the poor by her carefully staged charity. Her almoner's staff gave 5d. each to thirteen poor men every day at the palace gates; about £130 was handed out to the poor over Easter, as well as the formal gifts of Maundy money. In addition, she gave an average of about £240 a year in casual alms to the poor, especially on progress – perhaps one reason for the loyal crowds around her coach was that there was often money to be had. Elizabeth also showed her common touch quite literally, by touching victims of scrofula, the 'king's evil', in the hope of cure. She seems to have taken this up in the 1570s, perhaps to show that, despite the papal deposition, she really was still queen. She took some of the obviously Catholic prayers out of the ceremony, and had it translated into English, but she retained the essentials of the old rite. She seems to have touched at Whitehall at Easter, and on summer progress: we know she touched nine scrofula victims at Kenilworth in 1575, ten in 1596, and thirty-eight on Good Friday 1597. There were, however, attacks upon the custom, and in 1597 and 1602 books were published praising and publicising her touching as a sign of God's endorsement of her rule.

These were practical ways in which Elizabeth tried to demonstrate her love for her subjects, and the loving relationship between queen and people was a regular theme in her own speeches and in the work of her image-makers. She appears to have worked on the assumption that if she boasted of her devotion often enough, she would never have to do anything about it – and if she told her people often enough how much they loved her, they would actually do it. The theme of loving care was set out by Lord Keeper Bacon in the first parliamentary speech of the reign: the Queen would not rule selfishly, but in ways which would meet the needs of her people – she was a princess 'to whom nothing – what nothing? – no, no worldly thing under the sun is so dear as the hearty love and goodwill of her nobles and subjects'. In 1563 Elizabeth herself promised to be a 'natural mother' to the realm; in 1589 she told a parliamentary delegation of her 'great and inestimable loving care towards her loving subjects: yea, more than of her own self, or than any of them have of themselves'.[10] In 1588, she told a London crowd that 'You may well have a greater prince, but you shall never have a more loving prince', and in 1593 she claimed to be the most loving sovereign the English had ever had – with the pious exception of her own father. She was reported to have said in 1601 that 'A more wise [prince] they may have, but a more careful and loving they shall never have. For she esteemeth the safety and happiness of her good subjects more dear and precious unto her than anything under heaven'.[11]

Ruled by such a paragon of princely virtues, it is not surprising that the English loved Elizabeth in return – or, at least, they were regularly told that they did. At the close of the Parliament of 1576, the Queen delighted that 'yet still I find that assured zeal amongst my faithful subjects, to my special comfort, which was first declared to my great encouragement'. Ten years later, she gave God public thanks for a great wonder: 'Even this it is, that as I came to the crown with willing hearts of subjects, so do I now, after twenty-eight years' reign, perceive in you no diminution of good wills, which, if haply I should want, well might I breathe but never think I lived.'[12] Outside Parliament, too, Elizabeth's subjects were reminded of the mutual love of queen and people. Her speech to the army at Tilbury in 1588 is justly famous:

> I have always so behaved myself that, under God, I have placed my chiefest strength and safeguard in the loyal hearts and good will of my subjects; and therefore I am come amongst you, as you see, at this time, not for my recreation and disport, but being resolved, in the midst and heat of the battle, to live or die amongst you all, to lay

down for my God, and for my kingdom, and for my people, my honour and blood, even in the dust.

Speaking to Oxford students in 1592, she marvelled at the extent of popular devotion, forcing her audience to conclude that they were participating in some divinely inspired miracle:

Your love for me is of such a kind as has never been known or heard of in the memory of man. Love of this nature is not possessed by parents, it happens not among friends, no, not even among lovers, whose fortune does not always include fidelity, as experience teaches. It is such love as neither persuasion, nor threats nor curses can destroy. Time has no power over it. Time, which eats away iron and wears away the rocks, cannot sever this love of yours. It is of this your services consist, and they are of such kind that I would think they would be eternal, if only I were to be eternal.[13]

There is more than a hint of misplaced arrogance here, but there is a good deal of political astuteness too: she told her subjects that their devotion was boundless, and in doing so she made it at least half true.

In prayers, ballads, and speeches, the people of England were regularly informed of how lucky they were, and how successfully Elizabeth had ruled them. The addresses given by the recorders of the great provincial towns she visited on progress pounded the themes home. At Coventry in 1565, at Warwick in 1572, at Worcester in 1575, the sentiments are so similar, the wording at times identical, that one suspects there was a model version of the speech, sent out by the Council or passed around the Midlands mafia of recorders: the Queen had ruled with peace and mercy, unfortunately the town was in economic decline, but now Elizabeth's appearance had raised the people from their gloom – her visit 'doth both look and, as it were, prognosticate even unto us the reverse of all our adverse fortune into a more happy and prosperous state'. But the key theme was always Elizabeth's attributes and achievements: 'If I should speak of the singular and manifold gifts of nature and grace ingrafted in your royal person from your tender years, of your profound learning and policy, seldom to be found in any man comparable, much less in any woman, it would be a great deal harder for me to find an end than a beginning.'[14] These words were addressed to the Queen, but the real audience was the citizens of Coventry in 1565: Elizabeth knew she was a marvel – it was her people who had to be persuaded.

The Queen had a strong, almost mystical, sense of personal identity with her people. She bragged to foreign ambassadors about how much her subjects loved her, and, in a private prayer of about 1579, she gave thanks that 'The love of my people hath appeared firm, and the devices of mine enemies frustrate.' But Elizabeth I was a realistic politician, who took few chances. She knew this support could not be taken for granted, and that she had to work to keep it. In 1599 she asked John Harington's wife how she kept her husband's affection: the wife replied that it was by her own love and obedience, which persuaded him of her affection which he then reciprocated. Elizabeth confided that 'after such sort do I keep the goodwill of all my husbands, my good people, for if they did not rest assured of some special love toward them, they would not readily yield me such good obedience'.[15] Elizabeth had deliberately chosen the role of a loving queen, and she played it throughout her reign – but it was only a role.

Queen Elizabeth projected an image of herself as a loving virgin mother, devoted to the interests of her children, whose love was warmly reciprocated. It was an image which, after some early difficulties, seems to have been widely accepted: the English came to believe what they had been told. It was the virgin part of the image which proved most difficult to put over: partly because of general assumptions about the natural relationship of the sexes, and partly because of the Queen's own conduct, it was for some years generally assumed that she was Dudley's mistress. In 1560 and 1561 there were widespread rumours, from Essex across to Devon, that the Queen was pregnant by Robert Dudley, and when Dudley's wife was found dead there were persistent stories around London and the Midlands that he had poisoned her with Elizabeth's connivance. The Spanish ambassador reported the popular outrage at what was thought to be the Queen's disgraceful misconduct: 'The cry is that they do not want any more women rulers, and this woman may find herself and her favourite in prison any morning.'[16] The attempt to do a deal with Philip II in 1561 also leaked out, and seemed to show that Elizabeth and Dudley would sacrifice the Gospel to their own fleshly lusts. In the London area at least, Dudley took most of the blame, but the rumours did the Queen's own reputation no good and suggested that she was no more than the pawn of her paramour.

After 1561 the stories of sexual misconduct died down, but the allegations surfaced again from time to time. In 1563 a Suffolk man was in trouble for saying that Elizabeth was 'a naughty woman' kept by Dudley, and when she went to Ipswich she was said to look 'like one lately come out of childbed'.[17] There was a flood of similar tales in 1570–72: it was claimed in East Anglia and Kent that Leicester and Hatton were the Queen's lovers, that Elizabeth had had two children by Leicester, and that the nymphomaniac Queen sometimes forced herself upon unwilling courtiers, and chopped off the heads of those who, like Norfolk, would not co-operate. But such slanders were rare thereafter, and were isolated allegations rather than general rumours. A labourer at Maldon in Essex claimed in 1580 that Elizabeth had had two children, though in 1581 another man thought the number was five and suggested that the Queen only went on summer progresses to have her babies away from London. But these were only isolated tales, very different from the widespread rumours of 1559–61 and 1570–72.

After 1572 the scandals were less frequent and the image of the Virgin Queen seems to have had some impact. In 1568 a book on marriage had been dedicated to Elizabeth, but in 1581 Thomas Bentley dedicated his praise of virginity to her – he referred to her 'perpetual virginity', her role as 'natural mother and noble nurse' of the Church, and her position as 'spiritual spouse' of Christ.[18] The official image of Elizabeth as virgin mother of her people also seems to have been effective – even if it was taken too literally by some. In 1587 a madman named Miles Fry, who called himself 'Emmanuel Plantagenet', claimed to be the son of God and the Queen, taken from his royal mother at birth by the Angel Gabriel and given into the care of Mrs Fry of Axminster, Devon. By the 1590s, indeed, the virgin mother theme had been taken to its obvious conclusion, and a number of writers were explicitly associating Elizabeth with the Virgin Mary. But even then, not everyone wished to have Elizabeth as a virgin mother: for some, she was the sex-symbol of the age. The astrologer Simon Forman recorded a dream in July 1597 that he and Elizabeth went on a country walk together: they sat under a tree and flirted, and he offered to 'make this belly a little bigger' – but unfortunately he woke up at that point![19]

The images of Elizabeth which were projected to the popular

level appear to have generated a real devotion to her – though it is not easy to distinguish the spontaneous from the stage-managed. Communal enthusiasm was affirmed through the commemoration of 17 November, the Queen's Accession Day: as well as the official Court rituals, there were eventually town and parish festivities across the country. The Accession Day was marked by bell-ringing at Lambeth parish church from 1567, presumably encouraged by Archbishop Parker. Then the celebration seems to have spread spontaneously on 17 November 1570 as an expression of loyalty after the papal bull of excommunication and of relief that Catholic predictions that Elizabeth would not last for twelve years had been disproved. There was bell-ringing in several churches, especially in western England, and an academic commemoration at Oxford, organised by Vice-Chancellor Cooper – his efforts presumably did his career no harm at all, and he was nominated to the see of Lincoln two months later.

Oxford city council was not to be outdone by the University, and it marked 17 November 1571 with a sermon; in 1572 there was a sermon and a communion service; and in 1573 a sermon, communion, and fireworks. Cambridge, too, joined in, with bell-ringing at Great St Mary's from 1571, and thereafter more and more parishes participated in the festival – south coast and west country parishes led the way, with the South-east lagging behind. Within five or six years, however, the celebrations were geographically widespread and not restricted to bell-ringing: the mayor of Liverpool ordered bonfires on 17 November 1576, and many parishes organised dancing and ales to mark the occasion. After the defeat of the Armada in 1588, there were few districts which did not have some festivity on 'the queen's day', and many towns organised feasts, sermons, and civic rituals.

By then the state had moved in. In 1576, 17 November was added to the calendar of official festivals in the Church of England, and special service books were issued. A popular festivity was now turned into a propaganda occasion. The 1576 prayers gave thanks to God, but at the same time reminded congregations of the achievements of the reign:

O Lord God, most merciful Father, who as upon this day, placing thy servant our sovereign and gracious queen Elizabeth in the kingdom, didst deliver thy people of

England from the danger of war and oppression, both of bodies by tyranny and of conscience by superstition, restoring peace and true religion, with liberty both of bodies and minds, and hast continued the same thy blessings, without all desert on our part, now by the space of these eighteen years . . .

In 1585, Edmund Bunny published *Certain prayers and other godly exercises for the 17th of November*, and there were annual crops of Accession-Day ballads and printed sermons which claimed that Elizabeth had delivered the people from darkness. Perhaps the attempt to turn a popular festival into a national day of prayer was unsuccessful: it is notable that neither the official prayers of 1576 nor Bunny's private enterprise sold well, and 17 November became an excuse for a booze-up. But the Accession Day, and in some parishes the coronation anniversary too, became occasions of real celebration. In January 1595 the churchwardens of Wigston Magna in Leicestershire recorded, 'Paid 2d. for a candle on the coronation day of our gracious queen. God long continue her in health and peace to reign over us. So be it, Amen!'[20]

There is plenty of evidence of individual and communal devotion to the Queen. The exposure of real or alleged plots usually led to outbursts of emotional loyalty. In 1583, after the discovery of the Throckmorton Plot, Londoners knelt in the streets as the Queen passed, to give thanks for her safety. In 1586, when the Babington Plot was foiled, church bells were rung, there were bonfires in the streets, and there was dancing and music in celebration. Such occasions were seized upon by the state, with official prayers of thankfulness for the Queen's delivery from danger – but the safety of the Queen was by then identified with the security of the nation, and the relief was real. The ballad-writers also celebrated the Queen's deliverance and the punishment of her enemies. The execution of the Babington plotters was marked by 'A proper new ballad briefly declaring the death and execution of fourteen most wicked traitors, who suffered death in Lincoln's Inn Field near London, the 20 and 21 September 1586':

Rejoice in heart, good people all,
Sing praise to God on high,
Which hath preserved us by his power
From traitors' tyranny.

Six months later, the new releases included 'An excellent ditty made as a general rejoicing for the cutting off of the Scottish queen'.[21] This grisly offering probably sold well in London, where the news of Mary's execution was well received: the citizens had lit a bonfire outside the French ambassador's door, mocking his inability to prevent the beheading.

The emotional loyalty which individuals felt towards the Queen could be very intense. In 1585 a Sussex lawyer wrote on the flyleaf of the family Bible:

I heartily pray the Almighty God to send a long, prosperous and happy life and reign to our good Queen Elizabeth and send us all grace that we may all live in his fear as good and dutiful subjects to our said gracious sovereign lady and queen, and all die before the sorrowful days of England shall come if God take her from us before the end of the world. And for that if for our sins he shorten her days, as he did the days of good King Edward, and yet he will grant me the grace to die at her feet before her, and that at the end of all things which is at hand we may joyfully rise again to life everlasting with perpetual joy and felicity. Amen! Amen!

In 1589 a bored Westminster schoolboy doodled over his text of Julius Caesar: the name 'Elizabeth' is everywhere, and in a margin the couplet

The rose is red, the leaves are green,
God save Elizabeth, our noble queen.[22]

The mingling of patriotic and religious sentiments had become common, and, as in the case of the Sussex lawyer, devotion to God, devotion to England, and devotion to the Queen necessarily went together. This was a product of the highly influential image of the Queen as a Protestant heroine, the saviour of English religion, and defender of the Gospel. This was not an image created officially for the Queen, but one thrust upon her by her Protestant subjects. From the beginning of the reign the Protestants had presented Elizabeth as their queen, in the hope that she would grow into the role. At her accession, ballads and pageants portrayed her as 'Deborah, judge and restorer of the house of Israel',[23] and in 1563 John Foxe's *Acts and Monuments* told how she had been protected by God through the bloody reign of her sister so that she could restore true religion. Especially in the dangerous 1580s, Elizabeth was seen as the Protestant bulwark against Catholic plotting in England and Catholic armies in Europe: more than twenty Protestant books were dedicated to the Queen in that decade, many of them volumes of anti-Catholic polemic.

But the problem with the 'Protestant heroine' image was that Elizabeth did not always live up to it. London Protestants were horrified in 1561 when they heard of the plan to get Spanish support for a Dudley marriage by offering concessions on religion, and it took Elizabeth almost a decade to re-establish her Protestant credentials. Fortunately for her, the northern revolt of 1569 and the papal bull of excommunication made her again the darling of the Protestants. There was another public relations crisis in 1579, when the mask of the Protestant heroine slipped once more: there was a public outcry when it seemed that Elizabeth would marry Alençon, and the future of the Protestant religion again seemed in doubt. It is probably true that the popular agitation was master-minded by Leicester and his political allies, but there was plenty of support for it. John Stubbs's *The discovery of a gaping gulf* was so dangerous precisely because it showed that Elizabeth was not conforming to her Protestant image, and implied that she would lose the devotion of her Protestant subjects unless she did so. It was only partly an excuse when Elizabeth blamed her people for her refusal to marry Alençon: when it came to the crunch she had to play the Protestant role, even though she had not chosen it. She dared not shatter the image created for her.

Elizabeth had trouble when she did not live up to her unofficial image as the Protestant heroine – and she also had trouble when she was unable to live up to her official image as loving mother of her children. This was certainly true in the 1590s, when war, heavy taxation, harvest failure, and trade disruption combined to create economic crisis. The claim that Elizabeth ruled in the interests of all her subjects, and was the protectress of the poor, began to ring hollow, and her government was abused. In 1591 an Essex labourer was saying that the people should pray for a king, for 'the queen is but a woman, and ruled by noblemen, and the noblemen and gentlemen are all one, and the gentlemen and farmers will hold together so that the poor can get nothing' – 'we shall never have a merry world while the queen liveth'. In the following year, another Essex labourer was saying that 'this is no good government which we now live under, and it was merry England when there was better government, and if the queen die there will be a change'.[24]

It was argued in both Essex and Kent that Philip II would be a more solicitous ruler than Elizabeth, and that a Spanish invasion might be no bad thing. Even among non-Catholics, the reign of Mary was coming to seem like a golden age. In Middlesex, too, there was criticism of Elizabeth: in 1591 a yeoman 'desired and wished her dead', and in 1592 two sailors were complaining loudly against her rule. In 1602, when a constable warned a yeoman to obey the Queen's laws, he was told, 'Why dost thou tell me of the queen? A turd for the queen!'[25] In Staffordshire, county officers had difficulty in collecting wartime taxes, and there was contempt for the Queen and her laws. It is significant that scandalous stories about the Queen's sexual relationships surfaced again. In 1591 an Essex couple were saying that Elizabeth had had several children, but that Leicester had stuffed each of them up the palace chimney and burned them alive. In Dorset in 1598, Edward Francis claimed that Elizabeth had three children by noblemen, and England would have been better if she had been murdered twenty years before so the country could have been ruled by a king.

In her last years, Elizabeth was losing the devotion of her subjects. There was, at best, an amused tolerance of the old woman's doings, with few signs of real affection. There was criticism of the celebration of her Accession Day, as it became increasingly difficult to see 17 November 1558 as the inauguration of a new age of peace and plenty. As early as 1583 Archbishop Whitgift had to justify the festival in a sermon, and in 1601 Thomas Holland published a defence of the celebrations against charges of idolatry. Elizabeth's earliest biographers, Camden and Clapham, both testify to the mounting chorus of criticism of her rule from both nobles and people, and the French ambassador thought 'the English would never again submit to the rule of a woman'.[26] Attendance at Court declined, and Elizabeth was much angered by her aristocracy's neglect. The Queen no longer held the undivided loyalty of her subjects, who had found new – and male – heroes. There were bell-ringings and prayers for the exploits of the Earl of Essex, and in 1600 the Council had to prohibit the engraving of pictures of Essex and other nobles.

Above all, men looked to Scotland. 'There was much posting that way', reported John Chamberlain, 'and many run thither of their own errand, as if it were nothing else but first come first served, or that preferment were a goal to be got by footmanship.' Sir John Harington, Elizabeth's godson, complained that 'I find some less mindful of what they are soon to lose, than of what they may perchance hereafter get', but he too joined the clamour. For New Year 1603, he sent James VI a lantern, adorned with a crucifixion scene and inscribed with the words of the good thief on the cross – 'Lord, remember me when thou comest into thy Kingdom'.[27] Despite the impatience for the old Queen's death, there was a stunned silence in London when it was announced on 25 March 1603: she had been queen for forty-four years, and there was fear of the unknown future. But, by the afternoon, people were getting used to the idea of a world without Elizabeth, and they rather liked it. In the evening there were bonfires and street parties to celebrate the accession of James: 'We have a king!' the people cried.[28]

. . .

NOTES AND REFERENCES

1. Neale J E 1979 *Queen Elizabeth I*. Panther edn, p. 320
2. De Maisse A H 1931 *A Journal of All That was Accomplished by Monsieur de Maisse*. Nonsuch p. 110; Camden W 1675 *A History of the Most Renowned and Victorious Princess Elizabeth*, p. 555
3. Goodman G 1839 *The Court of King James the First* (2 vols). Bentley, vol. 1 p. 163
4. Firth C H 1909 The ballad history of the reigns of the later Tudors, *Transactions of the Royal Historical Society*. 3rd series, 3: 71, 95, 117–18
5. Wilson E C 1939 *England's Eliza*. Harvard, pp. 13, 36; Firth C H 1909: 96
6. Wilson E C 1939 p. 47
7. Nichols J 1823 *The Progresses and Public Processions of Queen Elizabeth* (3 vols), Nichols, vol. 1 pp. 59, 49
8. *Calendar of State Papers Spanish, 1568–69*, pp. 50–1
9. Nichols J 1823 vol. 2 p. 166
10. Hartley T E (ed.) 1981 *Proceedings in the Parliaments of Elizabeth I, 1558–1581*. Leicester, pp. 36, 95; Neale J E 1957 *Elizabeth I and her Parliaments, 1584–1601*. Cape, p. 213

11. Goodman G 1839 vol. 1 p. 163;   Neale J E 1957 p. 426
12. Hartley T E (ed.) 1981 p. 472;   Neale J E 1957 p. 117
13. Neale J E 1979 p. 302;   Smith L B 1975 *Elizabeth Tudor: portrait of a queen*. Hutchinson, p. 67, translating Nichols J 1823 vol. 3 p. 147
14. Nichols J 1823 vol. 1 pp. 196, 314, 547, 193-4
15. Haugaard W P 1981 Elizabeth Tudor's *Book of Devotions, Sixteenth Century Journal* 12: 99;   Harington J 1804 *Nugae Antiquae* (2 vols), Park T (ed.). Vernon & Hood, vol. 1 p. 178
16. *Calendar of State Papers Spanish, 1558-67*, p. 176
17. Wilson D 1981 *Sweet Robin: a biography of Robert Dudley, earl of Leicester*. Hamilton, p. 115
18. Bentley T 1581 *The Monument of Matrones*, The Epistle
19. Ellis H 1846 *Original Letters*, 3rd series (4 vols). Bentley, vol. 4 pp. 61-3;   Johnson P 1974 *Elizabeth I: a study in power and intellect*. Weidenfeld and Nicolson, p. 117
20. Clay W K (ed.) 1847 *Liturgical Services*. Parker Society, pp. 556-7;   Nichols J 1823 vol. 3 p. 369
21. Firth C H 1909: 93, 101
22. Hasler P W (ed.) 1981 *The House of Commons, 1558-1603* (3 vols). History of Parliament Trust, vol. 1 p. 474;   Morris C 1976 *The Tudors*. Severn House, p. 185
23. Nichols J 1823 vol. 1 p. 53
24. Emmison F G 1970 *Elizabethan Life: disorder*. Essex County Council, pp. 57, 58
25. Jeaffreson J C (ed.) 1886 *Middlesex County Records* (4 vols). Middlesex County Record Society, vol. 1 pp. 195, 204, 283
26. De Maisse A H 1931 p. 12
27. McClure N E (ed.) 1939 *The Letters of John Chamberlain* (2 vols). American Philosophical Society, vol. 1 p. 189;   Harington J 1804 vol. 1 pp. 321, 326
28. Read E P, Read C (eds) 1951 *Elizabeth of England: certain observations concerning the life and reign of Queen Elizabeth by John Clapham*. Pennsylvania p. 104

CONCLUSION

Elizabeth died unloved and almost unlamented, and it was partly her own fault. She had aimed for popularity and political security by projecting herself as the ever-young and ever-beautiful virgin mother of her people, bringing them peace and prosperity; she ended her days as an irascible old woman, presiding over war and failure abroad and poverty and factionalism at home. From 1558 to 1588, Elizabeth had successfully courted her politicians and entranced her people. She had made herself the focus of fervent devotion and earnest loyalty, the well-publicised source and guarantee of international safety and national stability. But her reign had been thirty years of illusion, followed by fifteen of disillusion. Peace with England's neighbours gave way to war in the Low Countries, in France, in Ireland, on the coast of Spain, and at sea – with no signs of successful conclusion. Domestic peace, and the occasionally uneasy co-operation of major politicians in the period from the death of Norfolk to the death of Leicester, gave way to bitter factional competition at Court and related conflicts in many counties. The economic prosperity which had, by its regular good harvests, showed God's favour to Eliza's England, gave way to the same appalling conditions of high food prices, high mortality, trade depression, and social instability which had discredited Mary Tudor in her last years.

As the gap between image and reality widened, so resentment spread, for the English had never loved the *real* Elizabeth – they had loved the image she created and the promises she had made. When the economic and military circumstances of the post-Armada years proved so difficult, the old image was tarnished and the old promises were shown to be hollow. But there was no new model of the Queen, no new vision of her contribution to

164

the nation's welfare. In the new and bitter world of the 1590s, Elizabeth was shown to be politically bankrupt. The only answer she and those close to her could provide seemed to be 'more of the same'. For her political style, this meant more resort to ill-temper as a tool of management, more reluctance to spend money on necessary policies, more reliance on and reward of a few trusted advisers. For her political image, this meant more extravagant praise of non-existent qualities, more far-fetched portrayals of idealised beauty, more frequent repetitions of the old slogans. The world in which Elizabeth had painstakingly built her model of female monarchy changed – but Elizabeth lived up to her motto, *semper eadem*, always the same. She was a ruler overtaken by events – 'a lady whom time had surprised', as Raleigh remarked.[1]

In only two respects did her style of government change in her last years. First, she allowed herself to become the prisoner of a faction. For most of her reign, she had tried to maintain a balance of counsel and to keep policy options open – she had even pursued conflicting tactics simultaneously. But in the 1590s, she threw in her lot with the Cecilians or was taken over by them: she promoted their allies and, in general, she espoused their policies. Essex and his followers had real grievances – and, after they had broken with the Cecil camp, so did Raleigh and Cobham. By 1597, Elizabeth had a Privy Council of only eleven members, and five of them were the sons (and another the stepson) of previous councillors. By her very conservatism, by her loyalty to the families of old servants and her reluctance to make new appointments, the Queen had narrowed the basis of her political support. She therefore drove the Essex group to revolt in 1601, as she had driven the northern earls in 1569, by exclusion. The failure of the Essex coup left her even more firmly under the control of Robert Cecil: he managed her Court entertainments as he managed her policy – and he even tried to tell her when to go to bed.

Second, Elizabeth became a much less public queen, described by Harington in 1602 as 'a lady shut up in a chamber from her subjects and most of her servants, and seldom seen but on holy days'.[2] It is true that she went off again on summer progress in 1599–1602, but she travelled short distances, kept away from towns, and made no real attempt to mix with her people. In her last progresses, she was showing herself she could still do it, rather than showing her subjects she was still queen.

Old Accession Day ballads were republished, and paintings and engravings reproduced old images (of a young queen), but Elizabeth herself now contributed little to her own public relations. She made her 'golden speech' to representatives of the Commons in 1601 – but it was an enforced attempt to re-establish herself as a caring ruler after the débâcle over monopolies, and its themes, like the Queen, were exhausted. In propaganda terms, Elizabeth had nothing new to offer – she was certainly not going to appear as grandmother of the nation. The tremendous popularity of Essex, and the appeal of Cumberland and Mountjoy, reflects not just a search for a new hero but the low profile of the old heroine.

At Court and in the counties, the political misogynism of the early years of the reign re-emerged. The ills of the times were ascribed to the rule of a woman. Henry Wotton claimed that 'A queen's declining is commonly even of itself the more umbratious and apprehensive', and Essex complained of the government's 'delay and inconstancy, which proceeded chiefly from the sex of the queen'.[3] This explanation by royal gender was attractive, for it held out the expectation that all would be well when the old lady died. Not least of the attractions of James of Scotland was that he was a man – though, in the event, not as much of a man as had been hoped. At Court, there was much personal mockery of the Queen: Elizabeth's ladies sniggered wickedly at her, foreign ambassadors reported on her weird ways, and John Harington, her godson, wrote pen-portraits of her as a silly old woman. She was a woman; she was certainly old, but if she seemed silly it was only because of the contrast between idea and reality. Elizabeth had failed to develop a new role: the aged actress looked foolish as she continued to play the part which had once made her famous.

In the last years, Elizabeth had irritated and embarrassed her leading subjects: they were 'very generally weary of an old woman's government', and they wanted a king. John Harington had laughed at his godmother, and waited expectantly for James – but the debauched celebrations of the visit of Christian IV of Denmark in 1606 persuaded him that the old girl had not been so bad after all. The 17 November observances were moved to 24 March, the Accession Day of James. But, wrote Bishop Goodman, after a few years, when we had experience of the Scottish government, then – in disparagement of the Scots and in hate and detestation of them – the queen did seem to revive. Then was her memory much magnified – such ringing of bells, such public joy and sermons in commemoration of her, the picture of her tomb painted in many churches; and, in effect, more solemnity and joy in memory of her coronation than was for the coming in of King James.[4]

It was, in fact, much more than hostility to the Scots. Elizabeth Tudor rapidly became a stick to beat the Stuarts, first James and then Charles.

Fulke Greville, former friend of Philip Sidney and follower of Essex, soon produced an analysis of Elizabeth's success which was a coded commentary on the defects of James's early rule.[5] By about 1610, Greville was praising as qualities of the Queen what had in her lifetime seemed defects – her frugality, her reluctance to create peers. She was dressed up in clothes she would hardly have recognised, to pose as a model for her successor: an idealist willing to put religion first, and an exponent of an activist, Protestant foreign policy. In direct comparison with James, she was praised for what she did not do – she did not search out precedents to extend her prerogative; she did not provoke Parliament to defend its liberties; she did not devise oppressive financial expedients; she did not allow favourites independence; and she did not intimidate councillors by firm statement of her own views. Some of this picture was accurate, some was gross distortion – but most of all it was a mirror reflection of James rather than a portrait of Elizabeth. A new image of Elizabeth was being created, as a weapon of early Stuart politics.

Fulke Greville's outline sketch of the Queen was given detail and substance by William Camden, whose history of her reign was written between 1608 and 1617. The themes were much the same: Elizabeth was a model of constitutional propriety, financial probity, and Protestant energy. The first three parts of Camden's *Annales* were published in Latin in 1615 and in English in 1625: they showed Elizabeth determinedly seeking religious purity, national security, and economic prosperity – she spent her money on defence and allies rather than on favourites. Book Four of the work, published in Latin in 1625 and English in 1629, dealt with the period between 1588 and 1603: by its stress on Elizabeth's military and naval successes against Spain, it posed a contrast with the supine and ineffective foreign policies of the Stuarts. To make the comparison clear to all, the 1625 English edition appeared with an illustrated title-page showing Elizabeth's naval glories – Drake's attack on Cadiz in 1587, the Armada victory of 1588, Cumberland's burning of San Juan de Puerto Rico in 1591, and the expedition to Cadiz in 1596. Elizabeth, most reluctant of combatants, was now the Protestant heroine, who had used English sea power to humble Catholic Spain – which is what the Stuarts were being urged to do.

Camden, like Greville, portrayed Elizabeth as a skilful tactician in domestic politics, struggling to contain factional competition at Court. By the 1630s, another former Essex henchman, Robert Naunton, saw her manipulation of factions as the key to her political success. He denied that Elizabeth had given Leicester a free hand, and claimed that by creating and balancing factions she had kept channels of communication open and run a broad-based regime. Again, a version of Elizabeth's rule was constructed as the antithesis of the Stuarts': Elizabeth had not allowed a Buckingham-like figure to monopolise patronage and policy, and she had not become isolated from alternative opinions. Naunton's queen, too, had dealt considerately with her subjects, taxed them lightly, and devoted herself to the establishment and defence of the Protestant religion. To Naunton, and to Sir John Eliot, Elizabeth had been all that Charles I was not – a popular monarch, a friend to Parliaments and the champion of international Protestantism.

In 1603, Elizabeth had seemed a foolish old woman, as men looked expectantly to a Stuart king. By 1630, when Stuart kings had proved rather a disappointment, she had become the paragon of all princely virtues – principled, as James had not been, and wise, as Charles had not been. But the perspective of 1630 was just as warping as the perspective of 1603: Elizabeth was no more of a Protestant heroine than she had been a crabby old dame. Elizabeth was a Protestant, but she had wished to do as little as possible about it. She had moderated her intentions in 1559 when confronted by aristocratic opposition in the House of Lords and popular opposition in the parishes. She had resisted all later attempts to remove the popish deficiencies of the English Church, and many of the efforts to impose penalties on Catholics. Above all, she refused to see foreign policy in terms of Protestant ideology – and her refusal led to long-running conflicts with her closest advisers. If Elizabeth allied with Protestant rebels – Scottish Calvinists in 1560, French Huguenots in 1562, 1589, and 1591, Dutch Calvinists from 1585 – it was not in pursuit of any ideological struggle with the forces of Antichrist. She did so only because it was sensible to sustain her enemies' enemies.

The Protestant enthusiasts of the early seventeenth century produced a picture of Elizabeth I which has proved attractive and influential. Like the approved pattern-portraits in her reign, the Protestant picture has been replicated many times in different clothes and against different backgrounds. The imperialistic historians of the late nineteenth century and the romantic English nationalists of the mid-twentieth both saw her as a sympathetic manager of the urgent aspirations of an energetic Protestant England – a midwife for the future. But Elizabeth had little enthusiasm for the growth of popular Protestantism, of parliamentary oversight, of continental alliances, and of maritime challenges to Spain. She did not lead advances from the front, she restrained them from behind: her reign was a constant struggle to avoid policies and contain forces which she disliked. Elizabeth was not a wise and powerful statesperson, implementing the constructive policies she knew her nation needed: she was a nervous politician struggling for survival.

Although it suited her purpose for them to be exaggerated, Elizabeth really did face difficult problems when she became queen – and some of them soon got worse. England was fighting a war on two fronts, a war made unpopular by military failure and economic distress. The Treaty of Cateau-Cambresis in 1559 and the intervention in Scotland in 1560 reduced the risk of invasion by French forces – but thereafter the civil wars in France weakened a counterbalance to the power of Spain. After the revolt of his Dutch subjects had prompted Philip II to send a Spanish army to the Low Countries in 1567, England ran the risk of invasion across the Channel if the Dutch should be defeated. Elizabeth then found herself under persistent pressure from her closest advisers to construct a league of Protestant states and Protestant rebels, and carry war to the Catholics in Europe. But the Queen was reluctant to legitimise religious revolt by supporting rebels against other princes, and feared that Protestant alliances would stimulate the Spanish hostility she sought to restrain. She thereafter offered only such minimum aid to foreign Protestants as would preserve them from defeat, while seeking agreements with foreign monarchs – a policy which appeared indecisive at home and duplicitous abroad.

In the sphere of religion, Elizabeth's political problems were equally severe. She was a Protestant herself, her trusted supporters were Protestants, and at the beginning of her reign there were sound political reasons for a Protestant religious settlement. Many Catholics regarded Elizabeth as the illegitimate offspring of a tyrant and a heretic, and Mary Queen of Scots had a respectable Catholic claim to the English throne (with some backing from Rome). If Elizabeth became a Protestant queen, she would undercut a rival interest, bind English Protestants to her throne, and dissociate herself from the tarnished causes of her sister's reign. But it proved impossible to achieve an authentic Protestant settlement in 1559, and parliamentary and parish opinions showed hostility to change. While her advisers and her Protestant bishops pressed for further measures of Protestantisation, Elizabeth herself saw the danger of alienating Catholic opinion. She therefore sought to maintain those features of the Church of England which Protestants found most offensive, to retain conservatives within the national Church.

In foreign policy, Elizabeth refused to choose between support for rebel Protestants and concessions to Catholic Spain: she tried to follow both strategies. In religion, she refused to choose between unequivocal Protestantism and hard-line Catholicism: she tried to construct a Church which offered inducements to conformity for all but the recalcitrants on both sides. There were solid political reasons for avoiding irrevocable commitments at the beginning of her reign – but it is also true that Elizabeth's own nervous indecision contributed to her initial fastidiousness, and maintained it thereafter. Indeed, it is far from clear that the Queen ever did pursue conscious policies of moderation in religion and foreign relations. Perhaps she vacillated between policy options, or followed all of them irresolutely, or muddled through by good luck, in ways which appear deliberately moderate only with the penetrating vision of hindsight. We know roughly what Elizabeth did, but she has not told us why she did it.

The political circumstances of Elizabeth's first decade as queen forced her into positions which entailed constant struggle. The new issues which developed – especially what to do about marriage, the succession, and Mary Queen of Scots – all raised the basic difficulties of foreign and religious alliances. Early in 1561, she seems to have considered a dramatic initiative to solve her dilemmas – she thought briefly of marrying Robert Dudley, seeking support from Spain, and making further concessions to English Catholics. She might thus have freed herself from restricting reliance upon Protestants, and attracted sufficient support from Catholics. But the hostility provoked at Court and in London by rumours of this plan must have convinced her that the 'Spanish strategy' would lead to civil war. There was really no practicable alternative to moderation (or muddling through) – and no practicable alternative to coexistence with her Protestant supporters. The Queen therefore faced a continuing barrage of advice and information from her Protestant councillors, designed to force her to adopt more determinedly Protestant policies.

The reign of Elizabeth therefore saw a constant testing of the political power and the political skills of a Tudor monarch. Her task could hardly have been more difficult. She had to resist the machinations of her councillors as they tried to draw her into their schemes. Her sources of intelligence were almost uniformly unreliable, and her own advisers and ambassadors, as well as foreign diplomats, fed her the information which suited them. The specific policies (or tactics) she pursued had little positive support, and the officers supposed to carry them out often did not believe in what they were doing. She could not trust her agents – whether they were administrators, ambassadors, local governors, or generals – to obey her orders without continued supervision. She had to buy co-operation from reluctant servants by offering attractive rewards – but the distribution of favour could lead to either monopoly by a patronage-broker or factionalism between competing groups. And she had to achieve all this despite an appalling political handicap; she was a woman in a man's world.

Elizabeth's gender raised three major difficulties in a patriarchal society, where there was no ideological foundation for female authority. First, it complicated the problem of the succession, for it was hard to find a father for her child without finding a master for herself. Sir Philip Sidney warned the

Queen not to marry Alençon, for when the Duke pressed her to change religion she would be torn between obedience to God and obedience to her husband. Second, it complicated her dealings with politicians: she had to make them willing to obey her, and convince them that she could know best. Third, it complicated her relationship to her subjects: she had to find an image of monarchy which was appropriate for a woman yet which invited obedience. Out of these difficulties came the image of the Virgin Queen, mother of her people. Virginity did not help much with the succession problem – but it did provide a positive justification for not solving it by marriage. The Virgin Queen was able to entrance her councillors and courtiers, and secure loving co-operation from some of her magnates. And the virgin mother could pose as the caring protectress of the interests of her children.

Elizabeth brought real dramatic talent to the role of Virgin Queen and mother, and freed herself from some of the restrictions of her sex. But the production in which she starred ran for forty-five years, she had no understudy, and she had to appear in every show: it was a constant strain. Her performances were not flawless: she disliked her part in the early years, when she hoped to marry Dudley; she was bored with it in 1579, when she thought of marrying Alençon; and she could not quite carry it off in her last decade. She fluffed her lines on important occasions – in her dealings with the Duke of Norfolk and the northern earls in 1569, and with Essex and his allies from 1596. She often alienated her Protestant fans by not wearing their costumes, in 1561, in 1565, in 1575, in 1579, and in 1584. She lost confidence in her interpretation of the part in 1585, and allowed her leading man to persuade her into a more aggressive version for foreign audiences. Her relationship with supporting actresses was always poor, she worked uneasily with young newcomers, and as an old trouper she was upstaged by the fiery talent of Essex. But hers was an award-winning performance, and what was missing in dramatic conception was more than made up for in sheer professional skill.

The metaphor of drama is an appropriate one for Elizabeth's reign, for her power was an illusion – and an illusion was her power. Like Henry IV of France, she projected an image of herself which brought stability and prestige to her country. By constant attention to the details of her total performance, she kept the rest of the cast on their toes and kept her own part as queen. Elizabeth made herself indispensable to her politicians, popular with her people, and reluctantly admired by her fellow princes. Though they might rage against the 'new Jezebel', the rulers of Europe had to recognise her skills. Pope Sixtus V was especially impressed. 'Just see how well she governs!' he declared in 1588; 'She is only a woman, only the mistress of half an island, and yet she makes herself feared by Spain, by France, by the Empire, by all!' Among her contemporaries, Catherine de Medici could not prevent civil wars in France, and Mary Stuart was hounded out of her kingdom after only seven years of personal rule. Francis Bacon drew the lesson: 'The government of a woman has been a rare thing at all times; felicity in such government a rarer thing still; felicity and long continuance together the rarest thing of all.'[6] For a female ruler, mere survival was a tremendous achievement.

But it was not only a queen who might find it wise to settle for survival. Philip of Spain, like Elizabeth, ruled for more than forty years, and for him, too, indecision was a tool of policy: when urged to deal rapidly with business, he replied wearily, 'I and time shall arrange matters as we can.'[7] Given the limited coercive power of early modern governments, unambitious goals were realistic ones and there was much to be said for masterly inactivity. Grand projects were, as Philip found with his three disastrous armadas against England, all too likely to come to grief. Elizabeth did not, after 1559, adopt any drastic policy initiatives: she resisted her ministers' attempts to force her into action, and the fates of English military expeditions showed that her caution was correct. Francis Bacon's praise of her was strikingly negative: she was to be commended for what she did not do, rather than what she did. The Queen was a tactician rather than a strategist – a born actress, and not a dramatist or a director.

Queen Elizabeth did not attempt to solve problems, she simply avoided them – and then survived long enough for some to go away. The rest returned to plague her successor, James I – but that was his problem, and she had never given much attention to what would happen after her death. Her refusal to tackle the succession issue, her sale of Crown lands to finance war, and her denial of place and reward to the Essex generation showed how limited was her concern for the future. This pragmatic approach to politics was possible because Elizabeth had a restricted conception of her role as queen. Though she spoke much of her duty to God and her care for her people, this was political rhetoric to justify her rule. After the ecclesiastical settlement of 1559, she felt no public obligation to do anything more – she did not reform administration, or purify the Church, or improve the lot of the poor, or colonise North America, because she saw no reason why she should. Elizabeth's objective as queen was to be queen; her exercise of royal power was not a means to a higher end, it was an end in itself. She would not have agreed with Philip II that 'the prince was created for the community', still less that monarchy was 'a form of slavery which carries with it a crown'.[8] Queen Elizabeth may have been God's servant, but she was certainly not her people's.

. . .

NOTES AND REFERENCES

1. Hurstfield J 1971 *Elizabeth I and the Unity of England.* Penguin edn, p. 196

2. Adams S L 1984 Eliza enthroned? The Court and its politics, in Haigh C A (ed.) *The Reign of Elizabeth I.* Macmillan, p. 77

3. Erickson C 1983 *The First Elizabethan.* Macmillan, p. 398;   De Maisse A H 1931 *A Journal of All That Was Accomplished by Monsieur de Maisse.* Nonsuch, p. 115

4. Goodman G 1839 *The Court of King James the First* (2 vols). Bentley, vol. 1 pp. 97–8

5. Greville F 1652 *The Life of the Renowned Sir Philip Sidney,* pp. 185–234

6. Pastor L von 1932 *The History of the Popes* Kerr R F (ed.). Kegan Paul, vol. 22 p. 34n;   Neale J E 1963 *The Age of Catherine de Medici and Essays in Elizabethan History.* Cape, p. 217

7. Pierson P 1975 *Philip II of Spain.* Thames & Hudson, p. 40

8. Pierson P 1975 p. 43

BIBLIOGRAPHICAL ESSAY

It is almost impossible to write a balanced study of Elizabeth I. The historiographical tradition is so laudatory that it is hard to avoid either floating with the current of applauding opinion or creating an unseemly splash by swimming too energetically against it. The marketing of Elizabeth began in her own reign, with the efforts of Protestants, official propagandists, and profit-seeking balladeers. Enthusiastic praise was turned into structured history by William Camden, who wrote his *Annales* in the 1610s. Camden formulated the historiographical agenda for the reign, and historians have usually followed his scheme: Elizabeth inherited chaos at home and threats from abroad, but by her own foresight and skill she imposed unifying solutions to national problems. The reign of Elizabeth was thus a golden age of progress, in which a careful queen inspired her people to greatness and checked any divisive militant tendencies. The 'Camden version' has dominated interpretations of Elizabeth over the past century: it was followed in most of the almost eighty biographies published since 1890. The best representatives of the modern romantic nationalist interpretation are: Neale J E 1934 *Queen Elizabeth*, Cape; Rowse A L 1950 *The England of Elizabeth*, Macmillan; Hurstfield J 1960 *Elizabeth I and the Unity of England*, Teach Yourself History Series; and Johnson P 1974 *Elizabeth I: a study in power and intellect*, Weidenfeld & Nicolson.

Critics of Elizabeth have been rare, and the grounds for their criticisms sometimes seem rather odd. Froude J A in his 1856–70 *History of England from the Fall of Cardinal Wolsey to the Defeat of the Spanish Armada* (12 vols), Macmillan, blamed Elizabeth for her lack of robust Protestantism and energetic nationalism. C H Wilson's 1970 *Queen Elizabeth and the*

Revolt of the Netherlands, Macmillan, bewailed her refusal to act as midwife for an independent greater Netherlands by offering determined support against Spain. Except for Catholics who damned her persecutions, Elizabeth has usually been condemned for what she did not do (or what she did not do with sufficient determination) rather than what she did, as if all options were open to her. But Carolly Erickson's 1983 *The First Elizabeth*, Macmillan, presents the Queen as unimaginative, indecisive, irritable, and thoroughly selfish. Although Erickson's account was heavily influenced by the gossip purveyed by foreign ambassadors and Bess of Hardwick, her perspective was in some respects more realistic. Her Elizabeth was at least a recognisable human being in a difficult situation, not a *dea ex machina* able to solve all problems if only she tried.

Elizabeth's political position now seems a good deal more complicated than it did when the romantic nationalist tradition was at its height. Studies of the reign of her father – especially Starkey D R 1985 *The Reign of Henry VIII: personalities and politics*, George Philip, and Ives E W 1986 *Anne Boleyn*, Blackwell – have shown how even a strong-willed and intimidating king could be manœuvred by Court factions. Loades D M in 1979 *The Reign of Mary Tudor*, Benn, has suggested that the rule of Elizabeth's sister began well, but foundered on the rocks of foreign war, religious division, inflation, and administrative weakness – problems Elizabeth was to encounter herself. The machinery of Tudor government now looks ramshackle and in some respects ineffective. Smith A G R in 1967 *The Government of Elizabethan England*, Arnold, Williams P H in 1979 *The Tudor Regime*, Oxford, and Elton G R in three essays on Tudor government: the points of contact (reprinted in his 1983 *Studies in Tudor and Stuart Politics and Government*, Cambridge, vol. 3), have shown how far rule was dependent upon the co-operation of local magnates, bought by patronage or enticed by propaganda. Monarchical power was not exercised by issuing peremptory orders to instantly obedient officials: rather, there was a constant struggle to keep the show of government on the road.

Studies of Elizabeth's rule have generally tackled her policies, and marked them good or bad, successful or failed. This judging procedure assumes that the Queen could do much as she liked: she could formulate answers to recognised national problems, and impose them through the machinery of government. But the information and the institutions which were available to the Queen do not justify such an approach. This book, instead, examines Elizabeth in terms of her power rather than in terms of her policies: it considers her relations with other politicians and with the institutions and groups of political life – it asks how she survived rather than how she solved. For it was not easy to be monarch of England – and it was especially difficult to be a queen regnant. First, Elizabeth had to establish herself as a worthy and independent ruler, despite her tainted origins and her gender. The perspective of Heisch A 1980 Queen Elizabeth and the persistence of patriarchy, *Feminist Review* 4, leads her to ask important questions, and there is useful material on marriage and the succession in Levine M 1966 *The Early Elizabethan Succession Question, 1558-1568*, Stanford; MacCaffrey W T 1969 *The Shaping of the Elizabethan Regime*, Cape; and 1981 *Queen Elizabeth and the Making of Policy*, Princeton. The contribution of Elizabeth's image to her dealings with politicians is discussed in works listed below in the paragraph on the Court.

Elizabeth's relationship with the Church is best approached through Haugaard W P 1968 *Elizabeth and the English Reformation*, Cambridge, though his discussion of the making of the 1559 legislation should be reinterpreted in the light of Jones N L 1982 *Faith by Statute: Parliament and the settlement of religion, 1559*, Royal Historical Society. The conflicting pressures to which the Queen was subject are shown by Collinson P 1967 *The Elizabethan Puritan Movement*, Cape (who stresses the evangelical demands for more Protestantism) and Haigh C A 1981 The continuity of Catholicism in the English Reformation, *Past and Present* 93 (who shows the extent of conservative resistance to change). Surveys of religion in the period are offered by McGrath P 1967 *Papists and Puritans under Elizabeth I*, Batsford, and by Collinson and Haigh in Haigh C A (ed.) 1984 *The Reign of Elizabeth I*, Macmillan. Elizabeth's own piety is considered by Haugaard W P 1981 Elizabeth Tudor's *Book of Devotions*: a neglected clue to the queen's life and character, *Sixteenth Century Journal* 12; how little it influenced her political calculations is illustrated by Cross C 1970 *The Royal Supremacy in the Elizabethan Church*, Allen & Unwin, and Heal F M 1980 *Of Prelates and Princes: a study of the economic and social position of the Tudor episcopate*, Cambridge.

Lawrence Stone's monumental 1965 *The Crisis of the Aristocracy, 1558–1641*, Oxford, is the starting-point for all discussions of the relationship between the Crown and the nobility. It may be that Stone mistakes changes in the bases of aristocratic wealth and power for decline, and the Tudors' necessary destruction of particular traitors for a general anti-noble policy. The continuing political significance of peers is well illustrated in Williams P H 1979 *The Tudor Regime*, Oxford, and Hasler P W 1981 *The House of Commons, 1558–1603*, History of Parliament Trust (3 vols) vol. 1. There is no thorough published treatment of the conspiracies and revolts of 1568–71: MacCaffrey W T 1969 *The Shaping of the Elizabethan Regime*, Cape, Read C 1955 *Mr Secretary Cecil and Queen Elizabeth*, Cape, and Williams N 1964 *Thomas Howard, Fourth Duke of Norfolk*, Barrie & Rockliff, give brief surveys, and my interpretation of the revolt has been much influenced by Taylor S E 1981 The revolt of the northern earls, University of Manchester Ph.D. thesis. There are hints on official attitudes towards nobles in MacCaffrey W T 1961 Place and patronage in Elizabethan politics, in Bindoff S T, Hurstfield J, Williams C H (eds) *Elizabethan Government and Society*, Athlone, and Hurstfield J 1958 *The Queen's Wards: wardship and marriage under Elizabeth I*, Cape.

The only sensitive discussion of the Privy Council and its role is Elton G R 1983 Tudor government: the points of contact. II the Council, in *Studies in Tudor and Stuart Politics and Government*, Cambridge, vol. 3. There is useful material in Pulman M B 1971 *The Elizabethan Privy Council in the Fifteen-Seventies*, California. There has been dispute between historians on the extent of disagreement and rivalry among councillors: Read C 1913 Walsingham and Burghley in Queen Elizabeth's Privy Council, *English Historical Review* 28, may have exaggerated the conflict, but MacCaffrey W T 1981 *Queen Elizabeth and the Making of Policy*, Princeton, and Adams S L 1984 Eliza enthroned? The Court and its politics, in Haigh C A (ed.) *The Reign of Elizabeth I*, Macmillan, seem to exaggerate harmony. The debates over foreign policy between councillors and Queen are discussed in: Thorp M R 1984 Catholic conspiracy in early Elizabethan foreign policy, *Sixteenth Century Journal* 15; Wilson C H 1970 *Queen Elizabeth and the Revolt of the Netherlands*, Macmillan; Adams S L 1973 The Protestant cause: religious alliance with the West European

Calvinist communities as a political issue in England, 1585–1630, University of Oxford D.Phil. thesis; Read C 1925 *Mr Secretary Walsingham and the policy of Queen Elizabeth* (3 vols), Oxford; Read C 1955 *Mr Secretary Cecil and Queen Elizabeth*, Cape; Read C 1960 *Lord Burghley and Queen Elizabeth*, Cape; Wernham R B 1980 *The Making of Elizabethan Foreign Policy*, California; Wernham R B 1984 *After the Armada: Elizabethan England and the struggle for western Europe, 1588–1595*, Oxford.

The importance of the Court in politics was made clear by Neale J E 1958 The Elizabethan political scene, in *Essays in Elizabethan History*, Cape. It may be that Neale exaggerated the factionalisation of the Court in the early 1590s: Wernham R B 1984 *After the Armada*, Oxford, suggests that Essex and the Cecils co-operated effectively in foreign policy matters. The most useful recent surveys of the Court are: MacCaffrey W T 1961 Place and patronage in Elizabethan politics, in Bindoff S T, Hurstfield J, Williams C H (eds) *Elizabethan Government and Society*, Athlone; Elton G R 1983 Tudor government: the points of contact. III the Court, in *Studies in Tudor and Stuart Politics and Government*, Cambridge, vol. 3; Williams P H 1983 Court and polity under Elizabeth I, *Bulletin of the John Rylands University Library* 65; Adams S L 1984 Eliza enthroned? The Court and its politics, in Haigh C A (ed.) *The Reign of Elizabeth I*, Macmillan; Loades D M 1986 *The Tudor Court*, Batsford. We need detailed scholarly studies of Court politics. The personal relationships of the Court can be examined through Williams N 1972 *All the Queen's Men*, Macmillan; Brooks E St J 1946 *Sir Christopher Hatton*, Cape; Wilson D 1981 *Sweet Robin: a biography of Robert Dudley, earl of Leicester*, Hamilton; Rowse A L 1962 *Raleigh and the Throckmortons*, Macmillan; and Lacey R 1971 *Robert, Earl of Essex*, Weidenfeld & Nicolson. Aspects of the culture and ritual of the Court are illuminated by: Yates F A 1975 *Astraea: the imperial theme in the sixteenth century*, Routledge & Kegan Paul; Strong R 1977 *The Cult of Elizabeth: Elizabethan portraiture and pageantry*, Thames & Hudson; Strong R 1987 *Gloriana: the portraits of Elizabeth I*, Thames & Hudson.

The classic account of Elizabeth's management of her Parliaments is Neale J E 1953, 1957 *Elizabeth I and Her Parliaments*, Cape (2 vols). But the Neale version, with its constant clashes between a puritan Parliament and a beleaguered government, has been undermined – if not demolished – by Elton G R 1984 Parliament, in Haigh C A (ed.) *The Reign of Elizabeth I*, Macmillan. The problems of parliamentary management are examined from a perspective very different from Neale's by Graves M A R 1980 Thomas Norton the Parliament man, *Historical Journal* 23; Graves M A R 1983 The management of the Elizabethan House of Commons: the Council's 'men of business', *Parliamentary History* 2. Elizabeth's own contribution is assessed by Heisch A 1975 Queen Elizabeth I: parliamentary rhetoric and the exercise of power, *Signs*, 1. In Elton G R 1986 *The Parliament of England, 1559–1581*, Cambridge, the workings of Parliament are given scholarly treatment, with detailed attention to the making of Bills and Acts. Elections to the Commons are dealt with (sometimes speculatively) by Neale J E 1949 *The Elizabethan House of Commons*, Cape, and Hasler P W 1981 *The House of Commons, 1559–1603*, History of Parliament Trust (3 vols) vol. 1. The importance of the House of Lords is obscured by a paucity of records – but it was probably much more significant than now appears.

The best discussion of Elizabethan England's limited military resources, and the problems of deploying them, is Cruickshank C G 1966 *Elizabeth's Army*, 2nd edn, Oxford, although Wernham R B 1984 *After the Armada: Elizabethan England and the struggle for western Europe, 1588–95*, Oxford, is much less pessimistic about achievements. The strategic options available to Elizabeth, and the difficulties of controlling commanders, are set out with insight and clarity by Wernham R B 1961 Elizabethan war aims and strategy, in Bindoff S T, Hurstfield J, Williams C H (eds) *Elizabethan Government and Society*, Athlone. Leicester's campaign in the Netherlands is assessed in MacCaffrey W T 1981 *Queen Elizabeth and the Making of Policy*, Princeton; the Essex campaign in Normandy in Lloyd H A 1973 *The Rouen Campaign, 1590–92*, Oxford; and the campaigns in Ireland in Falls C 1950 *Elizabeth's Irish Wars*, Methuen, and Falls C 1955 *Mountjoy, Elizabethan General*, Oldham. The importance of private enterprise in naval warfare is shown in Andrews K R 1964 *Elizabethan Privateering*, Cambridge; Andrews K R 1967 *Drake's Voyages*, Weidenfeld & Nicolson; Andrews K R 1972 Sir Robert Cecil and Mediterranean plunder, *English Historical Review* 87. Professor Andrews shows just how far private profit became an issue in the making and execution of policy.

Elizabethan public relations techniques have been widely studied. Political pamphleteering can be approached through Read C 1961 William Cecil and Elizabethan public relations, in Bindoff S T, Hurstfield J, Williams C H (eds) *Elizabethan Government and Society*, Athlone; pictures through Strong R 1977 *The Cult of Elizabeth: Elizabethan portraiture and pageantry*, Thames & Hudson, and Strong R 1987 *Gloriana: the portraits of Queen Elizabeth I*, Thames & Hudson; ballads and poetry through Wilson E C 1939 *England's Eliza*, Harvard, and Firth C H 1909 The ballad history of the later Tudors, *Transactions of the Royal Historical Society*, 3rd series, vol. 3; and progresses through Dunlop I 1962 *Palaces and progresses of Elizabeth I*, Cape, and especially Nichols J 1823 *The Progresses and Public Processions of Queen Elizabeth* (3 vols), Nichols. The effectiveness of such propaganda has been less often – and less well – examined: see Samaha J T 1975 Gleanings from local criminal court records: sedition amongst the 'inarticulate' in Elizabethan Essex, *Journal of Social History* 8. Some of the scandalous stories are reported in Erickson C 1983 *The First Elizabeth*, Macmillan, and the public relations disaster of 1579 is briefly discussed in MacCaffrey W T 1981 *Queen Elizabeth and the Making of Policy*, Princeton. Since Elizabeth's public appeal has generally been examined by her admirers, there is no systematic study of the decline in her popularity in her last decade. On this, as on many other aspects of Elizabethan political history, there is still much to be done.

LIST OF DATES

1533   Birth of Elizabeth

1536   Execution of Elizabeth's mother, Anne Boleyn

1547   Death of Elizabeth's father, King Henry VIII

1553   Death of Elizabeth's brother, King Edward VI

1558   Death of Elizabeth's sister, Queen Mary; accession of Queen Elizabeth; Cecil becomes Secretary of State

1559   Treaty of Cateau-Cambresis with France; Parliament petitions the Queen to marry; Acts of Supremacy and Uniformity restore 'Edwardian' religion, with emendations

1560   English military intervention in Scotland; death of Amy Dudley

1561   Robert Dudley's 'Spanish strategy' for marriage to Elizabeth; scandalous rumours about Elizabeth and Dudley

1562   Elizabeth almost dies of smallpox; Council in disarray on the succession; English military intervention in France by the 'Newhaven Adventure'; Dudley and Norfolk appointed to the Council

1563   Parliament petitions the Queen to marry and to settle the succession; Convocation approves the Thirty-nine Articles; Warwick's army withdraws from Le Havre

1564   Dudley made Earl of Leicester, as possible suitor for Mary Queen of Scots

1565   Elizabeth insists on uniformity in clerical dress; disputes at Court between Leicester and Norfolk

1566   Parliament petitions for regulation of the succession

1567   Enforced abdication of Mary Queen of Scots; accession of baby James VI as King of Scots

1568   Mary flees to England and is taken into custody; Elizabeth orders seizure of Spanish treasure *en route* to the Netherlands

1569   Court conspiracy for the overthrow of Cecil and the marriage of Norfolk to Mary Queen of Scots; Revolt of the Northern Earls defeated

1570   Executions in northern England; papal bull *Regnans in excelsis* declares Elizabeth deposed; renewed scandals about Elizabeth

1571   Act against bringing in bulls from Rome; Elizabeth vetoes the Bill on church attendance; 'Ridolfi Plot' and arrest of Norfolk

1572   Treaty of Blois with France; execution of the Duke of Norfolk; Elizabeth resists pressure to exclude Mary from the succession; Burghley becomes Lord Treasurer; 'Alençon courtship' begins

1573   Walsingham becomes Secretary of State

1574   Convention of Bristol settles some disputes with Spain; arrival of first Catholic seminary priests

1575   Grindal succeeds Parker as Archbishop of Canterbury

1576   Parliament petitions the Queen to marry; Elizabeth orders Grindal to suppress the prophesyings; he refuses; official celebration of 'Accession Day' begins

1577   Elizabeth herself orders suppression of the prophesyings; Grindal is suspended from the exercise of his office; councillors press Elizabeth to intervene in the Netherlands; Drake begins his voyage around the world; the first execution of a seminary priest

1578   Alençon marriage negotiations are resumed

1579   Alençon visits England; campaign against the proposed marriage; Stubbs publishes *The Discovery of a Gaping Gulf,* and Spencer *The Shepherd's Calendar*; revolt in Ireland

1580   Jesuit missionaries arrive in England; return of Drake

1581   Recusancy Act imposes heavy fines for absence from church; Alençon's second visit to England

1582   'Alençon courtship' abandoned

1583   'Throckmorton Plot' against Elizabeth; Whitgift succeeds Grindal as Archbishop of Canterbury, and seeks clerical conformity

1584   Death of Alençon, murder of William of Orange, and Treaty of Joinville (between Spain and the French Catholic League) weaken Elizabeth's international position; the 'Bond of Association' formed to protect Elizabeth

1585   Treaty of Nonsuch with Dutch rebels; Act against Jesuits and seminary priests prescribes death penalty for Catholic missionary priests and those who harbour them; English military intervention in the Netherlands, under Leicester

1586   Three 'moderates' appointed to the Council; 'Babington Plot' against Elizabeth; Parliament petitions for execution of Mary

1587   'Stafford Plot' against Elizabeth; execution of Mary Queen of Scots; Secretary Davison sent to the Tower; Hatton becomes Lord Chancellor; Drake's raid on Cadiz

1588   Negotiations with Parma; Spanish Armada defeated; Elizabeth addresses her army at Tilbury; death of Leicester

1589   English expedition to Portugal; English military intervention in Normandy under Willoughby

1590   Death of Walsingham; no replacement as Secretary

1591   Further English military interventions in France, under Essex in Normandy and Norris in Brittany; Robert Cecil appointed to the Council

1592 Elizabeth orders Essex to return home

1593 Parliament votes heavy war taxation; rebellion in Ireland; Essex appointed to the Council

1594 'Lopez Plot' against Elizabeth; bad harvest and high prices

1595 Calvinist 'Lambeth articles' are issued by Whitgift, but are not approved by Elizabeth; bad harvest

1596 Robert Cecil becomes Secretary of State; English expedition to Cadiz, under Howard and Essex; bad harvest

1597 'Islands Voyage' to the Azores under Essex and Raleigh; the Commons complain of abuses of monopolies; bad harvest

1598 Further heavy war taxation; codified Poor Law; death of Burghley intensifies power struggle between Cecil and Essex

1599 English military expedition to Ireland, under Essex; Cecil becomes Master of the Wards; after military failure, Essex makes a secret agreement with Tyrone and returns to Court

1600 Essex in disgrace; Elizabeth refuses to renew his monopoly of sweet wines

1601 Essex Revolt fails, and he is executed; further heavy war taxation; Commons debate on monopolies; Elizabeth's 'golden speech'; Lord Deputy Mountjoy defeats Tyrone

1602 Cecil prepares for accession of James of Scotland

1603 Death of Elizabeth

INDEX

William Parr, Marquis of, 59, 67
Northumberland, Earls of, 48
  Thomas Percy, Earl of, 52, 53–6,
    59, 61
  Henry Percy, Earl of, 64
Norwich, Bishops of, see Parkhurst,
    John; Scambler, Edmund
  city of, 47, 48, 147, 152
  diocese of, 43
Nottingham, county of, 88
Nottingham, Charles Howard, Earl
    of, 50, 59, 60, 63, 99–100, 134,
    135, 136, 137, 141, 185
Nowell, Alexander, 32

Oglander, John, 142
Old Sarum, 49
Onslow, Fulke, 114
Ordnance, Master of the, 62
Orpheus, 94
Oxford, city of, 147, 157
  county of, 151
  university of, 90, 154, 157
Oxford Earls of, 62
  Anne de Vere, Countess of, 61
  Edward de Vere, Earl of, 37, 44,
    58, 61, 63, 89, 93, 96, 99

Paget, William Lord, 13, 81, 88
Painter Stainers Company, 148
Papacy, Popes, 2, 13, 29, 30, 68, 78,
    109, 133, 144, 149, 157, 170,
    173
Paris, 53, 74
Parker, Matthew, Archbishop of
    Canterbury, 3, 32, 34, 35, 37,
    38, 39, 42, 60, 157, 183
Parkhurst, John, Bishop of
    Norwich, 39
Parliament, 3, 11, 17, 20, 29, 37, 71,
    99, 106–23, 150, 185
  and religion, 30–1, 34, 35, 36,
    115, 118, 119, 120
  elections to, 48, 49–50, 60, 90,
    111–13
  Elizabeth and, 11, 17, 18, 20, 21,
    28, 106–7, 108, 110, 113–23,
    129, 142, 153, 167, 183
  petitions of, 11, 17, 40, 182, 183,
    184

Parma, Alexander Farnese, Duke of,
    82, 130, 131, 132, 133, 138, 184
Parr, Katherine, 3, 16
Parry, Blanche, 97, 98
  Thomas, 8, 81
  William, 144
Patronage and rewards, 43–5, 57,
    61–3, 64, 82–3, 88, 89–92, 97,
    98, 102–3, 134, 171
Paulet, William, 60
Pembroke, Earls of, 48, 49
  William Herbert, Earl of, 8, 53,
    54, 55, 57, 59, 60, 67, 69,
    81, 83
  Henry, Earl of, 49, 96
Percy, family of, 48, 52, 55; see also
    Northumberland, Earls of
Perrot, John, 89; see also Lord
    Deputy
  Thomas, 96
Peru, 133
Peterborough, Dean and Chapter of,
    91
Petre, William, 8
Philip II, 10, 11, 13, 72, 118, 129,
    130, 133, 135, 137, 144, 155,
    161, 169, 173, 174
Pickering, William, 12
Plantagenet, Emmanuel, see Fry,
    Miles
plots, against Anne Boleyn, 1–2
  under Henry VIII, 3
  against Mary, 4
  against Elizabeth, 53–4, 56, 57,
    60, 72, 111, 144–5, 146, 158,
    183, 184, 185
Pluralities Act (1529), 91
Pole, Cardinal Reginald, 145
Pollard, A F, 16
poor law, 185
Popham, John, 111
Portugal, 133
  expedition to (1589), 134–5, 184
preachers, preaching, 7, 9, 17, 29, 35,
    36, 39–41, 42, 76, 77, 146, 157
prerogative, 35, 120, 121, 122, 167
Privy Chamber, 3, 21, 43, 50, 70, 78,
    91, 93, 94, 97, 98, 99, 145
Privy Council, 1, 13, 17, 19, 22, 35,
    40, 41, 44, 59, 60, 66–83, 88,